The "Other Tuscany"

The "Other Tuscany"

Essays in the History of
Lucca, Pisa, and Siena
during the Thirteenth, Fourteenth,
and Fifteenth Centuries

EDITED BY

THOMAS W. BLOMQUIST
AND MAUREEN F. MAZZAOUI

Studies in Medieval Culture XXXIV

Medieval Institute Publications

WESTERN MICHIGAN UNIVERSITY

Kalamazoo, Michigan — 1994

Cover design by Linda K. Judy

Library of Congress Cataloging-in-Publication Data

The "Other Tuscany" : essays in the history of Lucca, Pisa, and Siena
  during the thirteenth, fourteenth, and fifteenth centuries / edited
  by Thomas W. Blomquist and Maureen F. Mazzaoui.
      p.   cm. -- (Studies in medieval culture ; 34)
    Papers from the symposium "The other Tuscany ... " subsumed within
  the larger proceedings of the Twenty-second International Congress
  on Medieval Studies held at the Western Michigan University campus,
  May 7–10, 1987. Cf. p. 13.
    Includes bibliographical references.
    ISBN 1-879288-41-9. -- ISBN 1-879288-42-7 (pbk.)
    1. Lucca (Italy)--History--Congresses. 2. Pisa (Italy)--History-
  -Congresses. 3. Siena (Italy)--History--Congresses. I. Blomquist,
  Thomas W. II. Mazzaoui, Maureen Fennell. III. Series.
  CB351.S83   vol. 34
  [DG975.L82]
  940.1 s--dc20
  [945'.5]
                                                          94-4664
                                                          CIP

Printed and bound by CPI Group (UK) Ltd, Croydon, CR0 4YY

Contents

Introduction

THOMAS W. BLOMQUIST
AND MAUREEN F. MAZZAOUI

Studies of late medieval Tuscany have traditionally relied on historiographical premises derived from the experience of its intensely investigated capital city. Specifically, normative and quantitative data from Florentine sources have been employed to chart demographic, social, and economic trends within the present day province of Tuscany during the communal age and across the critical period of the Black Death and its aftermath. Changes in settlement and tenurial patterns in the countryside have been viewed through the prism of Florentine administrative and fiscal policies as they applied to its subject territories. The results have invited instructive comparisons with other regions within Italy as well as other parts of Europe. At the same time, however, the focus on Florence in its role as a metropolitan center belies the conceptual problems inherent in the modern definition of "region," applicable only with hindsight to medieval juridical and topographical boundaries. It also tends to overlook the specific nature of power hierarchies and socio-economic structures in primary and secondary urban centers within and outside the Florentine orbit and in separate rural communities, differentiated by widely disparate elements of human and physical geography. Over the past several decades, studies of urban and rural communes in various parts of Tuscany have revealed a diversity of local networks and territorial strategies that do not conform to the familiar Florentine model.[1]

1

The conference papers in the present volume are designed to offer non-Italian scholars a representative sample of current European research and a summary of recent debates regarding the historical evolution of those republics that posed the most formidable obstacles to the extension of Florentine hegemony: Lucca, the earliest Tuscan city to rise to prominence on the basis of overland trade; Pisa, the principal maritime city of central Italy; and, finally, the wealthiest and most powerful commune to the south, Siena.[2] While the essays cover a range of topics, they all provide evidence of the important resources available to scholars working in provincial Tuscan archives. One of the papers directly addresses issues regarding the formation and internal organization of archival collections, from the point of view of modern archival science. Other contributions testify indirectly to the breadth and chronological scope of the extensive deposits of private documents preserved in Tuscan archives. In the absence of a consistent body of official documentation, private records have proved invaluable in reconstructing the internal political and social processes of individual communes.

Lucca obtained the height of her power and prosperity during the latter half of the thirteenth century.[3] What would appear from all indications to have been a period of prolonged economic expansion during the Duecento, based primarily upon a thriving silk industry and an international network of mercantile-banking companies established in virtually all the major industrial and financial centers of western Europe, was dramatically interrupted in 1301 when the popular Black Guelph faction came to power at the expense of the "conservative," merchant dominated, White Guelphs.[4] Lucca did enjoy a recovery of sorts during the rule of Castruccio Castracani from 1316 until his death in 1328.[5] Castruccio's policies engendered territorial expansion and support of—and from—a mercantile oriented oligarchy; these policies allowed Lucca to challenge Florence for ephemeral leadership in Tuscany and to experience a brief period of economic rejuvenation.[6]

Following Castruccio's demise, the city entered upon a time of troubles that witnessed the undignified spectacle of her being sold to the highest foreign bidder on four occasions until 1342, when Pisa, out-duelling Florence militarily, captured her neighbor. Lucca remained under Pisan rule until 1369, when, after extensive negotiations with Emperor Charles IV, she finally obtained her freedom from foreign domination,[7] a political independence that would last for over four centuries, until 1799.

Freedom from external rule did not, however, bring in its wake internal stability. The period extending from the re-acquisition of Lucca's "liberty" until the end of the fourteenth century was characterized by domestic factionalism that ultimately led to the creation of the Signoria of Paolo Guinigi.[8] The overthrow of the Guinigi in 1430 opened once again a long period, on the face of it one of relative stability, but one nonetheless punctuated by virtually endemic efforts to overthrow established regimes.[9] Through the later fourteenth and fifteenth centuries, a relatively reduced Lucchese republic maneuvered between the twin perils of the Milanese state to the North and Florence in Tuscany.[10] The Lucchese learned, however, to play the diplomatic game of survival well; for despite the entrance of France and Spain upon the scene, Lucca continued to jockey successfully between the major players on the Italian diplomatic checkerboard and to maintain her tenuous independence.

Michael E. Bratchel, in his essay on the politics of the restored republic, looks more closely beneath the veneer of political life in Lucca from the fall of Paolo Guinigi to the descent of the French upon Italy in 1494. He finds there a dynamic animated by the self-conscious ambitions and rivalries amongst the city's more prominent and powerful families; families, re-enforced by clients and neighbors, often slugging it out for frequently narrow personal or familial reasons. He is at pains to point out that such familial clashes were seldom informed by any discernable programmatic or ideological aims. Furthermore, he fails to discern within the convoluted sectarian internal politics of fifteenth-century Lucca any significant sign of popular class consciousness. Lucca did not experience a Ciompi uprising, and artisans, tradesmen, and shopkeepers played out their political roles as clients and/or friendly neighbors to the magnates.

In another vein, Dr. Bratchel, in a measured fashion, addresses the issue of the degree and character of Florentine imperialism. Responding to Michele Luzzatti's objections that the Arno city's expansionism was not overly aggressive, and that, concomitantly, Lucca had not firmly turned inward to the protective and defensive posture that characterized her sixteenth-century diplomacy, Bratchel concludes that, indeed, while one should not read the sixteenth century backward into the fifteenth, nonetheless, Florentine foreign policy surely was menacing to Lucca (as were the foreign policies of the Milanese and the Este), and that Lucca was already adroit at balancing one threatening power off against another.[11]

Christine Meek moves us from the arena of communal politics to a consideration of the administration and workings of tax farming in fourteenth-century Lucca. Medieval Tuscan fiscal policies have been the object of considerable scrutiny, and Professor Meek herself has made significant contributions to this discussion.[12] Here, however, her concerns are primarily social rather than economic. After describing the process by which gabelles were auctioned off by communal officials, she turns to a consideration of who the farmers were and how they operated. She finds a fairly homogenous group drawn in the main from the ranks of "new men" from the *contado* or denizens of modest means. Many were notaries and many held communal administrative positions on numerous occasions. While some members of Lucca's more prominent families appear as tax farmers, Professor Meek points out the total absence of merchants from the list of those engaging in this activity. She indeed provides a fascinating glimpse into a world of what must have been small-time schemes and machinations aimed at hedging the commune's best efforts, at least in formal procedure, to assure an optimum and reliable return from its farmed gabelles. She demonstrates that cooperation verging upon collusion existed among tax farmers. Her analysis provides valuable insights into the functioning of communal finance and the ability to raise public monies, which was a matter of life or death, as it were, in medieval Tuscany.

The last two articles to deal specifically with Lucca consider various aspects of the documentary record available to modern historians of the medieval city.

Professor Antonio Romiti begins his essay on archival organization and administration by reminding us of the perils to the public record deriving from war, insurrection, and/or the desire of one regime to erase, or at least edit, the legacy of its predecessor. With regard to the preservation of public documents in medieval Lucca, his conclusions fall into a "bad news-good news" dichotomy. The bad news is that, as a consequence of the disorders of the first three decades of the fourteenth century, the toll upon public documentation was considerable. The good news is that, from 1329—the date of the sack of Lucca by Ludwig of Bavaria—onward, the record remains consistently complete. Professor Romiti then turns to a reconstruction of the principles involved in organizing and cataloging the material flowing into the Lucchese public archive based upon his close scrutiny of the inventory of holdings in 1344–45 as recorded by the notary Giovanni Barellia at the request of the *Anziani*. On the basis of this close examination, Romiti is able to argue for the existence of a conscious archival methodology, and he holds out the real possibility of further advances in our knowledge of Lucchese archival practices from additional research in the remaining two registers of inventories, the first dating from 1348 and the second spanning the period 1389–1440.

Dr. Giorgio Tori then turns to the brief and unhappy chancellorship of the *Anziani* of Coluccio Salutati in 1370–71.[13] More specifically, he undertakes a comparison of the official accounts, drawn up by Coluccio, of deliberations and decisions of various communal councils with the rough notes, *Minute*, that the Chancellor made while the proceedings were going forth. He unearths a number of significant discrepancies between the notes and the final public version that should put historians exploiting such sources on alert. He finds, for example, that, in drawing up the public account of meetings of the General Council, Coluccio for some unexplained reason omitted council records from the official version that he had duly noted on-the-spot. Furthermore, the Chancellor habitually lumped opinions expressed by various councillors together and attributed them in the final account to one individual councillor. These variances and idiosyncrasies are more pronounced when Dr. Tori collates the official with the rough accounts for meetings of the council of Thirty-Six. One may wonder, of course, if, given Coluccio's precarious public situation, the personal misfortunes that befell him while he was in Lucca, and his apparent job dissatisfaction, the great humanist were merely sloughing off. In any event, as Dr. Tori warns, *caveat lector* when relying upon the official register alone.

There are few events that can be compared to the Battle of Meloria (1284) in terms of its long-range implications for the political and economic fortunes of Pisa.[14] However, in the aftermath of the conflict, those implications were neither immediately obvious nor inevitable.[15] The defeat did not signal a sudden or drastic reorientation of the foreign or domestic policies of this leading Ghibelline city. Indeed, as Emilio Cristiani has demonstrated in his comprehensive study of Pisa's ruling elite, there was a basic continuity in the composition of the ruling regime and in the structure of political power through the early decades of the fourteenth century.[16] The drift toward signorial government, which became manifest after Meloria, culminated in the lordship of the Counts of Donoratico. Through the early 1320s the Pisan leadership staunchly embraced the traditional "inviolable" objectives of the city's foreign policy—an implacable hostility toward Florence and Lucca combined with an unwavering commitment to the retention of Sardinia—which commanded the adhesion of a broad segment of the powerful noble and mercantile classes.

Professor Cristiani's essay is devoted to the exploration of a further dimension of the complex political situation that arose in the wake of Meloria. He shows how the onerous terms imposed by the victors in protracted treaty negotiations encouraged the formation of an opposition faction drawn from the families of nobles held hostage in Genoa and from the ranks of exiled Pisan Guelfs who espoused a policy of accommodation with Genoa, Florence, and the Guelf League under the leadership of Pope Boniface VIII. New evidence suggests the strength of the economic as well as the political ties that developed between leading exile Guelf families such as the Gaetani and Rome. One outcome of this alliance was the creation by Pisa's pro-Guelf noble and some *popolano* families of new banking companies that were heavily involved in the financial operations of the Papacy. These initiatives were compromised by the death of Boniface in 1303 and the rejection of his policies by subsequent popes, which led the Gaetani to undertake a series of inconclusive military expeditions against Pisa. It was not until the Aragonese conquest of 1323 severed the last ties between Sardinia and the mainland that Pisa definitively abandoned its preoccupation with overseas territory in order to pursue a greater role in regional politics. This fundamental reorientation gradually led to the adoption of political and economic policies similar to those that had been unsuccessfully championed by the dissident pro-Guelf faction some forty years earlier.

Over the past several decades, scholars at the University of Pisa, including students working under the direction of Cinzio Vio-

lante and Gabriella Rossetti, have been at the forefront of research
on the origin and composition of the ruling elites of Tuscany in the
precommunal and communal periods. Utilizing a range of private
and public documents, including many unpublished texts, investiga-
tors have reconstructed the lineages of scores of consular families.
The resulting data have made it possible to chart the diverse economic and political strategies pursued by consorterial families of
varying rank and influence who shared, nevertheless, a common
cultural ethos.[17]

Professor Maria Luisa Ceccarelli-Lemut has been a major con-
tributor to this field.[18] Her essay is, in effect, a case study of two
little-known families—the Anfossi and the more prominent Ebriaci—who are in many respects representative of the middle ranks
of Pisa's consular class. Unlike many of the great comital houses
of Tuscany whose dynastic history can be traced continuously
across generations, the families of the lesser nobility are typically
characterized by brief or interrupted lines that reflect a high degree
of instability and the attendant risks of extinction in the male line.
However, even these incomplete genealogies, when combined with
other references, provide important clues to the connections of the
Pisan ruling elite to the city, the territory, and the sea.

In the case of the Anfossi, a pattern of public office-holding,
legal training, and extensive seafaring in actions against Genoese
ships culminated in the rise to prominence of the brothers Bulgarino and Alkerio in the twelfth century, following which the political fortunes of the clan declined. A much more visible role in communal affairs was played by the Ebriaci, who can be traced for several generations until the line became extinct in the fifteenth century. Notices regarding the Ebriaci reflect the importance of church
patronage, formal alliances, and marital unions in cementing ties to
the Archbishop, the most powerful consular families, and even to
the Sardinian royal house, although the Ebriaci ultimately lost out
to other families in the competitive struggle for possessions in Sar-

dinia. Their overseas ventures included participation in the Crusades and commercial expeditions to Constantinople. Despite the cohesiveness of consorterial ties and a strong network of alliances, they, too, like the Anfossi, suffered a relative eclipse as a result of the political and institutional restructuring of communal government in the thirteenth century.

Siena in the course of the thirteenth century experienced a demographic and economic expansion similar to the other towns of interior Tuscany. Toward the end of the century, Siena would appear to have been about on a par with Lucca, vying with her for the position of "Second City" within Tuscany behind a rapidly growing Florence.[19] Siena's prosperity was based largely upon the success of her merchant-bankers in the arena of international commerce and finance.[20] The network of international banking and commerce created by Sienese companies—such as those headed by the magnatial families of the Bonsignori, Tolomei, Squarcialupi, Forteguerri, and Gallerani operating throughout Europe and serving as favored bankers to the papacy—parallels the one built contemporaneously by Lucchese merchants and financiers. Indeed, the Bonsignori and the Ricciardi Company of Lucca may be regarded as Europe's most powerful international merchant-banking enterprises of the later thirteenth century.[21] And both failed in the early fourteenth century, setting off a ripple effect that brought down other international banking establishments in both communes. For Siena, the wave of bankruptcies permanently altered the face of her economy, and no new firms comparable to the Bonsignori or Tolomei emerged to take their places as the Bardi or Peruzzi rose to replace the collapsed Mozzi, Franzesi, Pulci, and Rimbertini of contemporary Florence. Following the failures of her premier international banking enterprises, Siena's economy became subsequently more regional in character.[22]

Siena, then, like Lucca, saw the end of her heroic period of economic growth in the first decades of the *Trecento* and a relative loss of her economic and political influence vis-à-vis Florence. Both Siena and Lucca did, however, manage to remain free of Florentine domination during the later Middle Ages. But while Lucca experienced a time of political woe during the first half of the fourteenth century, the City of the Virgin remained under the politically stable rule of the "Nine Governors and Defenders of the Commune and People of Siena": "i novi," "i noveschi," "the Nine."

Professor Mario Ascheri, drawing upon the fundamental works of William Bowsky as well as his own archival researches, assays a new look at the Sienese state, its governance, and its civic ideology during the pivotal near-seven-decade rule of the Nine.[23] He highlights the ability of the oligarchic Noveschi, drawn largely from the ranks of successful merchants and bankers, to keep at bay, on the one hand, the more popular Guelph elements and, on the other, the more fractious of the old nobility. Professor Ascheri is not quite as sanguine about the rule of the Nine as Professor Bowsky, however, who attributes the longevity of the regime to diligence unmarred by originality, perspicacity, and pragmatism; all informed by a strong sense of purpose and a high-minded civic idealism.[24] He instead points out "the fearsome face of the military and police power of an otherwise anonymous government" symbolized by the office of the General Captain of War. Similarly, Professor Ascheri tends to view the "culture" of the era of the Nine as a "cultural plan": a self-serving propaganda devised by and for the ruling circle of merchants. Professor Bowsky, on the other hand, imputes a more benign motivation to the Noveschi, who were "instrumental in developing a *civismo*, a civic spirit and a civic ideal" that served to remind the governors and governed alike of the constant "desire to maintain the good and pacific state of the city and people of Siena."[25]

Professor Ascheri goes beyond Professor Bowsky, however, in his examination of the Sienese territory. While the latter focuses primarily upon the fiscal relations between the central city and the country, Ascheri concentrates upon the juridical ties between the two. He underscores the welter of distinct judicial conditions qualifying the status of the various individual and corporate entities that made up the Sienese territory. Ultimately, these varying juridical arrangements defined the economic and social bonds between the city and the country. He also suggests the need for further, specific, investigation into the status of these different outlying bodies in terms of their relations with the urban center.

Professor Duccio Balestracci follows with a consideration of the Nine as urban planners and developers. Here again the Novi and their vision and competence show through. Balestracci demonstrates that the Nine not only rationalized town planning regarding street layout and water distribution but also executed their ideal of what a city run by and for successful businessmen should look like. Like Professor Ascheri for the political, he emphasizes the accomplishments of the oligarchy in the realm of civic planning in terms of what was to come. Art apparently followed life—or politics—in that in both—the political and architectonic—the future brought little to overshadow the work of the Nine.

From the city, Professor Gabriella Piccinni takes us into the country; to wit, Amiata and the Maremma. A major theme of the recent historical literature on the Tuscan countryside is the development from the twelfth century on of a silvo-pastoral system that was closely connected to the growth of an urban-based market economy. It was the city that mediated the gradual integration of formerly isolated mountainous and sparsely populated zones into a regional economy based on agricultural specialization and expanding commercial networks. The effect of these changes on the small landowners of the Appenines was reflected in a deepening pattern of subsistence agriculture (in which chestnuts rather than grains were the principal crop), the substitution of large-scale transhumance for independent stock breeding, and new conflicts over pastures and other resources that expanded the sphere of collective action of the rural communes.[26]

However, the process was far from uniform. In some cases, access to outside capital and the stimulus of export markets set in motion a train of economic changes that dramatically transformed the occupational and social structures of pastoral regions. One example is the unique ecological zone of Monte Amiata and the Maremma that has been extensively studied by Gabriella Piccinni.[27] What linked the mountain to the marshy plain below was the seasonal migration of laborers, indeed of entire families, who accompanied livestock between summer and winter pastures and who descended from their habitations in the wooded mountain areas to cultivate cereals in the plain. Similar to what occurred in other localities, the flow of urban capital into the region, combined with the systematic organization of transhumance created new ties of dependency between the shepherds tending flocks in the Maremma and Amiata and urban investors.

In all of the above respects, this micro-region conforms to the general profile of mountain dwellers in medieval Tuscany. However, what is unusual about the residents of Amiata is their economic flexibility and their capacity for adaptation that is documented in both the written sources and the archeological record. The exploitation of the rich natural resources of the area gave rise to a wide range of artisan and industrial activities connected to the transformation of forest products, the extraction of minerals, and the harnessing of hydraulic power for the smelting of iron ore. Large-scale enterprises required the financial backing of Sienese citizens who entered into partnership agreements with resident artisans. But individual initiatives by local craftsmen were also common. A number of villages were specialized in the production of export commodities such as charcoal, smoked meats, shoes, textiles, and arms. The expansion of the non-agricultural and non-pastoral sectors affected the distribution of wealth and introduced new grades of social stratification. However, it did not erase the deeply embedded cultural ethos of equality, homogeneity, and fierce independence professed by the inhabitants. Nor did it curb the endemic violence traditionally associated with mountain societies.

Finally, Professor Piccinni calls attention to a hitherto unsuspected industrial zone characterized by a high degree of technological innovation in a thinly populated and generally impoverished part of the Sienese district, and she suggests the need for additional research on the micro level in order to ascertain the full dimensions of the economic and social transformation of rural life in the later medieval period.

In conclusion, the editors wish to thank Professor Otto Gründler, Director of the Medieval Institute, for his generosity and geniality towards the participants in the symposium "The Other Tuscany: Lucca, Pisa, Siena, and Minor Centers in the Thirteenth, Fourteenth, and Fifteenth Centuries" subsumed within the larger proceedings of the *Twenty-Second International Congress on Medieval Studies*, which met on the campus of Western Michigan University, 7–10 May 1987. We similarly express our gratitude to him for providing a pleasant and stimulating venue for such an undertaking. Also we wish to acknowledge our debt to Professor Thomas H. Seiler, Managing Editor of Medieval Institute Publications, Western Michigan University, for his patience and assistance in seeing this book through the press. Further, we gratefully acknowledge Professor Christine Meek's help with translations. And we owe thanks to Phyllis Pleckham of the History Department, Northern Illinois University, who tirelessly typed and re-typed various redactions and revisions of those texts which led to an intermediate typescript of the volume.

NOTES

1. The literature on medieval Tuscany is, to understate the matter, extensive. Here we can only direct the reader to M. Luzzatti, *Firenze e la Toscana nel medievo: seicento anni per la costruzione di uno stato* (Turin, 1986), pp. 229–68; G. Pinto, *La Toscana nel tardo medioevo: ambiente, economia rurale, società*, 2nd ed. (Florence, 1982), pp. 455–76; and D. Herlihy and C. Klapisch-Zuber, *Tuscans and Their Families: A Study of the Catasto of 1427* (New Haven, 1985), pp. 365–96 for a bibliographical orientation.

On the problems of defining Tuscany, see the oft-cited and oft-criticized analysis of Tuscany by J. C. Russell, *Medieval Regions and Their Cities* (Bloomington, Indiana, 1972), pp. 15–52 who includes Orvieto and Viterbo within the "region of Florence"; P. Malanima, "La formazione di una regione economica: la Toscana nei secoli XIII–XV," *Società e storia*, 20 (1983), 229–69; P. Malanima, "Politica ed economia nella formazione dello stato regionale: il caso Toscano," *Studi veneziani*, n.s. XI (1985), 61–72; and M. Tangheroni, "Il sistema economico della Toscana nel Trecento," in *La Toscana nel secolo XIV: caratteri di una civiltà regionale*, ed. S. Gensini (Pisa, 1988), pp. 41–66.

Comparative studies of Tuscany with other regions include M. Mirri, "Formazione di una regione economica: ipotesi sulla Toscana, sul Veneto, sulla Lombardia," *Studi veneziani*, n.s. XI (1985), 47–59; and S. R. Epstein, "Cities, Regions and the Late Medieval Crisis: Sicily and Tuscany Compared," *Past and Present*, 130 (1991), 33–50.

2. On relations between Florence and her subject areas, see the papers of G. Chittolini, D. Herlihy, M. Luzzatti, and E. Magliozzi in *Egemonia fiorentina ed autonomie locali nella Toscana nord-occidentale del primo Rinascimento; vita, arte, coltura: Settimo convegno internazionale del Centro Italiano di Studi di Storia e d'Arte, Pistoia, 18–25 settembre 1975* (Pistoia, 1978). For a brief discussion of the problem, see J. C. Brown, *In the Shadow of Florence: Provincial Society in Renaissance Pescia* (New York, 1982), pp. xvii–xxv.

3. For the general history of Lucca in the Middle Ages, see A. Mancini, *Storia di Lucca* (Florence, 1950); and G. Tommasi, *Sommario della storia di Lucca*, published as *Archivio storico italiano*, X (1876). For aspects of medieval Lucchese ecclesiastical history, see D. Osheim, *An Italian Lordship: The Bishopric of Lucca in the Late Middle Ages* (Berkeley, 1977). Also see D. Osheim, *A Tuscan Monastery and Its Social World: San Michele of Guamo (1156–1348)*, published

as *Italia sacra: studi e documenti di storia ecclesiastica*, 40 (Rome, 1989).

4. The events of the uprising are described in *Tholomei lucensis annales* in *Monumenta germaniae historica*, ed. B. Schmeidler, *Scriptores rerum germanicorum*, n.s. VIII (Berlin, 1930), pp. 318–19. We are here accepting L. Green's dating rather than the traditional 1300: L. Green, *Castruccio Castracani: A Study on the Origins and Character of a Fourteenth-Century Italian Despotism* (Oxford, 1986), p. 25, n. 50; See also *ibid.*, pp. 18–29 for an analysis of the factional alignments animating the violence of 1301. For the Lucchese silk industry, see F. Edler, "The Silk Trade of Lucca during the Thirteenth and Fourteenth Centuries" (Ph.D. diss. University of Chicago, 1930).

5. Green, *Castruccio Castracani*, pp. 112–22.

6. Green, *Castruccio Castracani*, pp. 121–22.

7. See C. Meek, *The Commune of Lucca under Pisan Rule, 1342–1369* (Cambridge, Mass., 1980) for the Pisan occupation.

8. C. Meek, *Lucca 1369–1400: Politics and Society in an Early Renaissance City-State* (Oxford, 1978).

9. See herein M. Bratchel's article.

10. M. Berengo, *Nobili e mercanti nella Lucca del cinquecento* (Turin, 1965).

11. M. Luzzatti, "Politica di salvaguardi dell' autonomia lucchese nella seconda metà del secolo XV," in *Egemonia fiorentina ed autonomie locali*, pp. 543–82.

12. Meek, *Lucca*, pp. 48–76 with bibliographical references p. 51, n. 18, and *The Commune of Lucca*, pp. 63–85.

13. For references to Salutati's stay in Lucca, see herein Giorgio Tori's article, n. 1.

14. For an assessment of the consequence of Meloria, see the essays published in the commemorative volume *Genova, Pisa e il Mediterraneo tra Due e Trecento: Per il VII° centenario della battaglia della Meloria* published by the *Società Ligure di Storia Patria* (Genoa, 1984).

15. D. Herlihy, *Pisa in the Early Renaissance* (New Haven, 1958).

16. E. Cristiani, *Nobiltà e popolo nel comune di Pisa* (Naples, 1962).

17. A summary of recent research and a bibliographical orientation to the subject are provided in the six volumes of conference proceedings published under the auspices of the *Comitato di Studi sulla storia dei ceti dirigenti in Toscana*: I: *I ceti dirigenti in Toscana nell'età precommunale. Atti del I° convegno, Firenze, 2 dicembre 1978* (Pisa, 1981); II: *I ceti dirigenti dell'età communale nei secoli XII e XIII. Atti del II° convegno, Firenze 14–15 dicembre 1979* (Pisa, 1982); III: *I ceti dirigenti nella Toscana tardo comunale. Atti del III° convegno, Firenze, 5–7 dicembre, 1980* (Florence, 1983); IV: *Nobiltà e ceti dirigenti in Toscana nei secoli XI–XIII: Strutture e Concetti. Atti del IV° convegno, Firenze, 12 dicembre, 1981* (Florence, 1982); V: *I ceti dirigenti nella Toscana del Quattrocento. Atti del V° convegno, Firenze, 10–11 dicembre, 1982* (Florence, 1987); VI: *I ceti dirigenti nella Toscana del Quattrocento. Atti del VI° convegno, Firenze, 2–3 dicembre, 1983* (Florence, 1987).

18. In addition to numerous studies of Tuscan aristocratic families, Professor Ceccarelli-Lemut is the author of *Il monastero di S. Giustiniano di Falesia e il castello di Piombino (secoli XI–XIII)* (Pisa, 1972).

19. See Meek, *Lucca*, p. 1, who cites the fact that in a league of 1282 Florence was required to furnish 166 knights, Lucca 114, and Siena 104. Lucca, however, seems to have lagged somewhat behind Siena in terms of population: Malanima "La formazione di una regione economica," p. 254, gives figures of 50,000 for Siena and 30,000 for Lucca between 1290 and 1330. For a general survey of Siena in the thirteenth century, see D. Waley, *Siena and The Sienese in the Thirteenth Century* (Cambridge and New York, 1991).

20. E. English, *Enterprise and Liability in Sienese Banking, 1230–1350* (Cambridge, Mass., 1988) provides a recent history of the Bonsignori and Tolomei merchant-banking companies; for Sienese medieval banking in general, see the accompanying bibliography, pp. 117–25.

21. For the Ricciardi, see R. Kaeuper, *Bankers to the Crown: The Ricciardi of Lucca and Edward I* (Princeton, 1973).

22. On the Sienese economy in the fifteenth century, see D. Hicks, "Sources of Wealth in Renaissance Siena: Businessmen and Landowners," *Bullettino senese di Storia Patria*, 113 (1986), 9–41.

23. For Bowsky's work, see herein Professor Balestracci's contribution, n. 7.

24. W. Bowsky, *A Medieval Commune: Siena under the Nine, 1287–1355* (Berkeley, 1981), pp. 307–10. For shifting expressions of pietism as expressed in wills, see S. K. Cohn, *Death and Property in Siena, 1205–1800* (Baltimore, 1988).

25. Bowsky, *A Medieval Commune*, p. 314.

26. The standard references are by G. Cherubini, *L'Italia rurale nel basso medioevo* (Bari, 1984); *Signori, contadini, borghesi: ricerche sulla società italiana del Basso Medioevo* (Florence, 1974); *Una comunità dell Appennino dal XIII al XV secolo: Montecoronaro dalla signoria dell abbazia del Trivio al dominio di Firenze* (Florence, 1972); and G. Pinto, *La Toscana nel tardo medioevo: ambiente, economia rurale, società* (Florence, 1982). See also C. J. Wickham, *The Mountains and the City: The Tuscan Appenines in the Early Middle Ages* (Oxford, 1988). For a unique glimpse of peasant life and mentality in the fifteenth-century Sienese countryside, see D. Balestracci, *La Zappa e la retorica: memorie familiari di un contadino toscano del Quattrocento* (Florence, 1984).

27. Professor Piccinni's previous studies of the Tuscan countryside include *Seminare, fruttare, raccogliere: mezzadri e salariati sulle terre di Monte Oliveto Maggiore (1374–1430)* (Milan, 1982). She is also the editor of *Il contratto mezzadrile nella toscana medievale, III: Contado di siena 1349–1518* in *Accademia toscana La Colombaria, Studi 124* (Florence, 1992).

Lucca, 1430–94: The Politics of the Restored Republic

MICHAEL E. BRATCHEL

The years between the peace of Lodi in 1454 and the first French invasion of Italy in 1494 have traditionally been viewed as an era of marked, if relative, stability in the history of internal Italian politics. For the small Tuscan city-republic of Lucca, the abiding significance of the events of 1494 is hardly to be disputed. The rivalries of foreign powers that resulted directly from Charles VIII's Italian expedition drove Lucca, for her own self-protection, inexorably into the imperial camp—with lasting consequences for the domestic life of the republic, and for her economic and diplomatic relations with the wider world.[1] The peace of Lodi itself marks less of a watershed in the political history of Lucca than did the restoration of republican forms achieved two-and-one-half decades earlier. In August 1430 the rule of Paolo Guinigi, lord of Lucca since 1400, was brought to an end by a bloodless *coup d'état* planned and executed by a small band of patrician conspirators. Thereafter, and despite the challenges of the sixteenth century, Lucca was to regain her political independence, and the constitutional and administrative restoration of 1430 survived in modified form until the very end of the eighteenth century, when the city was occupied by forces of the French republic under Serrurier.

In the months between August and October 1430 the traditional organs of government were rapidly reconstituted. The college of *Anziani*, headed by a *Gonfaloniere di Giustiza*, was restored im-

19

mediately on 16 August 1430. The important Council of Thirty-Six was reinstated on 30 August, and the General Council began to meet again from 11 October. Extraordinary measures were necessary to deal with the war situation of the 1430s, particularly the appointment of a series of *balìe* endowed with wide-ranging powers. But by 1432, political life in Lucca had very largely returned to pre-Guinigi normality. This settlement was not to be preserved inviolate in the centuries to follow. In Lucca, as elsewhere, the fifteenth century saw the creation of a growing number of special magistracies with specific functions and jurisdictions. Moderate constitutional tinkering throughout the fifteenth century was followed by the more substantive reforms of 1531. Against the background of the revolt of the Straccioni, membership of the General Council was increased from 90 to 130, and no more than three representatives of any individual family were allowed to sit together in Council. The more aristocratic ethos of the later sixteenth century produced restrictions on the number of those eligible for political office. As in the century before the fall of the republic, these restrictions resulted in further constitutional modifications when it became impossible to find sufficient eligible candidates to fill vacant offices.[2] Despite these later vicissitudes, the reforming councils of the 1430s had done their work well. In recreating the political forms of the late fourteenth century, a pattern was established that, in all essentials, was to survive as long as the Republic itself.

The decades after 1430 imperfectly foreshadowed the city's future stability. The war with Florence continued until 1433 and was resumed in the summer of 1436. A number of Lucca's foreign stipendiaries were suborned by the Florentines; and some Lucchese citizens themselves sought personal advantage by entering into negotiations with the enemy.[3] In June 1436 Pietro Cenami, chief instigator of Paolo Guinigi's fall, was murdered in the palace whilst holding the office of *Anziano*. The following year ser Tommaso Lupardi was executed for plotting with Venice and Florence, allegedly with the ambition of attaining the lordship of Lucca for himself.[4] Peace was made with Florence in 1438. The challenge to Lucchese liberty came now from a new direction. Throughout the 1440s there was a series of attempts by Ladislao, son of Paolo Guinigi, to recover the political inheritance of his late father. These efforts were rendered the more dangerous by the support that Ladislao received from powerful external forces, and from Guinigi sympathizers both within the city of Lucca and in the *contado*. The peace of Lodi of 1454 is popularly supposed to have heralded both a new age of non-aggression and collective security, and also a more tranquil period in the domestic histories of Italian states. To a degree, no doubt, this is true. But in 1456 in Lucca, internal peace was threatened by the rivalries of two of her leading families: the Guidiccioni and the Arnolfini. These quarrelled over, among other things, the antiquity of their respective lineages. Throughout these years the Lucchese authorities remained acutely aware of the potential for escalating civil disorder that such quarrels presented. In 1460 Michele Guerrucci made a vain bid to establish himself as lord of Lucca in one of the most complex and obscure of all the fifteenth-century conspiracies. And as late as the 1490s leading Lucchese citizens continued to plot with the agents of Lorenzo de'Medici the means whereby Florentine forces might be best introduced into the city.[5]

All attempts to subvert the constitutional settlement of 1430 proved abortive. The principal conspirators were executed, or—more frequently—had the good sense to flee into exile when things began to go wrong. Their actions, as recounted in the court proceedings and in the political records, placed in context through the rich totality of archival sources extant for fifteenth-century Lucca, provide a good deal of material through which to explore the mechanics of party-formation and the nature of dissent in the restored republic. In the present paper I shall limit myself to locating a number of themes that seem to me important both for the history of Lucca and as a contribution to wider debates in current Italian historiography.

One of the most striking features that characterize the diverse incidents of political disturbance in Quattrocento Lucca is the clear strength of close local connections and neighborhood bonds. The men who ousted Paolo Guinigi in August 1436 were close neighbors whose houses were clustered in the northeastern parts of the city in the *contrade* of *S. Frediano* and of *S. Giovanni Capo di Borghi*.[6] Their plans were laid, and sealed by oath, in the church of *S. Frediano*—and specifically in the chapel of *S. Caterina*, which housed the bones of the ancestors of one of the leading conspirators.[7] Six years later, the murder of the *Anziano* Pietro Cenami was planned in the houses of the di Poggio: the murderers issued forth from the di Poggio labyrinth of the *contrada* of *S. Lorenzo in Poggio* behind leaders drawn from youthful members of the di Poggio family.[8] Throughout the 1440s the group of *parenti* and *amici* that continued to make the Guinigi a feared force in Lucchese political life were firmly centered in the *terziere* of *S. Martino*, to the south and west of the palace and houses of the Guinigi.[9] In all these cases, and in others, the limited geographical focus of political or quasi-political conspiracies is too marked to be explained convincingly merely by coincidence.

Christine Meek has shown how, in the late fourteenth century, the first Guinigi party attracted men in equal numbers from every part of the city.[10] In a study of fifteenth-century Florence, Samuel Kline Cohn has recently argued that the Florentine patriciate were increasingly abandoning the limited parochial attachments of the past and were rapidly achieving the self-identity of the ruling èlite of a united Florentine polity.[11] This image of the declining vitality of neighborhood links is not reflected in the domestic politics of fifteenth-century Lucca. It is perhaps not surprising that this should be so. The widely disseminated appeal of the Guinigi party prior to 1400 was rooted in that family's capacity to dispense patronage and to offer political advancement, particularly from the 1370s onwards.[12] The conspiracies punctuating the history of Lucca after 1430 were closeted political adventures that, by their very nature, demanded intimate knowledge and mutual trust. More generally, Cohn's vision of a Florentine ruling class that had, by the fifteenth century, "emerged from the vestiges of tower family formation and parochial solidarities"[13] has scarcely won universal acceptance.[14] Insofar as Cohn is right, the Lucchese patriciate largely escaped the fears and enticements of the Ciompi experience that may have encouraged contemporary Florentines to forsake traditional neighborhood ties and vertical alliances.

The political life of the restored republic shows rather the continued importance of local connections based on trust, familiarity, and good neighborhood, and cemented by the geographical divisions that permeated electoral procedures and office-holding. In Florence, indeed, it was electoral procedures and the choice of eligible citizens that gave to neighborhood ties much of their vital force.[15] Kent has shown how, in fifteenth-century Florence, geographical isolation from *consorti* was both a reflection and a consummation of political powerlessness and obscurity.[16] In Lucca eligibility for office was not determined by scrutiny councils, and it is by no means clear that, in the more open electoral system favored by Lucca, geographical cohesion was as fundamental a precondition of political survival. But there can be no doubt that the political pre-eminence of the di Poggio family and its clients within the *terziere* of *S. Paolino* was surely founded on the control of a district. In 1371, we are told, the residents of the *contrada* of *S. Lorenzo in Poggio* "sono tutti di Poggio salvo."[17] It was within the houses or in the tower of the di Poggio that the family met to settle the affairs of the *consorteria*, or to appoint rectors to the churches of *S. Lorenzo in Poggio* and *S. Donato in Balbano*.[18] It was from this local power-base that the di Poggio worked to ensure that they were adequately represented in political office; it was discontent in this regard that resulted in the rising of 1522. It was within their houses that the conspiracies of 1436 and 1522 were hatched and organized.[19]

Physical isolation in fifteenth-century Lucca might not mean political impotence, but it was likely to reflect differing interests and allegiances. Taddeo di Poggio, who was *Anziano* in the palace at the time of Pietro Cenami's murder and to whom no suspicion attached, appears regularly in office during these years for the *terziere* of *S. Martino*.[20] The argument is somewhat less persuasive in the case of Pietro di Nicolao Guinigi, a very distant kinsman,[21] whose murder was regarded as a necessary prelude to the restoration of a Guinigi *signoria*.[22] Pietro lived in the *contrada* of *S. Anastasio*, just a little to the south of the main complex of Guinigi houses.

Conversely, common interests and allegiances drew men together in physical space. By the late fourteenth century the Buonvisi were established in the parish of *S. Frediano* in the *terziere* of *S. Salvatore*.[23] Lorenzo di Neri Buonvisi rose to prominence in the service of Paolo Guinigi, and until July 1432 appears regularly in the records of the *Consiglio Generale, Riformagioni Pubbliche*, as holding office for the Guinigi *terziere* of *S. Martino*. But at the time of the rising against Paolo Guinigi in August 1430, Lorenzo Buonvisi was probably resident in the *contrada* of *S. Giovanni Capo di Borgi*, in close proximity to his fellow conspirators Pietro Cenami and Nicolao Streghi.[24] From July 1432 onwards Lorenzo Buonvisi appears always for the *terziere* of *S. Salvatore*. In his will of 1420 Lorenzo asked to be buried near his father in the church of *S. Romano*. By the 1440s Lorenzo was active in the service of *S. Frediano*, a church closely associated with the leading conspirators of 1430 and the center of that conspiracy. By the time of Lorenzo's will of 1447, he envisaged the acquisition of an *avello* in the church of *S. Frediano*; by his third will of January 1458 Lorenzo arranged to be buried in *S. Frediano* in the *avello* recently obtained, that had formerly belonged to the now-extinct Turinghelli family. From this period a close relationship developed between the Buonvisi family and the church of *S. Frediano*; and Lorenzo's son Benedetto became increasingly preoccupied with the establishment of the Buonvisi chapel still to be seen on the south side of the basilica.[25] The mid-fifteenth century also saw the erection of the present *Cappella Gentili* (*della Speranza e del SS. Sacramento*) and of the Cenami chapel of *S. Biagio*.[26] In these and other ways the small group of men who plotted the events of 1430, and who were to figure most prominently in Lucchese affairs in the decades thereafter, were drawn together both in life and death.

If one feature of political life in Lucca after 1430 was the continued importance of neighborhood bonds, equally striking is the highly personalized nature of those grievances that generated political strife. The old political labels of Guelf and Ghibelline remained part of the political vocabulary, and the cry of "Marzocho" was still being heard in the Lucchese countryside as late as the 1490s.[27] Maybe in the field of foreign policy alone it is possible to detect real divisions within the Lucchese political nation. But even here issues provide the most transparent cloak for personal ambitions and immediate advancement. In reality it is exceedingly difficult to locate genuine political ideologies or consistent political programs, whether within or beyond Lucca's boundaries. Rather, throughout the fifteenth century, conflict centered on slighted honor and personal feud.

The point can be illustrated conveniently through the Cenami murder of 1436. It has long been accepted that Pietro Cenami's death was the result of a personal vendetta.[28] The nature of this vendetta has not been fully explored. The affair began, it appears to me, when the wealthy banker Bartolomeo del Portico was banished from Lucca at the end of April 1434. Del Portico was taken ill shortly thereafter, and died in Pietrasanta in June.[29] According to tradition, he was poisoned—and the poisoning was the result of politico-personal rivalries.[30] These events took place when the government of Lucca was headed by Pietro Cenami; Cenami was *Gonfaloniere di Giustizia* for the months May/June 1434. The Del Portico family, and Bartolomeo in particular, had been closely connected with the di Poggio, to whom Bartolomeo appears to have pledged one of his daughters in marriage. In his will of 17 June 1434, Bartolomeo del Portico named his two daughters as his universal heirs. Pietro Cenami—*padre della patria* after Guinigi's fall—seized both girls and their inheritance, giving one daughter to his son and one to his nephew.[31] It was this insult that prompted the di Poggio to take to the streets in a vain effort to raise up the people in the summer of 1436.[32]

The Cenami affair is no isolated example. The political trials of the fifteenth century, and indeed the Lucchese criminal court proceedings generally, provide detailed descriptions of action but are a very inadequate tool with which to probe motivation. Again and again, however, they speak of an exile's desire to revenge himself upon his enemies; of a citizen's determination to redress injuries received. Vengeance was pursued even when it was explicitly perceived to be prejudicial to Lucca and to her continued independence. Private quarrels thus engendered were transmuted into events of true political significance in part because of the stature of the personalities involved, but more especially by the neighborhood divisions and clientage networks to which we have already referred. Tensions were heightened by the emotional bonds and practical implications of common ancestry; by a passionate sense of the *casa*, its traditions and its honor.

These conclusions prompt us to reflect briefly on the family itself as a unit of political action in fifteenth-century Lucca. As late as 1560, Martino Bernardini recorded and named forty towers built by noble Lucchese families that were still standing in the second half of the sixteenth century.[33] It is relatively easy to chronicle for individual families the formal, legal, institutionalized expressions of familial power and familial cohesion: the maintenance of a tower; the administration of common lands; the election of consuls; the building of a *loggia*. By contrast, the inner and private dimensions of familial and extra-familial relationships are much more elusive. This is particularly true for Lucca; the Lucchesi were much more reticent than other Tuscans about perpetuating their feelings through the medium of family diaries.[34] The fifteenth-century Lucchese examples of the *genre* are largely the work of the Guinigi.[35] This may distort our vision, for the Guinigi in the century after Paolo may hardly be viewed as a typical constituent of the Lucchese oligarchy. Nevertheless the Guinigi *ricordi* do offer a useful indictor of the strengths and limitations of familial sentiment.

In essence these writings seem to combine a passionate interest in the *casa* and its antiquity; a rousing defence of the interests of the lineage against the machinations of outsiders; and an almost obsessive animosity towards near paternal kinsmen who might pose a threat to the material welfare of the writer's immediate household.[36] The findings here are unremarkable. The political history of fifteenth-century Lucca is very much a history of the ambitions and interaction of the city's great patrician families. In a sense this becomes increasingly true as the century progressed. But the strength and the identity derived from wider familial associations did not preclude the bitterest intra-familial conflict before both the civil and the criminal courts. Nor did familial loyalties impel men to sacrifice themselves for the hot-blooded political indiscretions of young kinsmen. Just as in the more familiar environs of the sixteenth century the Burlamacchi succeeded in distancing themselves from the treachery of Francesco Burlamacchi,[37] so in 1436 did senior members of the di Poggio clan remain untainted by the murder of Pietro Cenami. Throughout the 1440s and 1450s, leading members of the Guinigi family in Lucca severed their connections with the exiled sons of Paolo in the (correct) belief that the family's future political rehabilitation dictated identification with the new regime. These conclusions mirror the findings of Christine Meek for Lucca in the decades before the establishment of the *signoria*[38] and echo Dale Kent's observation that, in contemporary Florence and within consorterial blocks, "positive hostility, the obverse side of strong family feeling and identification, appears to have been a powerful force determining the divisions of the 1430s."[39]

The political life of Lucca after 1430 has been viewed so far from the perspective of internal dynamics. But Lucca, certainly in the fifteenth century, cannot be treated in isolation. During the first ten years after 1430 all of Lucca's resources were channelled into the fight for survival. For much of this period Lucca's territories were overrun by armies in the pay of her neighbors. Thereafter she precariously co-existed with the small number of greater territorial powers among whom the Italian peninsula was now divided. Against this background, Lucchese chroniclers have stressed the continuing covert intervention of foreign powers, particularly Florence, in Lucchese affairs as manifested not only in the threat posed, periodically, to Lucchese territories but also in the undermining, throughout the fifteenth century, of Lucchese political stability. These assumptions have recently been questioned by the Pisan historian Michele Luzzati.[40] Luzzati argues that historians, influenced by later Florentine ambitions for a consolidated Tuscan state, have been inclined to superimpose sixteenth-century realities on the fifteenth-century world. Using the evidence of the *Colloqui*, Luzzati has questioned the image of fifteenth-century Florence as an inevitable aggressor. He questions further the view that fifteenth-century Lucca had already renounced any autonomous political initiative; that already the chief determinant of Lucchese policy was the desire passively to co-exist, in a spirit of renunciation, with her more powerful neighbors.

There can be no doubt that Lucchese malcontents looked towards Florence for support throughout the fifteenth century. In 1430 Nicolao di Lazzaro Guinigi plotted the handing over of Lucca to the Florentines in return for financial and other rewards.[41] The young di Poggio murderers of Pietro Cenami petitioned, and probably received, a payment of 100 florins from Cosimo de'Medici.[42] In 1460 Michele Guerrucci planned to make himself lord of Lucca with the aid of Cosimo de'Medici, whom Guerrucci described as "a man of standing in the world, who I believe would do anything for me."[43] And as late as the 1490s the factor of Lorenzo de'Medici fanned the private grievances of Andrea Mei and Nese Franchi into a plot to betray Lucca.[44] In reporting on the condition of Lucca's defenses, and in arranging for the taking of *Porta S. Pietro*, Andrea Mei claimed that he had just cause considering the many injuries that he had received within the city of Lucca from many citizens.[45] More generally the corpus of letters to the Medici preserved in the series *Archivio mediceo avanti il principato* reveals an intense correspondence between the Medici and leading Lucchese citizens, despite periodic attempts by the Lucchese authorities to prevent communication between private citizens and foreign princes. Obviously the danger of Florentine intervention in the political life of the restored republic was greatest at the beginning of our period, at a time of open warfare; the thread runs, however, throughout the period as a whole.

It is difficult to find any ideological motivation behind these incidents of collaboration. It is true that there were some genuine disagreements over issues of foreign policy. Some believed that Lucca after 1430 should tie her fortunes closely to those of Milan in gratitude for past help; others feared that such a policy would encourage the Florentines to seek retribution. Acton believed that in the conspiracy of 1437 ser Tommaso Lupardi was moved by a desire to see Lucca align herself with the three great Italian republics of Genoa, Florence, and Venice against the despotism of Milan.[46] I have found no concrete evidence to support this view. Humanist propagandists might have reduced contemporary Italian history to a continuing struggle between the forces of republican liberty championed by Florence and the forces of encroaching despotism typified by Milan. From the perspective of Lucca, Florence's image was somewhat more tarnished, and such grandiose political ideals would have made little sense. In every case, with the possible exception of ser Tommaso Lupardi's negotiations with Florence and Venice, conspirators looked no further than immediate personal advantage and the settling of scores. Even Lupardi seems to have been peculiarly unmoved by the prospects of rape and pillage that would inevitably have followed the admission of Sforza's troops into the city.[47]

Florentine interests in Lucca were probably equally uncomplicated. Luzzati is probably right in his claim that to see Florence in

the fifteenth century as implacably committed to the creation of a consolidated Tuscan state is grotesquely to rewrite fifteenth-century history in terms of sixteenth-century preoccupations.[48] But Luzzati's
image of Florence as an essentially benign neighbor seems to me
contradicted by a mass of evidence from both Florentine and Lucchese sources. Not only, as shown above, did Lucchese dissidents
consistently receive succor from Florence, and specifically from the
Medici, but throughout the century Florence periodically continued
to pose a threat to Lucca's territorial integrity. It may be doubted
whether Florence pursued any very coherent policy towards the Lucchese state after 1441, although she remained adeptly prepared to fish
in troubled waters. The conspirators of 1460 were fully alert to the
possibility that their plans to establish Michele Guerrucci as *signore*
might result rather in a Florentine seizure of the city.[49] For their part,
the Lucchese authorities were well aware of the potential danger and
always displayed an anxious determination to mollify Florentine
opinion, except on rare occasions of impossible provocation.

Nor in looking for external pressures should we look only towards Florence. The Este state to the north attracted a body of support in the Lucchese countryside that was an important ingredient in
the turbulent internal histories of the small communities of the *contado*. Of more immediate relevance to the affairs of Lucca herself,
longstanding associations between the Guinigi family, Milan, and
later Genoa—sealed by marriages contracted by Paolo Guinigi—provided Paolo's son Ladislao with a secure base and source of support.[50] Other Lucchese families, notably the Gentili and the
Ghivizzani, had very strong business and personal connections in
Milan. In 1439 Tiero Gentili was exiled for secret correspondence
with the Duke of Milan, deemed to have been prejudicial to the interests of Lucca and Florence.[51] A similar presumption "de tractare cosa
che non si aspectava a loro" was to lead to the banishment of Giovanni da Ghivizzano and of his son Jacopo in 1446.[52] The image in
some of the Lucchese chroniclers of Milan as a constant malign in-

fluence in the background working for the destabilization of the internal political life of the restored republic is no less a distortion than is the attribution of so formulated a role to Florence. This fact does not diminish the potentiality for mischief enjoyed by all of Lucca's more powerful neighbors.

The present analysis of Lucchese political life—and particularly of Lucchese political strife—has been entirely élitist. The paper has concerned itself with the interaction of Lucca's great families and with the issues and influences that generated conflict among them. Much recent Italian scholarship has been orientated towards explaining away popular involvement in terms of residential arrangements, clientage, and familial bonds. The difficulty in fifteenth-century Lucca is to locate popular involvement in the socio-political life of the city, whether to explain or to explain away. During the Florentine wars of the 1430s there were some sporadic acts of popular violence against Florentine property in Lucca.[53] Conversely, when Lucca was hard pressed by the Florentine siege of 1437, there was some fear within Lucca, according to Florentine sources, that the hardships of the seige might cause the common people to betray the city.[54] Popular anti-Florentine sentiment was easily contained by the Lucchese authorities, and in 1437 no more than an eloquent appeal to patriotism was required for the *plebs* to declare themselves willing to defend the liberty of Lucca with their lives. The Lucchese court records consistently present the crowd as a passive backdrop before which a series of political dramas unfolded. Young patrician bucks periodically rode through the streets of Lucca exhorting the multitude to support them against the iniquities of the regime. There is no evidence that these appeals ever struck a sympathetic chord; these spirited orations with monotonous regularity were followed quickly by the flight, death, or exile of the principals.

The series of Guinigi plots of the 1430s and 1440s, and later the attempt in 1460 of Michele Guerrucci to establish a *signoria*, alone provide some evidence, not of popular movements but of wider popularist support. This is less apparent within the walls of Lucca itself than in the countryside and in the small urban centers of the *contado*. A succession of *contadini* appeared before the courts, accused of uttering variously formulated versions of Voltaire's "I would rather be ruled by one lion than by a thousand rats." Popular sentiment was allegedly expressed by Giovanni di Matteo da Agnino when, looking back nostalgically to the days of Guinigi rule, he denounced the present Lucchese patrician oligarchy who treated the population of the *castello* of Castiglioni like dogs. "Al tempo del segnore avevamo uno S. hora tutti ce volgliono segnorigiare."[55] This raises problems of the relationship between city and state that we cannot look at here. It is sufficient to note that individual spokesmen for the countryside saw real advantages in a common subjection to a common lord. How far these sentiments were shared by the *popolo minuto* in the city is very unclear. We can locate individual artisans who greatly desired the return of the Guinigi.[56] To build general interpretations upon such evidence would be a perilous undertaking. At most we can reiterate that popularist forces are very difficult to find in post-Guinigi Lucca; where there are traces of a program of political change emanating from below, the objective appears to have been less a democratization of Lucchese office-holding than a reversion to the allegedly more even-handed rule of a despot.

It is much more difficult to explain passivity than to analyze action. The absence of any marked popular ingredient from the turbulent political life of the restored republic of Lucca should probably, in part, be explained by the theoretical "openness" of the Lucchese constitution. In Lucca eligibility for political office was determined solely by citizenship, subject to certain age requirements and to legitimate birth. In practice, high office, particularly membership of the college of *Anziani*, was largely monopolized by a relatively small group of prominent citizens. But conflict in Lucca was not institutionalized by constitutional restrictions and divisions, as for example between the respective representation of the greater and lesser guilds in Florence. If political office in theory was open to all Lucchese citizens, those who in practice dominated the ruling councils were well aware of the danger posed to civic order by food shortages and by erratic grain prices. Especially in the war years, popular discontent was averted by the sustained paternalistic concern of urban government to ensure adequate, cheap food supplies.[57] Finally, attention must be drawn again to the continued vitality in Lucca of "vertical" rather than "horizontal" social alignments. This theme in Italian historiography has become intensely politicized and polemicized. It is self-evident that vertical and horizontal divisions were not, and cannot be, mutually exclusive. One man in his time plays many parts. In the real world of fifteenth-century Lucca there is some evidence of men, willingly or reluctantly, rallying to the support of patrician patrons, employers, and neighbors. Thus the unfortunate weaver Bartolomeo del fu Jacopo was dragged most reluctantly into the di Poggio conspiracy of 1436 and was executed for his pains.[58] Of course, social stratification based on patronage and clientage does not preclude contemporaneous identification with peers and with economic equals, and against those whose interests are perceived to be different and hostile. It is merely stated that political and quasi-political conflict situations in fifteenth-century Lucca show some evidence of the former solidarities and no evidence of the latter.

The focus in the present paper upon conflict situations must, to a degree, have presented a distorted image of the politics of the restored republic. The remarkable achievement of the settlement of 1430 was its endurance, both in the short term and in the centuries to come. The years between 1430 and 1440 were very unsettled. Thereafter, challenges to the "pacifico et populare stato" were isolated and occasional. The succession of well-documented conspiracies offers, nevertheless, a useful instrument with which to explore the issues that exercised the minds of the Lucchese patriciate; the interests and loyalties that bound men together; and the internal and external pressures that drove men apart—even to the act of rebellion.

NOTES

My participation in the Twenty-Second International Congress on Medieval Studies at Western Michigan University was made possible by travel and subsistence grants from the University of the Witwatersrand, Johannesburg, and from the Human Sciences Research Council in Pretoria. Research for this paper was undertaken in Italy in 1985 and 1986 with the aid of a Senior Researcher Award from the Human Sciences Research Council. Themes raised in the present paper will be discussed in greater detail in a book that I am currently preparing on the history of Lucca, 1430–94.

1. Marino Berengo, *Nobili e mercanti nella Lucca del Cinquecento* (Turin, 1965), pp. 11–19.

2. A convenient summary of Lucchese government prior to 1400 appears in Christine Meek, *Lucca 1369–1400: Politics and Society in an Early Renaissance City-State* (Oxford, 1978), pp. 6–16. For constitutional arrangements after 1430, see A. N. Cianelli, *Dissertazioni sopra la storia lucchese*, published as *Memorie e documenti per servire all'istoria della città e stato di Lucca*, II (Lucca, 1814), pp. 151–217. More generally, Lucchese political structures are discussed in some detail in S. Bongi, ed., *Inventario del R. Archivio di Stato in Lucca*, 4 vols. (Lucca, 1872–88), 1:82ff.

3. Notably Nicolao di Lazzaro Guinigi, who in December 1430–January 1431 offered to rally his supporters in Lucca and in the Garfagnana in support of Florence; and Jacobo di Giovanni Viviani, who left Lucca for Florence in November 1432 and thereafter conspired with the Florentines against his *patria*. For Guinigi see, particularly, *Archivio di Stato dini Lucca* (henceforth A.S.L.) *Sentenze e bandi*, 159, fols. 166^r–67^v, 178^r–79^r. The affairs of Viviani may be traced in *Biblioteca Statale di Lucca* (henceforth B.S.L.) MS 1139; G. Vincenzo Baroni, *Notizie genealogiche della famiglie lucchesi*, fols. 225^r–48^r; A.S.L. *Bibliotecha Manoscritti*, no. 38, *Storia di Lucca scritta da Giuseppe Civitali e riordinata da Daniello De'Nobili, dall'origine di esse città sino al 1572*, fols. 389^r, 391^v; *Sentenze e bandi*, 160, fols. 127^r–28^r.

4. Both the Cenami murder and the conspiracy of ser Tommaso Lupardi are explored by Francesco Acton, *La morte di Pietro Cenami e la congiura di ser Tommaso Lupardi raccontate sui documenti dell'Archivio di Lucca* (Lucca, 1882).

Acton here provides an accurate and very detailed narrative of events, drawn from the court records and from the series *Riformagioni Pubbliche* of the *Consiglio Generale*. A clearer understanding of the issues and personalities involved rests on a multiplicity of incidental references in the rich notarial archives of Lucca, and among the Medici correspondence preserved in the *Archivio di Stato di Firenze* (henceforth A.S.F.).

5. See particularly the proceedings of 1490 against Andrea Mei, Nese Franchi, and others: A.S.L. *Cause Delegate*, 4, pp. 21–35.

6. Of the leading conspirators of 1430, Pietro Cenami, Nicolao Streghi, and Lorenzo Buonvisi were all apparently resident in the *contrade* of *S. Frediano* and of *S. Giovanni Capo di Borghi*. Tiero Gentili and Giovanni da Ghivizzano lived nearby in the *contrade* of *S. Pier Cigoli* and *S. Lucia verso Fillungo* (or *S. Lucia verso archo*) respectively. Only Nicolao Neri came from outside of the *terziere* of *S. Frediano*. Neri lived in the *contrada* of *S. Masseo* in the *terziere* of *S. Paolino*. The location of individuals can be gleaned from Baroni, *Notizie genealogiche*; from A.S.L. *Imprestiti*, 21, for the assessment of 1431; and from a host of incidental notarial references.

7. Baroni, *Notizie genealogiche*, MS 1113, fols. 315^r, 317^v; and A.S.L. *Archivio dei notari, Testamenti*, 11, ser Domenico Ciomucchi, fol. 65^r. If the Gentili had long possessed sepulchres in the chapel of S. Caterina, there are also a number of early references connecting both the Cenami and the Streghi with the church of *S. Frediano*.

8. The events of 1436 involved members of the di Poggio family; their dependents living amongst them in the person of Lorenzo Cattani and of Tommaso Mercati; and a member of the neighboring Burlamacchi family.

9. Gerardo di Stefano Spada, alone amongst those implicit in the Guinigi plots of the 1440s, was resident outside of the Guinigi *terziere* of *S. Martino*—in *S. Salvatore in prima ruga del borgo*. Of the leading Guinigi supporters, the Angiorelli and the Fornari appear to have lived to the west of the Guinigi in the *contrade* of *S. Maria in via* and of *S. Quirico* respectively; the Anguilla and Orlando della Piastra lived to the southwest in or around the *contrada* of *SS. Giovanni e Reparata*.

10. Meek, *Lucca 1369–1400*, pp. 194–236, 366–67.

11. S. K. Cohn, *The Laboring Classes in Renaissance Florence* (New York, 1980), pp. 43–63.

12. The point is made by Meek herself, *Lucca 1369–1400*, p. 214.

13. Cohn, *Laboring Classes*, p. 63.

14. Cohn's thesis is implicitly countered by F. W. Kent, *Household and Lineage in Renaissance Florence: The Family Life of the Capponi, Ginori, and Rucellai* (Princeton, 1977); D. V. and F. W. Kent, *Neighbours and Neighbourhood in Renaissance Florence: The District of the Red Lion in the Fifteenth Century* (New York, 1982). See also the thoughtful comments on the sources used by Cohn in Ronald F. E. Weissman, *Ritual Brotherhood in Renaissance Florence* (New York, 1982), p. 12

15. Nicolai Rubinstein, *The Government of Florence under the Medici (1434 to 1494)* (Oxford, 1966), pp. 63–65.

16. Kent, *Household and Lineage*, pp. 264–51.

17. B.S.L. MS 38, *Ricordi Storici di Martino Bernardini*, fol. 346ᵛ.

18. Baroni, *Notizie genealogiche*, MS 1128, fols. 1ʳ–183ᵛ; M. E. Bratchel, "The *consorteria* in Fifteenth-Century Tuscany: In Pursuit of a Historical Definition," *Unisa Medieval Studies*, I (1983), 19–24; B.S.L. MS 62, *Memorie diverse di Lucca*, pp. 378–79.

19. For the events of 2–3 June 1436, see A.S.L. *Podestà di Lucca*, 5229, no foliation. A detailed discussion of the di Poggio conspiracy of 1522 appears in Berengo, *Nobili e mercanti*, pp. 83–107.

20. Taddeo di Poggio was often absent from Lucca in Venice; see A.S.L. *Cause Delegate*, 2, passim; and *Archivio dei notari*, 705, ser Benedetto Franciotti, pp. 403–04. It is true that in 1431, whilst absent in Venice, Taddeo was assessed with other members of the clan in the *contrada* of S. Lorenzo in Poggio; see A.S.L. *Imprestiti*, 21, fol. 5ʳ.

21. The relationship of Pietro di Nicolao to the main branch of the Guinigi family

is clarified in A.S.L. *Archivio Guinigi*, 151, *memorie e note di Michele q. di Giovanni q. Michele q. di Lazari Guinigi, principate l'anno 1447*, fols. 60ᵛ–61ʳ.

22. A.S.L. *Cause Delegate*, 3, pp. 3–6, 11–28, 33–42.

23. Baroni, *Notizie genealogiche*, MS 1108, fol. 10ᵛ.

24. A.S.L. *Imprestiti*, 21, fols. 25ʳ, 28ʳ.

25. Baroni, *Notize genealogiche*, MS 1108, fols. 41ʳ, 49ʳ⁻ᵛ; A.S.L. *Archivio dei notari*, 374, ser Paolo di Michele ser Federighi Bianchi, fol. 183ʳ; *Archivio dei notari*, *Testamenti*, ser Benedetto Franciotti, I, fols. 248ᵛ–49ᵛ, 520ᵛ–23ᵛ; and II, fols. 119ʳ–21ʳ, 212ʳ–13ʳ, 309–13ʳ, 344ʳ–49ᵛ.

26. A.S.L. *Archiviio dei notari*, *Testamenti*, 11, ser Domenico Ciomucchi, fol. 65ʳ; Baroni, *Notizie genealogiche*, MS 1110, fol. 34ʳ.

27. A.S.L. *Podestà di Lucca*, 5362, fol. 175ʳ⁻ᵛ.

28. M. Luzzati, "Cenami, Pietro" in *Dizionario biografico degli italiani*, 23 (Rome, 1979), p. 502; "Le fonti spiegano il grave fatto di sangue come una vendetta privata di un giovane Poggio al quale il C(enami) avrebbe impedito il matrimonio con una ricca e nobile fanciulla della famiglia del Portico, di cui era tutore."

29. A.S.L. *Archivio dei notari*, *Testamenti*, 11, ser Domencio Ciomucchi, fols. 157ʳ–59ᵛ.

30. Nicolao Tegrimi, *Le vite di Castruccio Castracani de gl'Anteliminelli nelli Principe de Lucca* (Lucca, 1556), p. 111.

31. A.S.L. *Archivio dei notari*, 429, ser Domenico Arrigi, fols. 37ʳ–38ᵛ.

32. The interaction of individuals, the range of personal slights and animosities, were, in reality, very complex. I shall be treating the Cenami affair in much greater depth in my forthcoming book on fifteenth-century Lucca.

33. B.S.L. MS 32, *Ricordi Storici di Martino Bernardini*, fol. 423ʳ⁻ᵛ.

34. *Libri di ricordanze* have provided a particularly rich source for Florentine history. For a general survey of this material, see P. J. Jones, "Florentine Families and Florentine Diaries in the Fourteenth Century," *Papers of the British School at Rome*, 24 (1956), pp. 183–205.

35. Particularly A.S.L. *Archivio Guinigi*, 29, *Libro di ricordi e note di contratti di Girolamo quondam Giiovanni quondam Michele Guinigi, fatto e cominciato nel 1468, segnato AA—anzi in sua origine era segnato B—dell'archivio di nostra casa Guinigi*; and *Michele Guinigi*, 151; and *Memorie e note*.

36. My finding essentially agree with those of Vito Tirelli, "I 'libri di ricordanze' a Lucca," in *La Famiglia e la vita quotidiana in Europa dal '100- al '600: Fonti e problemi: Atti del convegno internazionale, Milano 1–4 dicembre 1983* (Rome, 1986), pp. 123–65. .

37. Tirelli, "I 'libri di ricordanze' a Lucca," pp. 129–31.

38. Meek, *Lucca 1369–1400*, p. 349.

39. Dale Kent, *The Rise of the Medici: Faction in Florence 1426–1434* (Oxford, 1978), p. 196.

40. M. Luzzati, "Politica di salvaguardi dell'autonomia lucchese nella seconda metà del secolo xv," in *Egemonia fiorentina ed autonomie locali nella Toscana nord-occidentale del primo Rinascimento; vita, arte, coltura: Settimo convegno internazionale del Centro Italiano di Studi di Storia e d'Arte, Pistoia, 18–25 settembre 1975* (Pistoia, 1978), pp. 543–82.

41. A.S.L. *Sentenze e bandi*, 159, fols. 166^r–67^v, 178^r–79^r.

42. A.S.F. *Archivio mediceo avanti il principato*, filza XI, 143.

43. "Una personal delmondo che credo faria (fare) per me ognio cosa": A.S.L. *Cause Delegate*, 2, fasc. IV, p. 753. Cf. pp. 769, 773.

44. A.S.L. *Cause Delegate*, 4, pp. 21–35.

45. In 1428 Andrea di Biagio Mei was banished from Lucca as a notorious malefactor whose scandalous life posed a threat to public order: see A.S.L.

Consiglio Generale, Riformagioni Pubbliche, 21, pp. 371–74.

46. Acton, *La morte di Pietro Cenami*, pp. 45–69.

47. A.S.L. *Sentenze e bandi*, 161, fol. 120^v: "E queste cose accadendo verosimilmente la città di Lucca poteva esser sottoposta al sacco, e sottomessa al perpetuo giogo dei Fiorentini, vi sarebbe seguita strage di uomini e di donne, e queste ultime sarebbero soggetto di violenze e di ratti."

48. Luzzati, "Politica di salvaguardi dell'autonomia lucchese," p. 545.

49. A.S.L. *Cause Delegate*, 2, fasc. IV, pp. 745, 749.

50. A.S.L. *Cause Delegate*, 3, pp. 3–6, 11–28, 33–42.

51. A.S.L. *Sentenze e bandi*, 161, fols. 226^r–27^v; *Podestà di Lucca*, 5253, fols. 18^r–19^v.

52. A.S.L. *Consiglio Generale, Riformagioni Pubbliche*, 16, pp. 576–78, 778.

53. A.S.L. *Anziani al tempo della libertà*, 5, fol. 51^{r-v}; *Consiglio Generale, Riformagioni Pubbliche*, 15, p. 317; *Sentenze e bandi*, 159, fols. 222^v, 247^r; and *Podestà di Lucca*, 5229, no foliation.

54. Niccolò Machiavelli, *Istorie fiorentine*, ed. Plinio Carli, 2 vols. (Florence, 1927), 2:18–21.

55. A.S.L. *Cause Delegate*, 3, p. 18.

56. A.S.L. *Cause Delegate*, 3, pp. 20–22, 25–28.

57. A.S.L. *Consiglio Generale, Riformagioni Pubbliche*, 14–15, passim.

58. Bartolomeo del fu Jacopo is a strangely obscure figure. He seems to be the same man who, with his brother Antonio, appears fleetingly in the records of the court of merchants for 1432 as residents in the *contrada* of *S. Giustina*; see A.S.L. *Corte de'mercanti*, 150, *Cause civili*, fol. 45^r. For his part in the di Poggio conspiracy see, particularly, *Podestà di Lucca*, 5229, no foliation.

Public Policy and Private Profit: Tax Farming in Fourteenth-Century Lucca

CHRISTINE MEEK

The ordinary revenues of the commune of Lucca in the fourteenth century, as in other Tuscan and North Italian communes, were based on a large number of levies on the import, export, or sale of different categories of goods, on various activities or transactions, or on particular categories of people. These levies are called *proventi* or gabelles in Lucchese documents. They include the *gabella maggiore*, or customs duty on the more valuable categories of imports and exports, the general gabelle on the import and export of less valuable goods, the gabelle on the import of wine, the monopoly of salt and levies on the sale or processing of foodstuffs, such as the butchering of animals, the grinding of flour or the retail sale of bread and wine within the city, along with similar levies in the Six Miles, that is, the area immediately surrounding the city, and in each vicariate. There were also dues on contracts and alienations of property, on rents and leases, on moneylenders and innkeepers, on market gardens and mills, on the monopoly of gaming tables, on prostitutes, who were confined to a *bordello*, and on the administration of the communal prisons.[1]

These levies produced widely varying sums, ranging from the *gabella maggiore*, the salt monopoly, and the retail wine tax in the city, which at times each yielded well over ten thousand florins a year, through levies such as a gabelle on contracts or on the *borghi* and *sobborghi*, which produced a maximum of about £6,000 *buona moneta*,[2] down to *proventi* such as the seal of weights and measures and the gabelle on mills or on market gardens, which at best yielded a few hundred pounds, with one gabelle—that on the weighing of straw and hay—producing no more than a maximum of £100 and a minimum of £15. Some of the most lucrative of these levies were always administered by the commune directly—the *gabella maggiore*, the other gabelles on imports and exports, the salt monopoly and judicial fines—but many *proventi* were regularly farmed out. The practice of tax farming thus applies to the vast majority of Lucchese *proventi* numerically, but because several extremely lucrative levies were always administered directly, less than half of the total revenues of the commune came from taxes that were farmed. It is these farmed *proventi* and the system under which they were administered which is the subject of this paper.

The practice of tax farming was firmly established by the time we first have information on the finances under Castruccio Castracani.[3] It continued with a possible interruption after 1362 when Lucca was under Pisan rule and Lucchese revenues were being administered by Pisa,[4] but after 1369, when Lucca regained her freedom, many of the most important of the *proventi* that had earlier been farmed began to be administered directly. Farming was then mainly confined to the gabelles of the vicariates and to some marginal *proventi*, such as those on the prisons, gambling, and prostitutes. This continued to the time of Paolo Guinigi and beyond.[5] From at least 1323 until about 1362 farming was the normal method of administration for many *proventi*. When such *proventi* were administered directly in this period it was because circumstances made farming impossible—during the siege of Lucca 1341–42;[6] after 1354 when losses sustained by the farmers of the retail wine gabelle meant that no one was prepared to take the risk of farming it;[7] or after 1362 when political difficulties again made it hard to find men willing to farm the *proventi*.[8]

Communal records stretching from the 1320s to the 1380s show exceptionally clearly how the tax farming system worked over a long period of time. Contracts to farm a particular *provento* were sold to the highest bidder at the public auction conducted by the *precones* in the *Consiglio Generale* with special efforts by the commune to induce bidders to offer as much as possible. The records of these auctions are preserved in the series *Proventi Incanti* in the *Archivio di Stato in Lucca*. They often include a figure written at the top of the left hand page. Although its significance is never explained, it always seems to represent the sum for which that particular *provento* had been sold in the previous year, and thus the figure at which the auctioneer should aim, but it was not a reserve price, and *proventi* were sometimes sold for lower sums. The sale of any particular *provento* was not normally achieved on a single occasion but stretched over several sessions. The procedure was as follows. The auctioneer first invited bids and a number would be forthcoming, the highest of them usually well below the figure that the commune hoped to achieve. At the same or at subsequent sessions the commune would begin to offer inducements in order to elicit higher bids. These inducements would initially be modest: 10s. would be offered to the highest bidder for each further £100 bid, then 20s. or 40s. per £100 bid, £3 and in some cases £4, £5, and £6 for each additional £100. In the final stages inducements were often in the form of so many *denarii* or *solidi* for each additional £1. Again these would begin at modest levels of 6d. or 1s. in the £1, but might rise to 5s. or even 10s. in the £1 for additional bids.

When these inducements had ceased to elicit any higher bids, the auctioneer proceeded to the final stage, which consisted of fixing on a sum well beyond any figure yet bid and then gradually bringing it down a little at a time until a sum was reached at which one of the bidders was prepared to take the *provento*. No further inducements were offered at this stage. The most striking aspect of the system is the persistence of the commune in its attempts to achieve quite modest increases in the selling price of *proventi*, even if this meant missing the date at which the tax farming contract had been scheduled to begin. In 1337 it took four further sessions of the auction of the gabelle on moneylenders and innkeepers between 4 and 15 January to raise the price by only £10 above the figure of £1,000, which Lucetto Sbarra had been prepared to pay on 3 January.[9] Belluccino Dombellinghi had bid £29,100 for the retail wine gabelle on 12 April, and strenuous efforts by Lucca in at least ten additional sessions of the auction only succeeded in raising this to £30,100 at the cost of missing the date of 1 May on which the sale had been due to begin. This meant that the gabelle had to be re-scheduled to begin on the date that a purchase agreement was reached, which in the event was not until 25 August.[10]

Contracts were almost invariably for one year only, which probably worked out to the benefit of the commune, allowing it to take advantage of any increase in the value of the *provento*, and probably made tax farmers willing to offer higher figures than they might have otherwise, since they were only committing themselves for one year at a time.[11] But tax farming in Lucca was organized in such a way as to offer a number of advantages to the farmers, limiting the amount of liquid capital that they needed to have at their disposal and reducing the risk of loss from unforeseen circumstances. This in turn offered benefits to the commune in that it reduced the likelihood of tax farmers defaulting on their obligations, thereby throwing the finances into confusion.

Tax farmers did not have to pay the purchase price in one lump sum. It was normally divided into twelve monthly installments called *paghe*. The farmer did not have to pay even the first *paga* on the day his contract began; they were payable in arrears. Until 1342 each *paga* was due in the middle of each month, and from 1342 onwards it was due on the last day of the month,[12] so that the farmer would not have completed his payment of the purchase price until the very last day of his contract. The advantage to the contractor of this system of payment by installments is obvious. He did not need to have large sums of capital to enable him to make payments to the commune before he had been able to collect something from the taxpayers. While some *proventi*, such as the seal of weights and measures or the gabelle on moneylenders, were seasonal, payable only once or twice a year, and the farmers of these may have needed to make some payments to the commune before they had received much from the taxpayers, most farmers would probably find that receipts covered all or part of the first *paga* by the time it fell due.

From the point of view of the commune, the system of tax farming with payment in twelve equal installments meant that the amount due from each *provento* would be fixed and known well in advance, it would be net of any salaries or other expenses and would be spread evenly throughout the year. While some tax farmers were a little late in making their payments or even fell seriously into arrears, there are far more examples of the system working smoothly. It was not at all uncommon for the farmers of the various *proventi* to pay each *paga* regularly as it fell due. The bi-monthly receipts of the *camarlingo generale* from each *provento* often add up to precisely the total of the two *paghe* due in those two months.

Lucchese tax farmers were protected against loss to some extent by a system that provided for compensation or discounts—*restauro*, as it was called—in certain circumstances. The most regular and most financially significant examples of *restauro* applied to the *proventus farine* or gabelle on flour. Certain ecclesiastics and religious houses were exempt from this levy,[13] but the quantities they imported were carefully recorded, and the buyers of the *proventus farine* were granted *restauro* for the appropriate sum month by month. Thousands of *staia* of flour at 2s. per *staio* could amount to discounts of hundreds of pounds off the agreed purchase price. It would obviously have been much simpler administratively to farm the *proventus farine* exclusive of the imports by ecclesiastics, but the more accurate, if more complex, form of calculation was preferred.

The tax farmers' contracts often provided for *restauro* in the event of military operations that affected receipts. If there was a general mobilization, certain *proventi* that would be affected by the absence of large numbers of potential consumers—the retail wine tax, the gabelle on meat, and, interestingly, the gabelle on gaming tables—were to revert to the commune for the duration of military operations, and their farmers would be compensated by being allowed to retain them for a corresponding period after the term of their contracts would normally have expired.[14] In the case of more limited military operations, the "proventuals" were allowed a discount, their loss usually being assessed by two men, one chosen by the commune and the other by the proventuals themselves, with provision for a third to be added if the first two were unable to agree.[15]

Given Lucca's checkered history in the fourteenth century, it was often necessary to grant *restauro* because political disorders or loss of control of part of Lucchese territory had prevented tax farmers from enforcing their rights. It would have been defeatist to provide for this in tax farming contracts, but the justice of claims to *restauro* in such circumstances was readily accepted.[16] The sales contracts did specify gabelle rates and other conditions, and any change in these to the detriment of proventuals would give them a claim to compensation. When Lucca reduced the gabelle on flour from 2s. 5d. to 2s. per *staio* in May 1339, the farmers of the flour gabelle and the gabelle on the sale of bread were allowed the corresponding discounts without even having to ask.[17] When there was a temporary prohibition on the sale of wine in Lucca, when mills in the Serchio were destroyed on the orders of the *Anziani*, when a temporary bridge was built across the Serchio to the detriment of the farmers of the ferry boat, the appropriate discounts were allowed.[18]

Since petitions for *restauro* were recorded only if they were successful, it is not clear how often proventuals petitioned in vain.

There are references to previous but unsuccessful petitions in some cases,[19] but proventuals could normally hope for at least a modest *restauro* if their receipts had been affected by military operations, political disorders, or reverses or changes in Lucchese policy with regard to gabelles. The compensation might have been less than they had requested, but it is unlikely that they had underestimated their losses in the first place.

The occasions on which *restauro* was granted did not by any means, however, cover all contingencies. Grants were made only in cases where the loss could be attributed to causes for which the commune was, broadly speaking, responsible. There are neither grants nor any record of petitions for compensation for losses that resulted from misfortune or from miscalculation on the part of the proventuals. There was no *restauro* if bad weather or a poor harvest reduced the takings of the flour gabelle, the retail wine tax, or the gabelle on market gardens; if murrain among flocks or disorders in the areas from which animals were imported reduced the yield of the tax on butchering; or if a decline in economic activity adversely affected the gabelle on rents and certain industrial activities. It was not possible to obtain compensation if a gabelle unexpectedly yielded much less than anticipated or fell short of the receipts of previous years. The proventuals themselves bore these risks and were expected to allow for these possibilities. Some reductions do seem to have been allowed in the quite exceptional circumstances of 1348, although information is meager, since Lucchese revenues were at that time being paid directly to Pisa.[20] Normally, however, the proventuals bore the risks, and some of them did take losses.

But if the commune was stringent in the matter of discount to tax farmers, it was surprisingly lavish in another respect; namely, in the payment of what was called *beneficium incantus*, the cash sums offered to bidders in order to induce them to pay higher prices in the course of the auction. Although these *beneficia* were offered in Lucchese *piccioli*, not the more valuable *buona moneta*, and were liable to a small deduction for gabelle,[21] they could be a great source of profit to bidders and tax farmers and a heavy charge on the commune. It was normal for the commune to incur such obligations in the course of the auction, although sales were occasionally conducted without the offer of *beneficia*. Also there was usually not just one *beneficium* payment on each *provento* but, often, two or three. Small *beneficia* of £5 or £10 were frequent and many were less than £50, but higher sums were not unusual, and occasionally an individual received several hundred pounds. A typical example of *beneficia* on a modest *provento* is the gabelle on the *borghi* and *sobborghi* for 1354. The selling price was £3,200 *buona moneta* and each *paga* was £322 4s. 5d. *piccioli*, but £133 of the first *paga* was to be deducted for *beneficia* of £9 9s., £47 4s. 6d. and £29 2s. for three unsuccessful bidders and £47 4s. 6d. for the buyer himself.[22] Higher sums were paid to buyers of other *proventi* the same year; £94 9s. on the gabelle on contracts and £226 13s. on the retail wine tax.[23] Sums over £100 were by no means unusual; £257 1s. 6d. were paid on the gabelle on butchering, two *beneficia* of £147 8s. 5d. and £206 7s. 3d. on the bread tax, and two of £188 13s. 6d. and £594 6s. on the retail wine tax in the city, all in 1342.[24] *Beneficia* were payable within a month and were disbursed in the form of a discount on the purchase price in the case of buyers of the *provento* in question, while unsuccessful bidders were paid their *beneficia* in cash. These cash payments were made by the commune if no sale of that particular *provento* had been concluded; otherwise they were paid by the buyer, who was then allowed a corresponding discount.[25]

Since any *beneficia* promised were always allowed off the first *paga* of a *provento*, they could make serious inroads into it and, in the case of a few minor *proventi*, could absorb the first *paga* completely and begin to eat into the second. In 1342 each *paga* of the gabelle on the *borghi* and *sobborghi* was £304 10s. *picc.*, but *bene-*

ficia of £87 16s. reduced the first *paga* to £216 14s.[26] The first *paga* of the most important *provento*, the retail wine gabelle, was reduced from £2,583 11s. 4d. to £1,749 12s. 4d. by five *beneficia* totalling £833 19s, and that of the bread tax was reduced from £776 15s. 9d. to £337 18s. 7d. by five *beneficia* totalling £398 17s. 2d.[27] *Beneficia* of £158 1s. 6d. absorbed all of the first *paga* of £88 9s. 5d. of the gabelle on moneylenders and innkeepers and reduced the second to a mere £18 17s. 4d.[28] The most remarkable case is the gabelle on certain court dues, where *beneficia* of £114 17s. 3d. totally absorbed the first two *paghe* of £55 13s. 6d. each and nibbled £3 10s. 3d. off the third.[29] These are exceptional and the *beneficia* perhaps disproportionate to the value of the *proventi*, but *beneficia* that absorbed half or more of the first *paga* were not uncommon.

Nevertheless, it is easy to see why the commune persisted with the system. The maximum the commune ever offered for a higher bid was 10s. in the £1 or 50%, and that only at the very final stage of the auction, and thus applicable only to the last few pounds bid. Offers of *beneficia* clearly did produce higher bids, although it could be argued that, since they were aware that the communal authorities would eventually offer *beneficia*, bidders may have held back once a certain stage of the auction was reached in order to await such offers. It would presumably have caused difficulties, at least temporarily, had the commune ceased to offer *beneficia*, but, in any case, there is no sign that it ever thought of doing so, and the offer of *beneficia* for higher bids remained part of the auction system well into the 1380s.[30]

From the point of view of the bidders and tax farmers the advantages of the system are obvious. There was a price below which the commune would not be prepared to sanction the sale of a particular *provento*, so buyers were being offered financial inducements for bidding sums that they would have had to offer in any case, if they seriously wished to buy that *provento*. This may have been the reason why Francesco di Parente Onesti kept increasing his offers for the gabelle on gaming tables in 1460, although there were no other bidders.[31] The *beneficium* was counted off the first *paga*, which was the point at which tax farmers were most likely to be short of cash, if they had not yet collected much from the *provento*. Nevertheless, it is difficult to see why ser Gerardo di ser Ugo, who had already bought the gabelle on *cittadini selvatichi* for £1,335 *buona moneta* in 1337, should have been prepared to pay £15 *picc.*, unless it was to win general good will.[32]

The advantages of the system for bidders who were not the eventual buyer of that particular *provento* were even greater, since they received their payments of *beneficium* in cash. It was thus possible to derive a profit from tax farming without actually buying a *provento*. And the sums involved could be considerable. Even £50 *picc.* was well over ten florins and would be the equivalent of several months' salary for many officials. Bettuccio Catrignella received £174 6s. 8d, or over 40 florins, from the retail wine tax in 1342, without being the purchaser. It was also possible to earn *beneficia* from several *proventi* at the same time. In 1342 ser Guglielmo Guidi obtained £188 13s. 6d. from the retail wine tax, £82 11s. 6d. from the gabelle of Camaiore, and £206 7s. 3d. from the bread tax, a total of nearly 120 florins, although he purchased only the last of these *proventi*. Belluccino Dombellinghi received £594 6s. and £147 8s. 5d. from the retail wine tax and the bread tax, as well as £158 1s. 6d. on the gabelle on money lenders, which he actually purchased—a total of nearly 220 florins. The amount he received as *beneficia* on the first two *proventi* would cover between eight and nine *paghe* of the *provento* that he did buy.[33]

Although the most obvious advantages accrued to bidders who earned *beneficia* without actually buying the *provento* in question, it is doubtful that bids were deliberately made with this in mind. It would have been a risky business, since bidders remained bound to their offers for a considerable period after that particular session of the auction was over. In 1342 this period was limited to a month, having earlier often been longer.[34] It was not uncommon for a *provento* to be knocked down to someone for a bid made at an earlier session of the auction. Virtually all those recorded as receiving *beneficia* were serious bidders, who formed part of the body of regular tax farmers. Frequently, while earning *beneficia* on a *provento* that eventually was sold to someone else, they bid successfully for another *provento* on the same occasion. Nevertheless, collusion among bidders to ensure the maximum *beneficia* for some of their number in the course of reaching a figure at which the commune would be prepared to sell the *proventi* cannot be ruled out.

Tax farmers were required to provide suitable guarantors. In a society in which not only all communal officials but also people dealing with the public in humble capacities, such as millers and washerwomen, had to give sureties,[35] individuals engaged in such an important activity as tax farming, in which they handled large sums of public money, naturally had to do the same. The ability to provide adequate guarantors was of the highest importance. If a man could not provide satisfactory guarantors, he could not act as a tax farmer, as Puccinello della Rocca found to his cost in 1354. He petitioned that he had bought the local gabelle at Cerruglio for 1354–55 for £1,555 *buona moneta*, but because of heavy losses he had sustained as farmer of the gabelle on meat the previous year, the citizens who had undertaken to act as his guarantors had backed out. When he was summoned by the major syndic to give guarantors, he had been unable to do so, with the result that he had been fined £1,555 *buona moneta*, and the gabelle of Cerruglio was put up for auction again. Since the amount of his fine corresponded exactly with the sum he had agreed to pay for the *provento*, he was in effect being held responsible for the price, even though the *provento* had been taken away from him.[36]

The provision of sureties as a *sine qua non* for tax farming is emphasized in the conditions imposed in the sale of the gabelle of the vicariate, Pomezana and Stazzema. Manuele Sbarra stood surety for Pomezana for half of the purchase price but agreed that, if Stazzema failed to find a guarantor, he would stand surety for the entire sum, and the whole *provento* would then belong to Pomezana. Clearly if Stazzema could not find a guarantor, it could not share in the purchase.[37] In 1356 ser Angelo di ser Giusto of Pistoia and a lady called Fiore from Florence, who were the associates or partners of the farmer of the gabelle on prostitutes, had deposited three women's tunics in the cote hardie style with silver buttons, until such time as they were able to give an approved guarantor, whereupon they got the tunics back.[38]

Guarantors had to be approved by communal officials as suitable and of sufficient resources for the sum in question. In the case of a *provento* of modest yield one guarantor might be given, although on occasions two or three sureties were given for sums as low as £200 or £300. Conversely there are examples of a single individual standing surety for thousands of pounds, although it would be more usual for several guarantors to be named. In the case of the financially most significant gabelles there would often be many guarantors. There were five guarantors for £7,230 for the bread tax in 1337, ten for £7,825 in 1340, and nine for £5,800 in 1344, although only two guarantors for £7,625 in 1340 and three for £9,000 in 1342.[39] There were between five and nine guarantors for the flour tax for sums between £15,000 and £18,440 between 1339 and 1345, although only two people guaranteed £20,00 in 1337 and the same sum in 1347.[40] The most important *provento* of all, the retail wine gabelle, which sold for between £24,500 and £34,210 between 1337 and 1353, normally had at least six guarantors; and in 1352 it had thirteen and in 1351 seventeen, although only three men had stood surety for £30,100 in 1337.[41] Presumably a larger number was preferred both by the commune and by the guarantors themselves in the case of the most important *proventi*. The guarantors would naturally want to limit their risk, and the commune would wish to have a larger number of men on whom it might call, should the tax farmer himself default. However, the correlation between the financial significance of the gabelle and the number of guarantors is only very approximate. The guarantee for trivial sums was sometimes shared among two or three men, while in other cases single individuals were prepared to guarantee several thousand pounds and were accepted by the commune as adequate to do so; or two or three men guaranteed tens of thousands of pounds, while on other occasions it took eight or ten or more to cover similar sums.

Where there were several guarantors, they might guarantee the whole sum jointly—*insolidum*—or they might each guarantee only a portion of it, either a fraction of the total or a specific maximum figure. Until about 1350 guarantees *insolidum* seem to have been more common, but after that date lists of guarantors sometimes specify the amount or the proportion for which each man committed himself. It is possible that the difference was only apparent and sprang from the way in which the officials noted the guarantee, but it seems more likely that it represented a real change; after all, the precise obligation that a guarantor was undertaking was an important matter, which needed to be recorded carefully. Joint guarantees with no fixed proportions continued, but there seems to have been a growing practice for each surety to guarantee only a proportion of the price for the most important gabelles.

The proportion for which each guarantor stood surety could vary, and the whole guarantee could become decidedly complicated. When Donato Boccansocchi guaranteed one half and ser Guglielmo Guidi and ser Bartolomeo Bonotelli each guaranteed one quarter of the sum of £10,350, which Nuccino Boccansocchi agreed to pay for the flour tax in 1359, this was a comparatively simple transaction.[42] In 1358 Ludovico Corbi guaranteed one sixth, ser Nicolao Barellia one eighth, ser Arrigo Sartoy, Giovannino Arnaldi, and Chelluccio Ugolini a half jointly, and ser Nicolao Barellia

another eighth and later another quarter of the sum of £6,610 that
ser Guglielmo Guidi was to pay for the gabelle on meat.[43] The
greatest complexities, however, are found in the retail wine tax.
The guarantee for £25,300 in 1351 was made up as follows: one
man guaranteed one fifth, and four men each guaranteed one tenth,
two of them later being said to have guaranteed one fifth jointly;
there were three men who each guaranteed one twelfth and
Castruccio del Veglio guaranteed one twenty-fourth; Nerio Cassiani
guaranteed one eighth and Geo Bovi one twenty-fourth, to be
counted in this eighth; Francesco Bottacci guaranteed £150 out of
the twenty-four for which Castruccio del Veglio had already stood
guarantor, and Chelluccio Ugolini joined Giovanni di Dino Onesti,
who had already guaranteed one twelfth.[44] The next year the sale
price was £24,500, for which two men guaranteed one fifth jointly
and two others one twentieth jointly; two men guaranteed one
twentieth each and one man one eighth and another one tenth. Two
groups, one of three men and one of four men, guaranteed one
quarter, while two other men acted as guarantors with no limit specified. As in the previous year, additional guarantors were sometimes added for a proportion of the price already covered. Baldo
Boccansocchi and Paolino Vinciguerra had stood surety for one
quarter of the price on 25 September; on 22 October they were
joined by Tottorino di Poggio as guarantor for this same quarter.
Ser Cione Guerci and Franceschino Dombellinghi had guaranteed
one quarter on 27 September; on 17 October ser Cinello Flammi
and on 25 October Dino Volpastri were added as additional guarantors for this quarter.[45] The initial guarantors may have been regarded as inadequate for the sums involved, and the additional
guarantors may have been provided at the insistence of the communal authorities, since it was only on 29 October that all the guarantors together received official approval. Whether it was at the
wish of the guarantors themselves or at the insistence of the communal authorities, the subdivision of the guarantee was clearly to

spread the risk and bring the sum guaranteed into line with the guarantors' resources.

Guarantors had to be approved by the Lucchese officials appointed for the purpose, the *approbatores fideiussonum*, who were responsible for approving all guarantors, not just those given by tax farmers. There seem to have been two *approbatores* in the 1340s and three in the 1350s, but some of them held office for several years at a time. Belluccino Dombellinghi was certainly *approbator* in 1342, 1345, and 1347–48, in which year he died, and he may well have held the office continuously from 1342 to 1348.[46] Orlandino Mordecastelli was *approbator* in 1342 and 1343,[47] and there are other examples of men holding the office for more than one year at a time.

The office of *approbator* was held by much the same category of men as engaged in tax farming, and this led to some curious duplications and apparent conflicts of interest. Belluccino Dombellinghi as *approbator* approved the guarantors offered by his brother Petro.[48] Coluccino di ser Ugo approved the guarantors his brother Gerardo offered for the gabelle on *cittadini selvatichi* in 1340 and approved his brother as a guarantor for another *provento*.[49] Belluccino Dombellinghi was a bidder for a number of *proventi* while *approbator*, and subsequently approved the guarantors offered by the eventual buyers of these *proventi* in the cases of the bread tax in 1342, the seal of the weights and measures, the gabelle on rents, on *cittadini selvatichi*, the *borghi* and *sobborghi*, and on the vicariate of Camaiore in 1345.[50]

Belluccino Dombellinghi himself was the buyer of the gabelle on moneylenders and innkeepers in 1342, although his guarantors were approved by the other *approbator* and not by himself.[51] He stood guarantor for a *provento* while *approbator* in 1343, as did Orlandino Mordecastelli while he was *approbator*. It is not recorded who approved them, but they probably did not approve themselves. Certainly when Bartolomeo Arnolfi stood guarantor for ser Nicolao de Ghivizzano in 1352, he was approved by the other *approbator*, Puccinello Galganetti.[52] Michele Accettanti did approve himself as one of the guarantors for the gabelles on meat and the sale of bread in 1359, as did Coluccino Peri for the purchase of the right to run a ferry boat on the Serchio in 1360, but they were also approved by their fellow *approbatores*. Their approval of themselves was probably the consequence of a regulation of 5 December 1358 that no one should act as a guarantor unless approved by three *approbatores*, although it was certainly contrary to the spirit of that regulation.[53]

The conflict of interest and scope for abuse, however, was probably less than might at first sight appear, because the *approbatores* themselves were held liable, should both the principal and the guarantors whom they had approved default.[54] They therefore had good reason to be cautious in whom they accepted and to not authorize any guarantees of doubtful reliability. When *approbatores* were accused of malpractice, it was for refusing to approve perfectly suitable guarantors, not for accepting doubtful ones.[55] *Approbatores* who formed part of the body of tax farmers were, of course, likely to be well informed about the financial resources and reliability of guarantors who were also drawn from the group of regular tax farmers and their kinsmen. The *approbatores* had themselves to give guarantors, the sum being fixed at £2,000 each in December 1358.[56] If the buyer of the *provento* or his guarantors failed to pay a sum due within a month, the *approbatores* and their guarantors became liable. This was no idle threat. On 6 October 1355 Nuccino Boccansocchi, as *approbator*, was compelled by the major official of the gabelle to pay the September *paga* of the gabelle on the prison, due from the buyer, Nicolao del Tepa and his guarantor, Franceschino Dombellinghi.[57]

While sales of *proventi* were almost invariably to a single named individual, that individual could, if he wished, share it with one or more partners, without any need for special authorization from the commune. Indeed contracts often specify that the sale is to the named buyer and anyone with whom he wishes to share it.[58] The names of partners were seldom given in documents concerned with tax farming. Since it was the buyer himself who assumed the obligations to the commune and since he required no authorization to sell part of his rights to others, there would be no reason, under ordinary circumstances, for the existence of partners to be recorded in official documents. Often the only indication that a tax farmer was acting as the head of a syndicate rather than as a single entrepreneur is the addition of the words *et sotii* after his name in the communal records. Partners were most likely to be mentioned by name in cases where the syndicate had difficulty in meeting its obligations or where disputes arose among its members, and most or the information about partnerships comes from such cases.

A dispute between Francesco Accettanti and Bettuccio Catrignella in 1342 over shares in the retail wine gabelle of the Six Miles, of which Bettuccio was the buyer, shows how complicated the position could become and how difficult it could be for the partners to keep track of the shares. Francesco swore that there were six partners: himself, Bettuccio, Coluccino Peri, Vanne del Ghiotto, Ciandoro Pantasse, and ser Guglielmo Guidi, each with one-sixth share, and four of the other five agreed on oath that this was so. But Bettuccio swore that there were seven shares, the seventh being held jointly by Nicolao del Lieto and Petro Carincione. Nicolao agreed that there were seven, but swore that he had had a full share, Bettuccio having had the seventh jointly with Petro Carincione, until Nicolao was warned by a friend, Veltrino Ciandori, not to share with Bettuccio, whereupon he gave up his share to Bettuccio. Petro Carincione also agreed that there were seven shares, but claimed that he had held one share jointly with Bettuccio and another jointly with Nicolao del Lieto, until Nicolao gave up his share to Bettuccio, whereupon Petro had asked for Nicolao's share and had given his to Bettucio.[59]

The exceptional circumstances of 1348 produced an interesting lawsuit, which illustrates both the complications of shares and sub-divisions in a *provento* and the overlap of personnel involved. Ser Guglielmo Guidi had brought the gabelle on contracts for the year beginning 1 October 1347, at the request of ser Gerardo Dati, to whom it had been knocked down at the auction. His guarantors were ser Gerardo Dati, ser Andrea Domaschi, Giovannino Arnaldi, and ser Francesco Accettanti. Ser Gerardo had, of course, also been a bidder. It is not clear why ser Guglielmo should have been acting as the purchaser, since he almost immediately sold five sixths of the *provento* to ser Gerardo and ser Andrea, that is, to two of his guarantors, keeping one sixth for himself. Ser Gerardo and ser Andrea subsequently sold ser Francesco Accettanti and Giovannino Arnaldi, the other two guarantors, one sixth of each. They did this without ser Guglielmo's knowledge, so it was clearly possible for some of the partners to sell part of their share without consulting the partner who was the nominal purchaser of the *provento*, but he was presumably on good terms with them, as his guarantors, and all might have been well in this example had ser Gerardo, ser Francesco, and ser Andrea not died in May 1348, in each case leaving heirs who were minors. Neither these heirs nor Giovannino, although he was still alive, were in a position to attend to the administration personally, and ser Guglielmo asked for a division, so that he would levy only his own sixth share.[60]

In this case ser Guglielmo clearly expected at least some of the partners to take an active part in the administration of the *provento*. Tax farmers must often have needed assistants or officials, especially if, as was frequently the case, they were farming several *proventi* at the same time or if they held *proventi* outside Lucca as well as others in the city itself. Since officials were employed by the proventuals themselves and the commune was not involved, they are rarely mentioned in official sources, but a dispute over the salary of an official in 1348–49 provides a rare glimpse of the internal administration of a farmed gabelle. Paolo de Carmignano was serving as one of three *familiari* of the gabelle on contracts in the vicariate of Camaiore at a salary of £4 per month. The tax farmer himself, ser Guglielmo Guidi, was acting as notary, and there was also a treasurer. The treasurer and two of the *familiari* died in the plague and ser Guglielmo fled, leaving no one except Paolo to act as treasurer, notary, and *familiare*, although ser Guglielmo offered him a higher salary to stay on. Ser Guglielmo tried unsuccessfully to find another *familiare* to send to Camaiore, offering a salary of £8 a month, but when the crisis was over refused to pay Paolo more than £4.[61] The resulting dispute reveals that this one *provento*, although it must have been one that was unusually difficult to administer, was employing five people in the vicariate of Camaiore alone. Since ser Guglielmo was farming this gabelle for the whole of Lucca and its territory, he must have needed to employ many more officials or have had a real need of the services of his partners.

The *provento* officials most frequently mentioned in the communal records are the *camerarii*, since it was often they who made the payments to the communal treasurer. Sometimes such men are specifically said to be the official or treasurer of that particular farmed gabelle; on other occasions they are said to be paying on behalf of the buyer from money they themselves have exacted from that gabelle, and can therefore reasonably be assumed to be acting as officials, probably as treasurers. Interestingly those acting as treasurers for others were often men who themselves engaged in tax farming as principals. Giovannino Arnaldi, the farmer of the gabelle on meat in 1355–56, acted as treasurer on behalf of ser Nicolao de Ghivizzano and his partners for the same gabelle the next year and was an unsuccessful bidder the year after that.[62] Ser Nicolao de Ghivizzano himself acted as treasurer of the gabelle on market gardens for Francesco di Parente Onesti in 1357.[63] Giovanni Mingogi acted as treasurer for the gabelle in the vicariate of Barga for Arrigaccio Castagnacci in 1357,[64] while Arrigaccio was acting as treasurer for the seal of weights and measures for ser Nicolao de Ghivizzano.[65] Ser Guglielmo Guidi, one of the most active tax farmers, served as treasurer for Paolo Corsini both for the bread tax in Lucca and for the tax on the *borghi* and *sobborghi* in 1357.[66] Geo Bovi served as treasurer for three different *proventi* for three different buyers in 1357–58.[67] There are examples of a treasurer serving in the same gabelle under two successive farmers and of two farmers serving each other as treasurers.[68]

Who were all these people? Who were the men who engaged in tax farming? First of all it is clear that, despite the appearance of a few men who only dabbled in tax farming and occasionally bought a *provento*, there was a body of men who regularly engaged in this form of investment. The existence of a body of regular bidders was recognized by the authorities. In 1338 the regular bidders were said to refuse to participate in the auctions until a time limit was set for them to be bound to their bids.[69] In 1358 regular buyers of the *proventi* were declared ineligible for certain offices.[70] Lists compiled from the records of auctions, contracts, and the *Camarlingo Generale* also make it clear that a number of men were regular bidders and buyers of *proventi*. Some of them engaged in this activity over long periods of time. Ser Guglielmo Guidi is first recorded as a tax farmer in 1336 and was still a tax farmer when he died in 1371 or 1372. Nicolao del Tepa's activities stretch from 1350 to 1371, those of Tottino de Bozzano from 1349 to 1383, ser Nicolao de Ghivizzano's from 1332 to the early 1360s, and Arrigaccio Castagnacci's from 1342 to the early 1360s. A number of men continued to be tax farmers until their deaths.

As with other forms of economic activity, there was a tendency for tax farming to run in families. Not only was ser Nicolao de Ghivizzano one of the most regular tax farmers of the 1330s, 1340s, and 1350s, but his father, ser Azzolino, was one of the earliest recorded tax farmers in 1323 and 1326, and ser Nicolao's two brothers, Petruccio and ser Lippo, also engaged in the business.[71] Both Petro and Giovanni, sons of Ciucco Tedaldini, were tax farmers, although not apparently another brother, Francesco. Several members of the Dombellinghi family engaged in the business.[72] There were five members of the Onesti family and five of the Peri family who were involved in tax farming.[73]

Before 1369 tax farming was overwhelmingly in the hands of Lucchese citizens. There was, however, no legal requirement that farmers should be citizens, and there are examples of non-Lucchese tax farmers. Bernardo Buti of Prato several times farmed the gabelle on prostitutes in the 1350s, as did Francesco, known as Borsa, of Pisa in 1356–57.[74] The gabelle on gaming tables was quite frequently farmed to non-Lucchese—Tegghia of Florence in 1338, Lanzelotto of Bologna in 1341, Bondo de la Barba in 1346, Nicolao di Bartolo Minutoli of Florence in 1361, and Giovanni Giusmanti of Pisa in 1362, but almost all of these were said to be resident in Lucca.[75] The sale of *proventi* other than those on gaming and prostitutes to non-Lucchese was rare. The various external rulers of Lucca between 1328 and 1369 did not mean crowds of tax farmers from Parma, Verona, or even Pisa. There were a few tax farmers who were Lucchese subjects, but not citizens, such as Paolo Corsini de Batona or ser Bartolomeo Bonotelli from Villa Basilica, although they, too, seem to have been settled in Lucca. There are few examples of sales of even local gabelles to local men before 1369, although it became more common after that date.[76] The tax farmers and the bidders, whether successful or unsuccessful, were overwhelmingly Lucchese citizens.

There seem to have been no social barriers to prevent men of distinguished family from engaging in tax farming. Several members of the di Poggio family did so—Ciomeo di Nicolao, Guerra di Guido, Corraduccio, and Tottorino, the latter of whom also served together with another Lucchese with claims to nobility, Puccinello de'Quartigiani, as a captain-general of an army sent against

Capraia.[77] Lemmo Bovi and his son, Geo, who were both tax farmers, were members of the Antelminelli *consorteria*. Tottino and Ghetto, sons of Bettuccio di messer Buonaccorso, were nobles of Bozzano. Members of other well-established and distinguished families, such as the Carincioni, Dombellinghi, Sbarra, and Onesti, also engaged in tax farming.[78]

But other tax farmers were of humbler origin and seem to be classic "new men." Ser Guglielmo Guidi originated from Ponte S. Pietro in the *contado*. He was granted citizenship in 1335, his brothers and other kinsmen remaining in their native village.[79] There seem to have been a number of other tax farmers of the same type—relatively modest or *contado* origin—establishing themselves in the city and making their fortune there: ser Bartolomeo Bonotelli of Villa Basilica, ser Iacobo Michelini of Pescia, Zubbino Buoni of Pistoia, Paolo Corsini of Batona, and perhaps even ser Azzolino de Ghivizzano.[80]

The leading Lucchese merchants were conspicuous by their absence from the lists of tax farmers. There were no Guinigi, Rapondi, or Forteguerra among the tax farmers, no Benettoni, Busdraghi, Moriconi, or Rossiglioni. Even a cursory examination of the personnel of tax farming suggests that, although they included men of distinguished and well-established families, some of them of sufficient status to serve as *Anziani* and councillors or as vicars in the *contado* or envoys, and although some of them must have been men of wealth, as a whole they represented the second rank rather than the first rank of Lucchese society. Louis Green argued that for the period of Castruccio, tax farmers were the second rank of merchants.[81] In the succeeding period it is doubtful whether many tax farmers were merchants at all, although a few of them were bankers. Many of the tax farmers seem to have had an administrative background, which was important to them if they were to administer the gabelles they farmed in person. It is striking how many of the most important tax farmers were notaries, whether they were "new men" or belonged to more established families—not just ser Nicolao de Ghivizzano, ser Guglielmo Guidi, or ser Giovanni Barellia, but also ser Francesco Accettanti, ser Nerio Dombellinghi, ser Arrigo di Guido Sartoy, or ser Gerardo Sbarra.

These men, and a number of others who were not notaries, combined tax farming with the holding of communal offices, especially offices concerned with finance. In a few cases men who served as tax farmers also held the important office of *camarlingo generale*, as Bartolomeo Sbarra did in 1331 and 1335 and Nuccino Boccansocchi, Donato Panichi, Fredo Martini, Francesco di Parente Onesti, and Giovanni Anguilla in the 1350s.[82] However, these were not among the most important tax farmers, with the notable exception of Francesco di Parente Onesti. He was *camarlingo generale* continuously from August 1352 until the end of September 1355, and although he had previously only bought one very minor *provento*, from that date onwards he became one of the most active tax farmers, continuing until his death in 1362.[83] It seems to have been his involvement in financial office that brought him to tax farming, and the same applies on a lesser scale to Fredo Martini and perhaps Nuccio Boccansocchi. But on the whole tax farmers served in less important, more technical offices, although Coluccino Vinciguerra and Puccinello della Rocca both served as treasurers of the salt gabelle, the latter several times.[84] Ser Orso Barsellotti, ser Nicolao de Ghivizzano, and ser Guglielmo Guidi served as notaries of the *camera*, ser Nicolao de Ghivizzano, and ser Arrigo Sartoy as notaries of the *gabella maggiore*.[85] A number of tax farmers appear as *ragionieri*, or communal auditors: ser Orso Barsellotti, Prinze Peri, Coluccino Savini, Giovanni Anguilla, ser Nicolao de Ghivizzano, and ser Opizo and Petro Dombellinghi. Ser Bartolomeo Bianchi began a career of communal office holding that was to stretch over almost fifty years at much the same time as he began to engage in tax farming.[86]

Above all, the tax farmers appear as treasurers of *proventi* on behalf of the commune, when for some reason these were being administered directly and not farmed. Ser Opizo Dombellinghi was treasurer of the gabelles on *cittadini selvatichi*, salaries, mills, and wine sold retail in the Six Miles in the last months of 1348, and other *proventi* were being administered for the commune by Francesco and Michele Accettanti, Petro Dombellinghi, Geo Bovi, Guerra di Poggio, Coluccino Vinciguerra, and Francesco di Parente Onesti in the year or two after 1348, when there were problems farming them.[87] In 1362 when political difficulties caused a number of *proventi* to revert to the commune, their erstwhile farmers continued to exact them, acting now on behalf of Lucca, and it is indicative of the close connection between tax farming and communal administration that Francesco di Parente Onesti was the farmer of two *proventi* and communal treasurer of another five when he died in 1362.[88]

These men must have embodied a fund of experience and professional expertise that could equally well be developed on behalf of the commune or for their own profit. It adds point to ser Guglielmo Guidi's desire in 1349 to separate his share of the gabelle on contracts, because his one surviving partner and the heirs of the other and their guardians were not *ydonei nec sufficientes . . . et quia non sunt instructi nec docti* in the administration of this gabelle, unlike the dead partners, who had been *plene instructi*.[89]

There is no sign of any specialized category of men acting as guarantors, certainly no indication that bankers or any other group had a monopoly on this activity, or that they charged for it.[90] Guarantors seem to come from much the same background as their principals. Some of them are obviously kinsmen—brothers, fathers, sons, cousins, who share the same surname as their principal. No doubt there are other cases where the kinship is less apparent because they had different surnames—uncles, nephews, cousins, fathers-in-law, sons-in-law, brothers-in-law. The other most obvious category among the guarantors is that of men who themselves acted as tax farmers, or kinsmen of those who did so. This is very striking. The names of men familiar as tax farmers crop up in large numbers as guarantors for others. There can have been few of the regular tax farmers who did not also act as guarantors. An examination of the lists of guarantors suggests that tax farmers found their guarantors from much the same sources as did men needing sureties for other purposes—from their relatives, business associates, friends, and, perhaps, neighbors.

In at least some cases these guarantors were also partners in that *provento*. Although partners were relatively infrequently recorded by name, there were nevertheless several clear examples of overlap between partners and guarantors. When ser Forteguerra Toringhelli bought the retail wine tax of Lucca for £28,550 in 1340, his guarantors were ser Gerardo Dati, ser Michele di Provinzale Proficati, Bettuccio di ser Lando Giunte, Arrigo de Gallo, Bartolomeo Sbarra, Lemmo Catrignella, and ser Brunetto Scandaleoni, incidentally almost all of the men who themselves acted as tax farmers. A chance survival of the names of the partners in a petition for *restauro* gives these same seven men as partners for one seventh each.[91]

The communal authorities may not have been fully aware of the fact that guarantors also had shares in a particular *provento*, but there would probably have been no very serious objection. A guarantor undertook to ensure that the purchaser observed the terms of his contract and, in particular, that he paid the installments of the purchase price as they fell due, failing which the guarantor was to pay them himself, if necessary from his own resources. From the commune's point of view the aim was to reduce the risk of loss by involving other persons of sufficient resources against whom the commune could have recourse, should the principal default. The risk was to be reduced by involving more men in the obligation. In one case ten men of Cerruglio were permitted to farm the gabelle there without giving guarantors, on the grounds that they were themselves sufficient to guarantees payment.[92] In normal cases, once one or more guarantors had been provided and accepted as having sufficient resources to fulfill the buyer's obligations in case of default, the internal arrangements between buyer and guarantor were not of primary concern to the commune and could be regarded as a private matter. Since the guarantors already had obligations to the commune in that capacity, the commune did not concern itself with their obligations as partners.

More serious from the commune's point of view and with more sinister implications is the fact that unsuccessful bidders at the auction sometimes later turn up acting as guarantors for the buyer or as partners in the *provento*, or both. Many examples could be quoted, although the names of those involved are not always recorded. Ser Arrigo Sartoy's three sureties for the gabelle on the *borghi* and *sobborghi* in 1359 included Giovanni Tedaldini, one of the unsuccessful bidders.[93] Petro Dombellinghi and Petro Carincione, two of Gaymo Macchi's three guarantors for the gabelle on *cittadini selvatichi* in 1346, had been rival bidders.[94] Ser Opizo Dombellinghi bid for the bread tax of the Six Miles in 1339 and then stood as sole guarantor for the eventual buyer, Tomuccio Overardi.[95] On occasions a *provento* was sold to one man at the wish of another, who then stood guarantor for the buyer. Ser Gerardo Dati did this for Bettuccio ser Lando Giunte in 1339 and ser Guglielmo Guidi in 1347 for the gabelle on contracts, and Giovannino Arnaldi did it for Michele Accettanti for the retail wine gabelle in the Six Miles in 1359.[96] No doubt in these cases the undertaking to act as guarantor was part of the agreement between them, although that, too, argues a degree of trust and cooperation between supposedly rival bidders.

Bidders even sometimes bid on each other's behalf. On 26 September 1358 Francesco di Parente Onesti, one of the main bidders for the gabelle of Camaiore, declared that he had in fact been bidding on behalf of ser Nicolao de Ghivizzano and that the £157

10s. *beneficium incantus* therefore belonged to ser Nicolao.[97] On 23 October 1358 Francesco bought the gabelle of the vicariate of Valdilima and ser Nicolao stood guarantor for him. But ser Nicolao himself had been a bidder through another proxy: for Puccinello della Rocca declared on 29 October that he had been bidding on behalf of ser Nicolao, who should therefore have the *beneficium incantus* of £15, which these bids had earned.[98] In the early stages of the auction for the gabelle of the vicariate of Barga on 6 October 1358, ser Nicolao had been a bidder in person, although the main competitors were ser Biagio Mariani, ser Arrigo Sartoy, and Francesco di Parente Onesti. But by 15 October ser Nicolao had reached an understanding with ser Biagio Mariani, for the latter declared that he was bidding partly for himself and partly for ser Nicolao and that half the *beneficium incantus* of £132 10s. belonged to each of them. The next day the *provento* was sold to ser Biagio *pro se et illis quibus partem dare voluerti*, which was the usual formula. It is not specifically stated that ser Nicolao had a share, but he probably did.[99] Ser Nicolao de Ghivizzano was, therefore, on terms of familiarity and confidence with Francesco di Parente Onesti, ser Biagio Mariani, and Puccinello della Rocca, at any rate in September and October 1358; and the reality of competition between them may be doubted, although Puccinello della Rocca was bidding on ser Nicolao's behalf against Francesco di Parente Onesti for the gabelle of Validilima and Francesco was one of the bidders against ser Biagio Mariani, also acting partly on ser Nicolao's behalf, for the gabelle of Barga.

Of course such examples of cooperation among men engaged in tax farming do not mean that there were no rivalries and enmities among them; Veltrino Ciandori's warning to Nicolao del Lieto not to share in a *provento* with Bettuccio Catrignella in 1342 is sufficient to show that there were.[100] Perhaps even men who could hope for a share in the farm of a gabelle if it were sold to a rival bidder would have preferred themselves to have been the buyer and be, thereby, in a position to determine the distribution of shares. But the understanding and cooperation among those engaged in tax farming must have worked to the disadvantage of the commune. There is no reason to postulate any particular scruples on the part of tax farmers. There are complaints of the extortions and oppressions that they practiced on Lucchese subjects,[101] and they were equally likely to attempt to do down the commune. Ser Guglielmo Guidi, aided and abetted by Francesco Dati and Michele Accettanti, had taken advantage of the disorders of 1355 to break into the Lucchese *camera* and steal two books of the records of the gabelle on contracts with the intention of defrauding the commune. And Guglielmo's exclusive concern with his own interests is clear from his dealings with his partners and employees in the same gabelle in 1348.[102] Francesco di Parente Onesti and his kinsman, Giovanni di Dino Onesti, had gone to the *bottega* of a creditor and threatened to slash his face if he did not pay them the two florins they claimed he owed.[103]

It is impossible to be certain at what point an understanding was reached between the eventual buyer and the unsuccessful bidder in an auction. It cannot necessarily be assumed that they had been in agreement from the very beginning to share a purchase. Auctions were frequently prolonged, with a number of sessions spread over several weeks, and agreement between two or more bidders might be reached at any point in this period. Had two men been in agreement from the very beginning, it might seem unnecessary for more than one of them to bid at all, although it has to be borne in mind that the commune would not, in fact, sell the *provento* if the bids were considered to be too low. It is possible that on occasions two bidders were in agreement from the outset, bidding against each other in collusion until the figure was just high enough for the commune to agree to the sale. But it is likely that the chief effect of understandings among bidders was at the very final stages of the auction, when the commune was trying, by offers of *beneficia incantus* and every other means at its disposal, to induce bidders to offer a little more. Even where there was no prior agreement, the knowledge that the loss of a *provento* to a rival bidder did not preclude the possibility of a share in the venture, or even the fact that two bidders were on sufficiently good terms for the loser to act as guarantor for the winner, probably took the edge off their rivalry. Competition for *proventi* was probably often less than cutthroat.

Bidders probably knew exactly what a particular gabelle was likely to bring in. They were on terms to stand surety for each other, sometimes bid on each other's behalf or in partnership, and act as officials for each other. When a *provento* was sold to one man, rival bidders sometimes appeared as partners or guarantors or both. It is difficult to avoid the conclusion that the relationships to each other were likely to be more important to tax farmers than their relations with the commune. It seems likely that while the communal authorities were striving to maximize revenues by auctioning the *proventi* to the highest bidder, holding the auction in public, carefully noting the sum that had been paid the previous year, offering *beneficia* to men to bid a little higher, and insisting on sureties from tax farmers, there were other factors of cooperation, understanding, and, perhaps, collusion among the bidders, which worked equally or more strongly against communal interests.

NOTES

My work on Lucchese finances in general and this study in particular has been greatly facilitated by grants from the Twenty-Seven Foundation towards visits to the *Archivio di Stato in Lucca* and from the Arts and Social Sciences Benefactions Fund of Trinity College Dublin towards the purchase of microfilm. I would like to express my gratitude for this assistance.

All documents cited are to be found in the Archivio di Stato in Lucca.

1. Lucchese *proventi* for 1335–36 are described in *Proventi* 1, which is discussed by S. Bongi, ed., *Inventario del R. Archivio di Stato in Lucca*, 4 vols. (Lucca, 1872–88), 2:22–29. For gabelles in other communes, see W. M. Bowsky, *The Finances of the Commune of Siena, 1287–1355* (Oxford, 1970), pp. 114–65, esp. pp. 114–15 on the difficulty of defining gabelles; C. M. de la Roncière, "Indirect taxes or 'gabelles' at Florence in the fourteenth century," in N. Rubinstein, ed., *Florentine Studies* (London, 1968), pp. 140–92; de la Roncière, *Prix et salaries à Florence au XIVe siècle, 1280–1380* (Rome, 1982), pp. 33–60; A. Molho, *Florentine Public Finances in the Early Renanissance, 1400–1430* (Cambridge, Mass., 1971), esp. pp. 45–59; M. B. Becker, "Economic change and the emerging Florentine territorial state," *Studies in the Renaissance*, 13 (1966), pp. 7–39; E. Fiumi, "Fioritura e decadenza dell'economia fiorentina," *Archivio Storico Italiano*, 117 (1959), pp. 447–52; D. Herlihy, "Direct and indirect taxation in Tuscan finance, ca. 1200–1400," in *Finances et compatabilité urbaines du XIIIe au XVIe siècle, Colloque Internationale*, Blankenberge, 6–9 IX 1962, *Actes* (Brussels, 1964), pp. 385–405; and G. L. Bosini, "Note sulle pubbliche finanze di Reggio Emilia nell'epoca comunal (1306–1326)," *Nuova Rivesta Storica*, 47 (1963), 458–96.

2. Sales of *proventi* were normally in *buona moneta*, which was a money of account valued at 58s. to the florin. Actual payments were made in Lucchese *piccioli*, which varied in value from about £3 10s.–£4 7s. to the florin in the 1340s and 1350s and £5–£5 3s. after 1369.

3. *Proventi Contratti*, 13, records sales for 1322–23 and 1325–26; discussed in Christine Meek, "Le finanze e l'amministrazione finanziaria di Lucca al tempo di Castruccio," in *Castruccio Castracani e il suo tempo*, published as *Actum Luce*, vols. XIII–XIV (Lucca 1984–85), pp. 157–72. There are also records of sales for 1316, 1319, and 1320; see L. Green, *Castruccio Castracani: A Study on the Origins and Character of a Fourteenth-Century Italian Despotism* (Oxford, 1986), p. 119. For tax farming in other communes, see Bowsky, *Finance*, pp. 120–24; de la Roncière, "Indirect taxes," pp. 176–77; Fiumi, "Fioritura e decadenza," pp. 447–49; and Bosini, "Pubbliche finanze," pp. 469–70.

4. *Anziani avanti la libertà* [hereafter cited as *Anz. av. lib.*] 41, fol. 52^v, 9 June 1361; *Anz. av. lib.* 42, fols. 44^r, 30 May, 46^r 7 June 1362, 109^r, 10 Feb. 1363; and *Anz. av. lib.* 44, fols. 10^v–12^r, 29 Nov. 1366. For Lucchese finances in the 1360s, see Christine Meek, *The Commune of Lucca under Pisan Rule, 1342–1369* (Cambridge, Mass., 1980), esp. pp. 84–85, 106–11. Other communes turned to

direct administration rather earlier; see de la Roncière, "Indirect taxes," pp. 182–85; and Herlihy, "Direct and indirect taxation," p. 400.

5. For auctions of the *proventi* under much the same system as before 1369, see *Proventi contratti*, 30 (unfoliated); *Minute di Riformagioni, Anziani al Tempo della Libertà* [hereafter cited as *Anz. temp. lib.*] 2, fols. 139^r–61^v (1378 and 1379); and *Anz. temp. lib.* 3, pp. 399–415 (1385). There are arrangements for the auction of *proventi* in general terms; see *Consiglio Generale* [hereafter cited as *Cons. Gen.*] 1, fols. 24^r, 24 Aug. 1369, and 29^v, 22 Aug. 1369; *Cons. Gen.* 3, fol. 57^v, 19 Nov. 1371; *Cons. Gen.* 4, fol. 39^v, 24 March 1374; *Cons. Gen.* 6, fol. 58^v, 6 May 1378; *Cons. Gen.* 7, fols. 12^v, 4 Feb. 1379, and 217^r, 4 Jan. 1380; and *Cons. Gen.* 13, fol. 21^v, 20 Jan. 1397. There were discussions on whether or not to farm the *proventi* and which ones should be farmed (*Cons. Gen.* 1, fol. 47^r, 11 Sept. 1369; and *Cons. Gen.* 2, fol. 69^v, 4 Nov. 1370), but the arrangements for the administration of *proventi* that had not been sold (see *Cons. Gen.* 3, fol. 239^v, 19 Jan. 1373; and *Cons. Gen.* 4, fol. 80^v, 4 Aug. 1374) suggest that this was because of a failure to find buyers rather than a decision by Lucca that they should not be farmed. This impression is confirmed by the many inconclusive sessions of the auctions in *Anz. temp. lib.* 2 and 3.

6. *Anz. av. lib.* 16, fols. 8^r, 25 Oct. 1341, 24^v–25^r, 5 Dec. 1341, 32^v–33^r, 19 Jan. 1342, 35^r–36^r, 30 Jan. 1342, 40^v–41^r, 6 Feb. 1342; and *Anz. av. lib.* 18, fol. 28^r, 21 Sept. 1342. There is a break in the records of sales of gabelles between *Proventi Incanti* 9 (for 1347–48) and 10 (for 1352) and *Proventi Contratti* 24 (for 1347–48) and 10 (for 1352) and *Proventi Contratti* 24 (for 1345–46) and 25 (for 1351–52). *Ragionieri* 3 records many *proventi* being exacted by Lucchese officials between April 1341 and Nov. or Dec. 1342.

7. For the difficulties of Neiro Cassiani, buyer of this *provento* for 1354–55, and his *fideiussores*, when several of them were having their goods seized and auctioned to cover their obligations, see *Camarlingo Generale* [hereafter cited as *Cam. Gen.*] 54, fols. 51^r–^{v}; *Cam. Gen.* 56, fols. 51^r–^{v}; and *Cam. Gen.* 60, fols. 51^r, 126^r–27^v. The wine gabelle was not apparently sold between 22 Oct. 1355 and 1 June 1360; see *Proventi Contratti* 26, fols. 90^r–94^v. *Proventi Contratti* 29, fols. 121^r–24^v, *Cam. Gen.* 51, fol. 51^v; and *Cam. Gen.* 58–68 show it being administered directly by Lucchese officials.

8. *Anz. av. lib.* 41, fol. 52^v, 9 June 1361; *Anz. av. lib.* 42, fols. 37^v, 13 May 1362,

44^r–45^r, 30 May 1362, 46^r, 7 June 1362. *Cam. Gen.* 76 (unfoliated) records payments of salaries to a number of officials exacting the *proventi* on behalf of the commune on 6 Aug. 1362.

9. *Proventi Incanti*, nos. 2–12 for 1337–60.

10. *Proventi Incanti* 2, unfoliated.

11. Compare Siena, where contracts for longer periods were common (Bowsky, *Finance*, pp. 121–22); also for Florence (de la Roncière, "Indirect taxes," pp. 177–78); and Reggio (Bosini, "Pubbliche finanze," p. 469). There were some two- or three-year contracts in Lucca after 1369 (*Cons. Gen.* 8, fols. 120^r–20^v, 28 Aug. 1382; *Cons. Gen.* 10, fol. 61^r, 29 July 1388; *Cons. Gen.* 12, fol. 67^v, 3 June 1392; and *Proventi Contratti* 30, unfoliated).

12. *Anz. av. lib.* 19, fol. 15^r, 26 Oct. 1342. For attitudes elsewhere, see de la Roncière, "Indirect taxes," pp. 177–78; and Herlihy, "Direct and indirect taxation," pp. 399–400.

13. *Anz. av. lib.* 19, fol. 16^r, 26 Oct. 1342. A similar system was applied to the gabelle on rents, from which buildings rented by the commune for its officials were exempt. The amount due was calculated and the proventuals were allowed the appropriate discount, although this was much less significant financially than that for the flour gabelle; see *Cam. Gen.* 53, fol. 59^r, 10 Jan. 1355.

14. Examples include *Anz. av. lib.* 1 (unfoliated), p. 36, 30 April 1330, p. 108, 8 Aug. 1330, p. 204, 18 July 1331; *Anz. av. lib.* 15, fols. 4^v–5^v, 12 Aug. 1341; *Anz. av. lib.* 22, fols. 5^r–6^r, 20 Jan. 1344, 22^r, 23^r, 24^r, 8 April 1344; and *Cam. Gen.* 56, fol. 57^r, 5 Aug. 1355. In some of these cases the *restauro* took the form of money, not an extension of time.

15. Examples include *Anz. av. lib.* 2, fol. 141^r, Oct. 1330; *Anz. av. lib.* 15, fols. 2^r–^{v}, July 1341, 4^v, 12 Aug. 1341; *Anz. av. lib.* 19, fol. 11^r, 26 Oct. 1342; *Anz. av. lib.* 37, fols. 69^r–70^r, 15 Sept. 1354, 8 Oct. 1354; and *Anz. av. lib.* 39, fols. 88^r–89^r, 28 Sept. 1358.

16. General provision to that effect may be found in *Anz. av. lib.* 19, fols. 15^r–^{v}, 26 Oct. 1342. Examples include *Anz. av. lib.* 5 (unfoliated), p. 183, Jan. 1334,

p. 198, 24 Feb. 1334; *Anz. av. lib.* 7, fol. 50^v, 8 Nov. 1334; and *Anz. av. lib.* 22, fols. 31^{r-v}, 26 May 1344. For comparable discounts in Siena, see Bowsky, *Finance*, pp. 134–39.

17. *Anz. av. lib.* 14, fol. 19^r, 28 April 1338, 33^{r-v}, 16 June 1339. Where a rise in the gabelle produced increased receipts, the proventuals were allowed a portion, but not the whole, of the benefit; see *Anz. av. lib.* 35, fol. 3^r, 11 Jan. 1353. In another case the proventuals were not allowed either to lose or to gain from gabelle changes; see *Cons. Gen.* 11, fol. 95^v, 10 Dec. 1389.

18. *Anz. av. lib.* 2, fols. 55^v, 11 Jan. 1331, 61^r, 11 Feb. 1331 (wine); *Anz. av. lib.* 35, fols. 21^{r-v}, 8 March 1353 (mills); and *Anz. av. lib.* 42, fol. 43^r, 24 May 1362 (bridge). For compensation when outside rulers made regulations prejudicial to proventuals, see *Anz. av. lib.* 5 (unfoliated), p. 37, 19 Jan 1334; *Anz. av. lib.* 16, fols. 10^v–12^r, 16 Nov. 1341, 37^r–38^r, 31 Jan. 1342; *Anz. av. lib.* 21, fols. 5^{r-v}, 19 July 1343; *Anz. av. lib.* 22, fols. 7^{r-v}, 18 Jan. 1344; *Anz. av. lib.* 26, fols. 17^r–18^r, 15 Feb. 1347; *Anz. av. lib.* 34, fols. 14^{r-v}, 6 March 1352, 48^{r-v}, 6 Aug. 1352; *Anz. av. lib.* 35, fol. 4^v, 18 Jan. 1353; and *Anz. av. lib.* 39, fols. 38^v–39^v, 25 April 1358.

19. *Anz. av. lib.* 34, fols. 48^{r-v}, 6 Aug. 1352; *Anz. av. lib.* 41, fols. 87^v–88^r, 16 Aug. 1361 (for a gabelle year ending 10 Oct. 1360), 93^v–94^v, 6 Sept. 1361 (for a gabelle year ending 10 Oct. 1358).

20. Lucca took over control of her own revenues only on 1 October 1348, so proventuals seeking relief for losses before that date had to negotiate with Pisa. Lucca made some grants of relief for the period after 1 October. The flour gabelle had been sold for the year beginning 21 November 1347 for £20,000 *buona moneta*, equivalent to £24,166 13s. 4d. *picc.* The buyer owed Lucca a total of £3,356 10s. 9d. for October and November; the rest was payable to Pisa. He had paid £1,261 of the sum owed to Lucca, but £2,095 10s. 9d. was still owing in May 1349. £14,260 18s. 6d. had been collected from the gabelle and £13,586 8s. 6d. paid to Pisa, but £8,222 13s. 11d. was still outstanding. On 19 May 1349 Lucca waived three quarters of the amount still owing to her, so that the buyer only had to pay £523 17s. 8d. *picc.*; see *Ragionieri* 5, unfoliated. *Curia de'Rettori* 16, pp. 251–52 shows that Pisa also granted a reduction of the debt owed to her in February 1349 but does not make it clear what proportion of the total this represented. Lucca also made similar reductions of the arrears of other *proventi*; see *Cam. Gen.* 32, fols. 84^r–87^v. For discounts in other communes in 1348, see

Bowsky, *Finance*, pp. 134–39, and de la Roncière, "Indirect taxes," pp. 178–79.

21. The gabelle on *beneficia* was fixed at 2s. in the £1 (*Anz. av. lib.* 29, fol. 15^v, 26 Oct. 1342) but in practice was lower throughout the 1340s and 1350s, so that a *beneficium* of £10 produced an actual payment of £9 9s. and one of £50 a payment of £47 4s. 6d.

22. *Cam. Gen.* 52, fol. 56^r.

23. *Cam. Gen.* 52, fols. 55^r, 57^r.

24. *Anz. av. lib.* 19, fols. 32^r–33^r. The £594 6s. is the highest individual *beneficium* payment I have seen.

25. *Anz. av. lib.* 19, fols. 16^v, 26 Oct. 1342, 39^r, 28 Nov. 1342. The *Camarlingo Generale* records contain innumerable examples of this system in action.

26. *Anz. av. lib.* 19, fols. 33^{r-v}.

27. *Anz. av. lib.* 19, fols. 32^r–33^v.

28. *Anz. av. lib.* 19, fol. 36^r.

29. *Anz. av. lib.* 19, fol. 35^r.

30. *Anz. temp. lib.* 2, fols. 149^r–61^v, 357^r–407^v; *Anz. temp. lib.* 3, pp. 399–415; *Proventi Contratti* 30 (unfoliated); and *Ragionieri* 13 and 14.

31. *Proventi Incanti* 12, fols. 54^r–55^v. Giovanni Tedaldini did likewise for the *provento* of the *borghi* and *subborghi*, see *Proventi Incanti* 11, fols. 6^{r-v}, Sept. 1358.

32. *Proventi Incanti* 2, unfoliated. Puccinello della Rocca stressed the high prices he had been prepared to pay for *proventi* in the past, when asking for the mitigation of a fine; see *Anz. av. lib.* 37, fols. 25^{r-v}, 24 March 1354.

33. *Anz. av. lib.* 19, fols. 32^v, 33^r, 35^v–36^r.

34. *Anz. av. lib.* 19, fol. 15ʳ, 26 Oct. 1342; and *Anz. av. lib.* 13 (unfoliated), p. 120, 19 Aug. 1338. *Proventi Incanti* 3 (unfoliated) for 1339 specifies periods for which bidders are to be held to their bids, usually for between one month and about six weeks.

35. *Anz. av. lib.* 13, p. 13, 27 Feb. 1338; and *Anz. av. lib.* 26, fol. 14ᵛ, 25 Jan. 1347.

36. *Anz. av. lib.* 37, fols. 25ʳ⁻ᵛ, 24 March 1354. In the event his fine was reduced to £50 and the episode proved to be no more than a very temporary check on his career as a tax farmer.

37. *Proventi Incanti* 6, fols. 43ʳ⁻ᵛ. Stazzema did find a surety in Geo di Lemmo Bovi. For guarantors for tax farmers in Reggio, see Bosini, "Pubbliche finanze," pp. 469–70.

38. *Cam. Gen.* 61, fol. 150ᵛ, 13 April 1356. They were probably not very well known in Lucca. Fiore was the daughter of the late Rossellino of Florence and the widow of Rosso of Florence, but there was some confusion in Lucchese documents as to which of these two very similar names was that of her husband and whether or not he was dead. The buyer of the *provento* was Bernardo Buti, but Fiore made some of the payments from money she had exacted and seems to have been acting as an official. In *Cam. Gen.* 58, fol. 90ʳ, she is said to be one of the buyer's *fideiussores. Cam. Gen.* 59, fol. 35ʳ, notes that she advanced him £18 15s. *picc.* to pay a fine for a brawl, 9 Dec. 1355.

39. *Proventi Incanti* 2 and 4, unfoliated; *Proventi Incanti* 5, fols. 5ʳ⁻ᵛ and 30ʳ⁻31ᵛ; *Proventi Incanti* 6, fols. 45ʳ⁻ᵛ.

40. *Proventi Incanti* 2–4, unfoliated; *Proventi Incanti* 5, fols. 4ʳ⁻ᵛ, 39ʳ⁻40ʳ; *Proventi Incanti* 6, fols. 9–10ʳ; *Proventi Incanti* 8, fols. 54ʳ⁻ᵛ; and *Proventi Incanti* 9, fols. 16ʳ⁻ᵛ.

41. *Proventi Incanti* 2, unfoliated (1337); *Proventi Incanti* 10, fols. 19ʳ⁻21ᵛ (1351), 19ʳ⁻21ᵛ (different foliation) (1352). It is doubtful whether *fideiussores* were required to have such sums at their disposal, which would indeed have been difficult given the amounts involved. On 23 Jan. 1382, when *proventi* were being levied directly, the amounts for which the *camerarii* had to provide sureties were

laid down and were substantially lower than the yield of the *proventi* in question, see *Cons. Gen.* 8, fols. 23^r–^{v}. These sums in any case seem to represent a considerable increase on what had previously been required; see *Cons. Gen.* 8, fol. 146^v, 11 Oct. 1382. It may be significant that Nicolao Bolgarini attempted to obtain exemption from this requirement by arguing that he had already given a *fideiussore* sufficient for £800, which was the maximum sum that could ever come into his hands, since receipts had to be handed over to the *camarlingo generale* each week; see *Cam. Gen.* 8, fol. 26^v, 30 Jan. 1383. The exactor was obliged to proceed within a month against any tax farmer who was in arrears with his payments, and the resources that guarantors were required to possess may have been based on the amount that could be outstanding at any one time rather than the full purchase price of the *provento*.

42. *Proventi Incanti* 12, fols. 3^r–4^r.

43. *Proventi Incanti* 11, fols. 18^r–19^v. Not only was this complicated, but it covers one and one sixth times the purchase price.

44. *Proventi Incanti* 10, fols. 19^r–21^v.

45. *Proventi Incanti* 10, fols. 19^r–21^v (different foliation).

46. He appears regularly in this capacity in *Proventi Incanti* 5–9 for these years. He is referred to as dead in *Curia de'Rettori* 16, pp. 251–52, February 1349.

47. *Proventi Incanti* 5 for 1342–43. He appears less frequently than Belluccino.

48. *Proventi Incanti* 9, fols. 4^v, 16^v. He approved his brother as a *fideiussore* for the flour gabelle, but he and his brother are referred to as purchasers of a third of this *insolidum*; see *Curia de'Rettori* 16, pp. 251–52.

49. *Proventi Incanti* 4, unfoliated.

50. *Proventi Incanti* 5, fols. 5^r–^{v}, 20^r–^{v}, 30^r–31^r, 45^r–^{v}; *Proventi Incanti* 6, fols. 6^r–^{v}; *Proventi Incanti* 7, fols. 16^r–^{v}; and *Proventi Incanti* 8, fols. 3^r, 8^v.

51. *Proventi Incanti* 5, fols. 17^r–^{v}.

52. *Proventi Incanti* 5, fol. 46^r; *Proventi Incanti* 6, fols. 11^r–12^r; and *Proventi Incanti* 10, fols. 17^r–^{v}.

53. *Proventi Incanti* 12, fols. 18^r–19^r, 47^r–^{v}; *Anz. av. lib.* 39, fols. 104^r–05^r, 5 Dec. 1358.

54. *Anz. av. lib.* 39, fols. 104^r–05^r, 5 Dec. 1358. In *Anz. av. lib.* 1 (unfoliated), p. 146, 17 Dec. 1330, an *approbator* is apparently being held responsible in default of the buyer and his *fideiussore*.

55. *Anz. av. lib.* 18, fol. 5^v, 14 Aug. 1342.

56. *Anz. av. lib.* 39, fol. 104^r–05^r.

57. *Cam. Gen.* 58, fols. 82^r–^{v}; but *Cam. Gen.* 57, fol. 82^r, 25 Sept. 1355, reports that Nuccino was a *fideiussore* and Franceschino one of the buyers.

58. "Pro se et illis quibus partem dare et assignare voluerit." The practice of assigning shares goes back at least to the time of Castruccio; *Archivio de'Notari* 93, i, pp. 38–40, 16 Feb. 1317 (purchase 10 Nov. 1316) names four partners of the buyer of the retail wine gabelle in the Six Miles. *Archivio de'Notari* 93, ii, p. 148, 10 Dec. 1319 is an assignment of four shares in a *provento* by the original buyer, both quoting the phrase above. Similar assignments of shares are reported on pp. 165–68, 207–11, Jan. and March 1320. I owe these references to Dr. Louis Green.

59. *Anz. av. lib.* 19, fols. 25^r–27^r, 14–17 Dec. 1342. The decision went in favor of Francesco. None of this is recorded in the *Proventi* records, where the purchase is in the name of Francesco Accettanti, and of the others only Coluccino is mentioned—as an unsuccessful bidder; see *Proventi Incanti* 5, fols. 7^r–^{v}, 28^r–29^r.

60. *Curia de'Rettori* 15 (unfoliated), pp. 145–53; *Anz. av. lib.* 25, fols. 26^r–28^v; and *Proventi Incanti* 9, fols. 6^r–^{v}. This gabelle, which applied to all transfers of property, including inheritances, must have been one of the very few *proventi* to be favorably affected by the plague, but it had also been thrown into confusion—indeed the case began only in March 1349, although the purchase year had come to an end on 30 Sept. 1348. The fairness and even practicability of distinguishing Guido's sixth share from the rest seems doubtful. Unfortunately, the

outcome of the dispute is unknown; the other parties challenged the competence of the Rectors' court to deal with the matter, since it only had jurisdiction over *forenses* and mercenary soldiers, and all the parties to the case were Lucchese citizens.

61. *Curia de'Rettori* 15, fols. 17^r–^{v}. There are some references to actual elections of officials by partners in *proventi* in *Archivio de'Notari* 93, i, pp. 38–40, 16 Feb. 1317, 152–55, 12 Dec. 1319.

62. *Cam. Gen.* 62, fol. 54^v; *Cam. Gen.* 63, fols. 29^r, 27^v; and *Cam. Gen.* 64, fol. 29^r.

63. *Cam. Gen.* 64, fol. 36^r.

64. *Cam. Gen.* 64, fol. 39^r.

65. *Cam. Gen.* 63, fol. 39^r.

66. *Cam. Gen.* 62, fol. 53^v, 56^r–^{v}; *Cam. Gen.* 63, fols. 28^r–^{v}, 30^r, 31^r; *Cam. Gen.* 64, fols. 29^v, 30^r (all these volumes have several sets of foliation).

67. For the gabelle on meat for ser Guglielmo Guidi, the bread tax for Petro Dombellinghi, and the gabelle on the *borghi* and *sobborghi* for Paolo Corsini, see *Cam. Gen.* 64, fols. 29^r, 30^r, 31^r.

68. *Cam. Gen.* 67, fols. 36^r–38^r, 37^r–^{v}, 66^r–^{v} (various foliation).

69. *Anz. av. lib.* 13 (unfoliated), p. 120, 19 Aug. 1338.

70. *Anz. av. lib.* 39 (unfoliated), pp. 3–5, 29 April 1358.

71. References are too numerous to be given in detail, but are to be found in *Proventi Incanti* 2–12, *Proventi Contratti* 13–30, and the series *Camarlingo Generale*, *Anziani Avanti la Libertà*, and *Consiglio Generale* for the period. Tax farmers also included a ser Stefano Nosi de Ghivizzano and his son, Iacobo, but it is not certain that they were related. Ghivizzano was the name of a village in the Lucchese *contado*, as well as being the surname of ser Azzolino and his descendants.

72. Coluccino, son of Giuntoro Dombellinghi, in 1326; Bonagiunta Dombellinghi in the 1330s and his son Franceschino in the 1350s; Belluccino and Petro or Petruccio, the sons of Francesco Dombellinghi, in the 1330s and 1340s, Petro continuing in the 1350s after his brother's death in 1348; ser Nerio in the 1320s, who is presumably the same person as the ser Ranerio of the 1330s; and ser Opizo, son of Bernardo Dombellinghi, from 1331 to the late 1350s.

73. Parente Onesti in 1331 and his son Francesco 1351–62; Francesco di Riccardo Onesti 1338; Nicolao di Benetto, known as Bresciano, Onesti in 1339; and Giovanni di Dino Onesti 1350–72. Cosciorino di Giuntino Peri in 1332; Prinze di messer Moncello Peri 1326–47 and his son Nicolao in 1344; Coluccino di ser Ghianduccio Peri 1334–61; and Moncello di Vanni Peri 1346–47; there was also an Angelo Peri, who served as an official for Coluccio in 1355.

74. *Proventi contratti* 26, fols. 85^r–86^r; *Proventi Contratti* 28, unfoliated; *Proventi Contratti* 29, fols. 134^r–^{v}; *Cam. Gen.* 52, fol. 78^r; and *Cam. Gen.* 59, fols. 91^r–^{v}.

75. *Proventi Contratti* 19, fols. 9^r–12^r; *Proventi Contratti* 21, unfoliated; *Proventi Contratti* 23, fols. 132^r–34^r; *Proventi Contratti* 29, fols. 110^v–11^r, 112^r–12^v; and *Cam. Gen.* 18, fol. 219^r.

76. Examples include *Cons. Gen.* 8, fols. 120^r–20^v, 28 Aug. 1382, 36^v (different foliation), 25 Feb. 1383; and *Cons. Gen.* 10, fol. 61^r, 29 July 1288. Also *Proventi Contratti* 30, unfoliated.

77. *Anz. av. lib.* 39, fols. 32^r–33^r, 16 April 1358. He was also vicar of Camaiore in the second semester of 1352; see *Cam. Gen.* 47, fol. 19^v. A number of other Lucchese tax farmers served in important and honorific offices such as *Anziani*, vicars in the *contado*, or ambassadors.

78. Giovanni and Petro, sons of Coluccio Cristofani de'Carincioni 1337–48; Lucetto Sbarra 1337–39; Bernabò di ser Guido Sbarra 1337–43; Bartolomeo Sbarra 1340; and ser Gerardo di ser Guglielmo Sbarra 1353–55. Michele di Bartolomeo and Ciomeo Sbarra served as officials for proventuals in the 1350s. For the Dombellinghi and Onesti, see nn. 72 and 73 above.

79. *Anz. av. lib.* 9, fol. 10^v, 19 Jan. 1335.

80. Batona and Villa Baslica were in the Lucchese *contado*. Ser Iacobo Michelini and Zubbino Buoni were from outside Lucchese territory, although ser Iacobo was a Lucchese citizen. Ser Azzolino derived his surname from a village in Lucchese territory, but it is difficult to ascertain whether he himself was an immigrant.

81. Green, *Castruccio Castracani*, p. 119. He is mistaken in believing that Vanni Rapondi and Puccino Galganetti were tax farmers. They were appointed commissioners to fix the rates of customs duties on certain goods, and the document he cites to support his argument is their declaration of these rates, *Archivio de'Notari* 65, fol. 138^r, 28 May 1316.

82. Their accounts are to be found in *Ragionieri* 1, 6–9 (various foliations and some unfoliated) and in more extended form in the *Camarlingo Generale* records.

83. His accounts are in *Ragionieri* 6–8 and the *Camarlingo Generale* records. He had farmed the gabelle of the vicariate of Valdriana and Villa Basilica for £1,100 *buona moneta* in 1351–52; see *Cam. Gen.* 37, fol. 65^r. For his many other purchases between 1352 and 1362, see *Proventi Incanti* 10–12, and *Proventi Contratti* 26–29; for his death, see *Anz. av. lib.* 43, fol. 31^r, Sept. 1362.

84. *Cam Gen.* 29, fol. 75^r; and *Ragionieri* 6, fols. 5^r–9^v, and 8 (unfoliated).

85. *Cam Gen.* 31, fol. 1^r; *Cam. Gen.* 51, fols. 1^r, 106^r; *Cam. Gen.* 97 (unfoliated); and *Ragionieri* 7, fol. 1^r.

86. *Ragionieri* 3, fol. 1^r; *Cam. Gen.* 47, fol. 44^v; *Cam. Gen.* 53, fol. 113^v; and *Cam Gen.* 58, unfoliated. For ser Bartolomeo Bianchi as official 1352, see *Ragionieri* 7, fol. 13^r; as tax farmer 1353, see *Cam. Gen.* 47, fol. 59^v. He was still holding communal offices in the late 1390s.

87. *Cam. Gen.* 30, fols. 56^r–^{v}, 62^r; *Cam. Gen.* 31, fols. 48^r, 50^r, 57^r, 61^r, 70^v; *Cam. Gen.* 32, fols. 28^r–29^r; *Cam. Gen.* 33, unfoliated; and *Ragioniere* 6, fols. 4^r–5^v.

88. *Anz. av. lib.* 42, fols. 44^r–45^r, 30 May 1362; *Anz. av. lib.* 43, fol. 31^r, Sept. 1362; and *Cam. Gen.* 72, unfoliated, 6 Aug. 1362.

89. *Curia de'Rettori* 15, pp. 146–47.

90. Bowsky, *Finance*, p. 125.

91. *Proventi Incanti* 4, unfoliated; *Cam. Gen.* 20, fols. 214^r–15^r. This seems to mean that ser Forteguerra had either sold out or had been a front man. For partners as guarantors in Reggio, see Bosini, "Pubbliche finanze," pp. 69–70.

92. Individual tax farmers were also allowed to stand guarantor for each other; see *Proventi Incanti* 11, fols. 6^v, 12^v. However, when ser Orso Barsellotti, who had stood surety for half of the £3,940, for which Ludovico Corbi had bought the gabelle on contracts in October 1348, became a partner for this half, he provided new guarantors. The list of sureties, nine in all, clearly distinguishes those acting for ser Orso from those acting for Ludovico, but this seems to be unusual; see *Proventi Incanti* 11, fols. 20^r–21^v.

93. *Proventi Incanti* 12, fols. 6^r–^{v}.

94. *Proventi Incanti* 7, fols. 16^r–^{v}.

95. *Proventi Incanti* 3, unfoliated.

96. *Proventi Incanti* 3, unfoliated; *Proventi Incanti* 9, fols. 6^r–^{v}; and *Proventi Incanti* 12, fols. 14^r–15^r.

97. *Proventi Incanti* 11, fols. 16^r–17^v. It was eventually sold to ser Nicolao, and Francesco acted as one of his guarantors.

98. *Proventi Incanti* 11, fols. 23^r–24^r.

99. *Proventi Incanti* 11, fols. 25^r–26^v. Ser Nicolao de Ghivizzano, ser Biagio Mariani, and Puccinello della Rocca were also bidders for the gabelle on rents 6 and 8 October 1358, although the eventual buyer was Ludovico Corbi, fols. 27^r–^{v}.

100. *Anz. av. lib.* 19, fols. 26^r–^{v}, 15 Dec. 1342.

101. *Anz. av. lib.* 10, fol. 14^r, 1 June 1336; *Anz. av. lib.* 13, unfoliated, p. 77, 10 June 1338; *Anz. av. lib.* 26, fols. 117^v, 21 Nov. 1347, 125^v, 28 Nov. 1347.

102. *Cam. Gen.* 59, fols. 28^r, 7 Nov. 1355, 31^v, 16 Nov. 1355. See above

pp. 58–59 and nn. 60 and 61 above.

103. *Cam. Gen.* 48, fol. 18^r, 3 Jan. 1354. Since Francesco di Parente Onesti was *camarlingo generale* at the time, he paid the fine to himself. He was fined for another quarrel in which he struck Nerio Cassiani and drew his sword upon him. He subsequently failed to prove an accusation against him; see *Cam. Gen.* 66, fol. 11^r, 26 May 1358, paid 5 June of the same year.

Archival Inventorying in Fourteenth-Century Lucca: Methodologies, Theories, and Practices

ANTONIO ROMITI

The first three decades of the fourteenth century were a particularly distressed period for Lucca and its surrounding territory. As a result of a series of political upheavals, major changes were wrought in the political and administrative structures of the state. These disturbances began with the creation of a régime "a popolo" at the end of the thirteenth century, which gave rise in turn to the subsequent return of the "White" elements with Uguccione della Faggiuola and the sudden rise to power of Castruccio Castracani, the crashing fall of the structure built up by the Lucchese *condottiere* and political leader, the surrender of the city to mercenary soldiers, and its ultimate delivery into the hands of a sequence of ephemeral lordships.[1] These were thirty agitated years, especially as far as political changes were concerned.

Like other Italian cities that had achieved their own political and juridical autonomy in the communal period, Lucca preserved its public records with great care, since these represented the collective memory of the city's origins, subsequent development, changes in juridical stature, and the new rights obtained, consolidated, and recognized. Very frequently, however, a political change led to pillaging of the records that contained evidence of the policies of those who had held power in the previous government. This type of behavior was the rule rather than the exception, since the most effective way of destroying an adversary lay not only in defeating him but also, and more particularly, in cancelling out the record of his public actions.

The first thirty years of the fourteenth century witnessed the irreparable destruction of Lucchese public records; so few documents survived that Salvatore Bongi was led to assert:

> If some books and documents older than 1329 survive today in the archive, their salvation must be attributed to the fact that they were located in a place which by chance was spared from the sack or fire; or, because they were hidden from these pillagers they later resurfaced.[2]

On 14 June 1314 Uguccione and Castruccio led the sack of Lucca, among other things burning both public and private records and "in that fury to burn and pillage which lasted for some days they destroyed the major part of the citizens' houses." In addition, Uguccione appropriated documents belonging to the bishopric, but some two years later, as a result of pressure from the Roman Curia—although we do not know whether or not he did so in full—he thought it wise to return them.[3] Another particularly unfortunate date for Lucca was 19 March 1329 when, after the death of Castruccio, the forces of Ludwig of Bavaria sacked the city and once more sought to destroy its records, setting fire to a large part of the documents, mainly those produced during Castruccio's rule.[4] A new incursion, this time by Castruccio's sons, was carried out on the night of 25 September 1333. They again destroyed archival material pertaining to the *Camera Librorum* in an effort to locate the *Libro dei Banditi*, which contained the sentences passed against them.[5]

Other documents were said to have been destroyed periodically in the period of Pisan domination (1342–69), presumably because the Pisans, who ruled Lucca at the time, sought out the most significant evidence regarding Lucca's past in order to destroy it.[6] It is certain that the awareness of the loss of its documented past was a cause of concern and regret in Lucca. The *Anziani* at their meeting on 5 October 1334 asserted that: "since because of the fire set in the city of Lucca on 19 March in the year of the Lord 1329 many books, indeed nearly all, and the writings of Camera, Commune and Lucchese gabelles were burned and ruined."[7]

The archival items that survived the critical times described above were indeed decidedly limited in number. Examining some of the series of documents described in the *Archivi Pubblici*, which will be the particular subject of this study, it is possible to gain a preliminary idea of, first, how much has survived and, second, how much the *Camera Librorum* contained in 1343. This procedure will allow us to gauge the losses of pre-1329 holdings; that is, the records existing before the second decisive sack of Lucca.[8]

The *Curia del Podestà* contains one volume for 1324 and one for 1327; the records then begin again with five items for 1329, to continue very regularly until 1344. The *Curia dei Foretani* possesses two volumes for 1327 and three for 1328. The *Curia Nova di Giustizia* numbers four volumes for 1328 and continues with five items for 1329.[9] As far as the *Curia dei Treguani* is concerned, only two volumes remain for 1328 and two for 1329, while neither the *Curia delle Querimonie* nor the *Curia dei Castaldi* possesses any records earlier than 1329.[10] If the situation with regard to the *Curia del Maggior Sindaco e Giudice degli Appelli* was more favorable with five volumes for 1327 and seven for 1328, the *Curia dei Vicari* has even earlier records with one item for 1323, one for 1326, one for 1327, and two for 1328.[11] One register of 1324 was assigned to the *Curia della Dovana* and one for the year 1328 was attributed to the *Cancelleria*.[12] The *Curia dei Malefici* possesses two items for 1328, while the *Curia de' Ribelli*, the *Curia della Gabella*, the *Curia del Fondaco*, the *Curia della Taglia delle Cinquantasettemila*, the *Camera Maggiore*, and the "series" dealing with the *Proventi* have records dating only from 1328.[13]

This sample makes it clear that we are faced with an extreme scarcity of archival material and confirms how far-reaching were the destructive effects of the upheavals we have discussed. Other more or less fortuitous events occurring in subsequent centuries had far less pernicious effects. A brief survey of the records at present preserved in the *Archivio di Stato in Lucca* provides further clarification of the situation with regard to the fourteenth-century inventory. Although this kind of analysis is outside the scope of the present essay, we may note by way of example how, in 1344, the presence of two registers for the *Curia del Podestà* was certified, one from 1324 and the other from 1327. Bongi, describing the series *Podestà, Curia Civile* in the printed inventory, notes: "only two books prior to 1329 survive, saved by chance from the sack of that year. But from 1329 on the collection is preserved almost in its original form."[14] We may safely conclude that other series, too, are largely identical with those of the first fourteenth-century inventory, although there are some inevitable gaps, due to accidental losses or to the chance survival of material preserved in a safe place and brought together with the rest in later periods.[15]

In addition to the above indicators, we possess other information that enables us to determine the quantity of surviving recorded material and the organization of the Lucchese archives in the fourteenth century, thanks to the existence of a number of registers of *Inventari* preserved in the *Archivio di Stato in Lucca* in the series *Archivi Pubblici*, as numbers 1, 2, and 3, which respectively bear the dates 1344–45 for the first, 1348 for the second, and 1389–1440 for the third. All three concern the public offices and magistracies of the city and its territory.[16]

On this occasion we will analyze only the first of these registers numbered 1 which was begun on 6 September 1344 and has entries that continue until 1345.[17] The heading reads: "Liber repertorii seu inventarii facti de libris et scripturis omnibus existentibus in Camera seu Archivio librorum Camere lucani Comunis, sub custodia discreti viri ser Nicolai, filii quondam ser Tedaldini Lazarii de Luca, notarii et dicte Camere librorum etc. Custodis," allowing us to establish that the responsible post of keeper of the communal archive was entrusted to a notary in the person of ser Nicolao del fu Tedaldino Lazari.

The register consists of 298 folios, to which are to be added another 12 placed at the beginning and containing a "rubric of books and writings existing in the current book or inventory of books presently in the Camera of the Commune of Lucca under the custody of Ser Nicolao Tedaldini of Lucca, notary and custodian of the said books of the Camera" that continues to fol. iv. It is, in effect, an index that records the series title and the folio on which the description of that particular series begins, with a brief definition: "Libri Curie domini Maioris Sindici et Iudicis Apellationum incipiunt ad fol. XXIIIIor."[18] It is interesting to note that the post of *Custos Camere Librorum*, or keeper of the public records, in the first few years of the fourteenth century had been held by ser Tedaldino Lazari Gay before he passed it to his son Nicolao, thereby establishing a kind of hereditary succession not uncommon to other posts as well.[19]

The heading continues with the information that the register in question was "written, copied and transcribed from the original Inventory of the said books and writings made, edited and systemized by the discreet sire Giovanni Barellia of Lucca, notary especially deputized by the Lords Anziani for the compiling of the said Inventory in the year of our Lord 1344 and partly in 1345" ("Scriptus, copiatus et excemplatus ex originali Inventario de dictis libris et scripturis facto, edito et ordinato per discretum virum ser Iohannem Barelie de Luca, notarium ad dictum Inventarium faciendum per dominos Antianos etc. spetialiter deputaum. *Anno n. D.* MCCCXLIIII *et partim anno* MCCCXLV"). The register we have is, therefore, a copy of the original, since lost, drawn up by the notary, ser Giovanni Barellia, on specific commission of the *Anziani*.[20]

The *Camera Librorum et Scripturarum*, or public archive, had the task of preserving the documents produced by the public officials and magistrates who, in their turn, were required to deposit them there within a brief time limit, in accordance with the Statute of the Commune of 1308:

> all books of the deliberations and letters of the Commune of Lucca must be deposited each year within the first eight days of January with the *Camera* of the Lucchese Commune by the Chancellors possessing them; and if the above said notaries should not comply, each of them failing to observe the aforesaid shall be fined twenty-five pounds by the Major syndic and the said books are nonetheless to be deposited.[21]

This disposition, which provided for a centralized *Archivio Pubblico*, complete and up-to-date so that it could be consulted quickly, also rendered the archive liable to a more total destruction, which, as we have seen, in fact happened. If the various "series" had been kept in different buildings at the time of the "sack" of the city, it would very probably have been possible to save a larger number of items. Centralization made destruction more likely and more total.[22]

The clerk-notaries were, in practice, very careful to obey the regulations. Looking at the "series" described in the "inventory" one sees that the records for the most recent years are nearly complete. It is typical that the *Curia del Podestà* had already deposited its records up to 1344, the *Curia del Fondaco* up to 1344, the *Curia Nova di Giustizia* up to 1344, the *Curia dei Treguani* up to 1343, the *Curia delle Querimonie* up to 1343, the *Curia dei Castaldi* up to 1344, the *Curia del Maggior Sindaco e Guidice degli Appelli* up to 1343, and so on with a few exceptions, some of them accidental, such as the *Camera Maggiore*, which had deposited its records up to 1341, and the *Vicario di Coreglia*, which had stopped at 1333.[23] It is by no means impossible that this conscientiousness in effecting the deposits was encouraged not only by the penalty laid down in the Statute but also by an awareness of the project for an inventory of the material that took shape in the last months of 1344. Some delays occurred in the case of the magistracies outside the city for understandable logistical reasons.[24]

The archival material that came in from the clerks of the various offices was already arranged organically, and the *Custos Librorum et Scripturarum* was required to maintain this original arrangement of the items, respecting the principle of "provenance" and keeping the "series" together, according to the standards normally applied in the medieval period. The individual "series" were kept "open," so as to receive the new acquisitions each year within the time limits laid down in the statutory regulations already quoted. It is not possible to determine what the physical arrangement of the "series" in the storerooms of the *Camera delle Scritture* was like. One can, however, hypothesize that the listing of the archival material in the Inventory may have corresponded to physical reality; that is, that the compilation of the documents took account of the actual arrangement of the series in the storerooms. One can nevertheless affirm that in the course of the description the "nature" of the records was respected: first, by keeping each "series" together in obedience to the principle of provenance; and, second, by place, linking together several magistracies that had common characteristics as far as the institutional structures of the political and administrative organization of the Commune were concerned.

A first group of records is represented by the "series" concerned with those magistracies with a strictly judicial character, that is the civil and criminal courts, and by the records belonging to courts, which we may define as "mixed," comprising magistracies that had administrative duties that also extended into the judicial sphere.[25] A second group can be defined as the complex body of records stemming from offices dealing with financial and economic affairs. These ranged from the books of the *Camera Maggiore* of the commune to the wide category of "proventi" and the other offices that administered the revenues and resources of the Commune. The resulting structure was extremely complicated as a consequence of the fragmentation of official duties in this delicate ambit of the public service.[26] A third group brings together the records produced by the bodies operating in the territory outside the city itself, comprising both magistracies of a judicial character and those which were more strictly administrative, ranging from the *Curia Vicariarum* to the *Gabelle Vicariarum* in a multiplicity of offices.[27] A fourth group comprises documents from offices that could not be included in the groups already mentioned operating both inside as well as outside the city. Among these we may mention the office that produced the registers concerned with measurements of lands in order to determine the *Estimo*, as a basis for the subsequent imposition of taxation.[28]

The work of ser Giovanni Barellia was carried into effect and completed within the space of about one year. The task of compiling an inventory certainly gave rise to problems of method, which in view of the complexity of the work, were no light matters. Examining the nature of Barellia's listings, it is possible to isolate in each individual entry two types of elements: fixed and variable. The former are present in each entry, however concise; the latter may or may not be there, without compromising the technical validity and the standardized method of the Inventory.[29]

Analyzing the fixed elements, we have the following schema:

1) The first element that we can distinguish is the definition of each archival item, which is almost invariably effected by an analytical description, "piece by piece." We may quote by way of example: "Unus liber inquisitionum et processuum Curie lucani Fundaci"[30] or "Una Vacchetta denuntiationum et accusationum et aliorum extraordinariorum et cetera."[31] More rarely we find several items together, but in these cases, too, there are analytical descrip-

tions, always "piece by piece" after the main citation: "Duo quaterni sine cuberta in cartis realibus, quorum primus incipit . . ." and there follows a very full *intitulatio* before passing on to the *secundus quaternus dicti registri* with an equally full recording of its heading.[32] Further on we find another very significant example: "Quaternuli decem in quibus sunt reddite date in scriptis Nove Gabelle," and after other information of a general character there is added "videlicet, primus Comunis Corporis dicte Plebis, secundus comunis Sancte Marie Ley Iudicis, tertius Cappelle sancti Petri de Meata" and so on to the last one, "decimus Cappelle Sancti Michaelis de Scheto."[33] Thus, even in special cases consisting of descriptions of several items linked together, there is always immediately afterwards an analytical listing of individual pieces.

2) The second element, always included, is represented by the indication of the quality of each archival item, an absolutely necessary distinction, following that of quantity, noted above. In the Inventory as a whole these appear as various alternative types, distinguishable according to their nature, from *liber* to *filsa*, from *vacchetta* to *quaternus*, from *quaternulus* to *memoriale*.[34] One also finds the use of *registro* in a rather unusual form of spelling, which nevertheless represents a significant stage of development in the use of terms.[35]

The terminology used for archival items at various points in the Inventory merits particular attention. The type most commonly found consists of the *liber*, which is used for the item commonly called a "register." Unless there are specific indications to the contrary, items indicated as *libri* consisted of paper and were quarto in format. At the same time, the thickness of each single item in the inventory is indicated with great precision. In the first place a *liber* consisted of one or more *quaterni*, and the archivist never failed to indicate the number of *quaterni* of which each *liber* was composed. This information would not have been enough in itself, since the *quaternus* was not always made up of the same number of folios

or sheets. Indeed, one can say that variations in the number of
folios from one *quaternus* to another were a given. Thus we find
quaterni of eighteen folios, or of twenty-two folios or of nine
folios.[36] We may note further one *quaternus* of ten folios, of ten
folios again, and later of twelve folios.[37] We could continue to
quote examples without managing to find an average. We can also
quote an example of a designation that is by no means uncommon:
"Unus liber . . . quaterni quinque, quorum primus est foliorum
XXV, secundus foliorum X, tertius foliorum VII, quartus foliorum
VIIII et quintus foliorum XVII," illustrating variations in the
thickness of *quaterni* even within the same *liber*.[38]

If the *quaternus* did not always have the same thickness, the
problem was overcome in the course of inventorying by means of
specifying on each occasion the number of folios in the various
quaterni, thus providing accurate information on the number of
folios or sheets in every *liber* described in the inventory. Normally
a *liber* was made up of several *quaterni*, but it could also consist
of a single *quaternus*: in this case both words were used as alternatives "unus liber sive quaternus."[39] We also quite commonly find
references that repeat both terms "unus liber sive quaternus
introitus omnium denariorum . . . quaterni unius."[40]

Besides the term *quaternus*, the designation *quaternulus* was
frequently used. The difference between the two terms is by no
means clear. Since the *quaternulus* is most commonly found inside
a *filza*, which, as we shall see, was made up of loose sheets, one
might suppose that a *quaternulus* was nothing more than an un-
bound *quaternus*; that is, an entity corresponding to the modern
fascicule: "Item una filsa bonorum datorum ser Tedaldino per con-
sulem et iudicem Comunis Cappelle Sancti Laurentii Plebis Turris
et Comunis Galliani et Comunis Montis Catini dicti pleberii, in
anno MCCCXXXII in tribus quaternulis."[41] And further on one
reads: "Item una filsa in qua est solus quaternulus bonorum dicte
Plebis Lammari."[42] Nevertheless, one cannot completely exclude

the possibility that *quaternulus* may indicate a *quaternus* of a different size, or a small format, which did not, however, take the form of a *vacchetta*, even if other entries in the inventory seem to cause one to opt for the first hypothesis.[43]

The term *vacchetta*, while not that widely employed, does appear with some frequency in the Inventory. In this case one can give a more precise definition, since the term is still used today to mean a register with a particular format long and narrow in appearance. One frequently finds, in connection with references to this particular type of record, an indication of the type of paper from which it was made, such as a *vacchetta in cartis realibus*.[44] This form of appellation is always found in symbiosis; apart from *vacchetta in cartis realibus*,[45] one also finds *vacchetta in cartis regalibus*.[46]

The term, *in cartis realibus*, appears to indicate a particular format of paper, longer and narrower, which is connected to the particular shape of the *vacchetta*. In exceptional cases this expression is also found in the description of archival items, such as "unum memoriale in cartis realibus ad modum vacchette."[47] This description seems to reflect the need of the individual who made the entries to solve a technical problem, since in each case he was dealing with account books, which were kept in registers of this particular format. One also sometimes finds a description indicating that a document is *in cartis realibus* without any reference to it being a *vacchetta*, but these seem to be anomalies where the specification that it is a *vacchetta* has simply been left out.[48]

For the *vacchetta*, as for the *liber*, the number of pages of which it was composed is always specified, with the aim of supplying a useful suggestion of its thickness. In some cases, especially with regard to *carte reales* one finds the word *carta* used instead of folio. Again, besides a form such as "una vacchetta in cartis realibus ... quaterni unius, que est foliorum XXV,"[49] there may be the indication "una vacchetta in cartis regalibus ... quaternorum duorum quorum primus est foliorum XII et secundus foliorum XIII,"[50] but also entries such as "una vacchetta memorie . . . esse cartarum XX"[51] and "una vaccheta in cartis realibus . . . Quaternorum trium, qui videuntur esse cartarum CXLVI,"[52] which gives us the number of pages in total, but not by *quaternus*.

In the Inventory under consideration there are more frequent references to *filsa*, a term which gives rise to fewer problems of interpretation than others, since the descriptions make it clear that it was a container holding a number of *quaterni* or loose pages. Many examples of this could be quoted. After he had indicated the existence of a "filsa mandatoriarum factarum Iohanni Pagani camsori depositario pecunie bladi Fundaci lucani Comunis et aliis occasione dicti officii Fundaci et aliarum scripturarum pro ipso officio, et sunt mandatorie XXV" making it clear that it contained other documents or pages originally not bound, the archivist adds "item ibidem infilsa est exitus expensarum extraordinariarum pro mandatoriis per Rustichinum, in foliis tribus," adding that this involves another three loose sheets.[53] The entry then continues, indicating the presence of other loose papers, removing any doubt about the precise meaning of the term *filsa*, which already had its modern sense in the medieval period.

Ser Giovanni Barellia undoubtedly had to face the technical problem of foliating the *filze*, an operation that would certainly have taken up an excessive amount of time. In describing some of them he does not give either the number of folios or the number of pages. In view of the heterogeneous character, the fragmentary nature, and the quantity of the material, the picture that he gives is not particularly precise: "una filsa bonorum de pleberio Vurni et cappelarum et contractarum eius datarum, scripto anno MCCCVIII."[54] These imprecisions in the entries are not very frequent, but they would seem to indicate that in a major undertaking such as the work of ser Giovanni Barellia there could be variations of method, frequently caused by the presentation of new archival problems inherent in the documentation that was deposited in the *Camera Librorum.*

3) The third element consists of a specification of content. Taking the Inventory as a whole, this element appears unevenly. In the first part of the Inventory the specification of content is very concise and limited in extent. As the work proceeds, however, the analysis of content is progressively expanded. In the early phases of the work, the archivist was very probably worried by the considerable volume of the material to be inventoried and had opted for a method that was analytic or "piece by piece," but limited as far as specifics of content was concerned. As the work proceeded he chose, albeit if not always on a regular basis, a more detailed and precise analysis.

If we sometimes find simply "liber introitus et exitus," this may indicate that since the material was subdivided by "series" or the offices from which it originated, there was no need to repeat that it belonged to the particular office that had already been described in detail at the beginning of the "series."[55] Further on we read: "Unus liber provisionum stipendiariorum peditum existentium ad stipendia lucani Comunis mensium novembris et decembris infrascripti anni,"[56] and later still "unus liber mensure seu mensurationis terrarum positarum in territorio Comunis Fibbialle, mensuratarum per Nardinum Nacchi de Piscia, agrimensorem, et scriptarum per Ser Michelem quondam Conforti de Sorana, notarium et cetera."[57] This third fixed element was supplemented from time to time in the course of the work by other variables, which we will discuss in more detail later. It seems sufficient for the moment to have suggested the possible variations within this particular category.

4) The fourth element is concerned with the thickness of the archival items, which for almost all the entries is given quite fully and accurately. We find "quaternus unus qui est foliorum XVIII," or "quaternorum duorum quorum primus est foliorum V et secundus foliorum XII," or "quaterni unius qui est foliorum VIIII." However, one also finds examples of very simplified descriptions,

such as "quaterni unius," without any further elaboration.[58] There are also exceptional situations, which are faithfully indicated with notations such as

> unus liber terrarum mensuratarum . . . quarternorum trium, quorum primus est foliorm XXV, secundus foliorum XXIIII est tertius foliorum CCV. Et nota quod in dicto secundo quaterno est unum folium legatum et confictum inter cartas LVII et LVIII, secundum quod dictus quaternus signatus est.[59]

revealing the presence of a pre-existing foliation already written on the individual archival items. In another case the lack of a precise description of thickness arises from the nature of the document itself, since having indicated "unus liber exitus denariorum solutorum pro salariis quorundam officialium . . . quaternorum duorum" there is noted "cum filsa mandatoriarum conficta in cuberta dicti libri, scripti manu dicti ser Aytantis."[60]

To these four fixed elements, which can be regarded as fundamental to the work of description, there are added others, which may be defined as variable in that their appearance is sporadic and is very frequently concerned with the nature of the documents themselves and whether or not they lent to a rapid and easy description. The presence of an *intitulatio* in a *liber* could be a sufficient incentive to make a full description of it, facilitating its interpretation in the inventory. It is clear that items that had a full heading were treated differently from those which only had a partial one or none at all. To suggest some of the main variable elements we may note:

a) the indication of the name of the official who held a particular post at the time a document was compiled: "existente camerario Franceschino Riccardi de Honestis,"[61] "unus liber inquisitionum et processuum Curie lucani Fundaci, tempore ser Iohannis Ferrandi de Vico,"[62] "existente Franceschino Acceptantis et Ser Iohanne Genovesis, provisoribus castrorum";[63]

b) the indication of the names of the higher political and administrative authorities, clarifying the historical period in which a document was complied: "tempore domini Comitis de Octhinghen, imperialis Vicarii in Tuscia";[64]

c) the indication of the name or names of those who produced material from which the *liber* was compiled: "unus liber mensure seu mensurationis terrarum positarum in territorio Comunis Fibbialle mensuratarum per Nardinum Nocchii de Piscia, agrimensorem";[65]

d) the indication of the name or names of those who actually wrote the document: "et scriptarum per ser Michelem quondam Conforti de Sorana, notarium";[66]

e) the indication of chronological dating regarding the document: "unus liber fulcimentorum . . . factus sub anno nativitatis Domini MCCCXXIIII,"[67] sometimes including the day and the month of composition: "unus quaternus sine cuberta requisitionum . . . factarum dies XXVIIII aprilis,"[68] sometimes providing a complete dating clause: "unus liber mensurationum . . . scriptarum per dictum ser Michelem, sub anno nativitatis Domini MCCCXXXII et partim anno Domini MCCCXXXIII, indictione prima, inceptus in kalendis decembris suprascripti anni";[69] and

f) the indication of the *incipit* as an additional element illustrating the content: "Item unus alius quaternus requisitionum . . . et incipit de banneria Guardacanis balistarum qui incipit servire die XXVIIII martii et inceperunt requisitiones fieri die VIIII aprilis."[70] Then: "item unus alius quaternus requisitionum balistrariorum . . . et incipit de banneria Francischi Matasse de Cappella Sancti Viti in Battefolle, Pisis, et requisitiones inceperunt fieri die XXV martii."[71] Such entries began to detail the operations that were the actual subject of the document.

Leaving aside a few other minor and exceptional cases, it seems desirable to make a few brief remarks about the external appearance of the documents. When there was nothing special about it, the Inventory makes no mention of the external appearance of a piece; in the other cases it gives exact details. Thus we find "unus liber cuius cuberta est in totum quasi rubes," which details a particularity in the color of the binding.[72] We also find "unus quaternus sine cuberta," which was said to be composed of nineteen *folii*,[73] and another "quaternus in cartis realibus qui . . . est dictus quaternus sine titulo et sine cuberta,"[74] composed of forty pages. There is no information with regard to the materials used for the *cuberte* of the registers, let alone what the outside part of the *filza* was made of.

Among the other details that might also be included, it is necessary to consider those regarding:

i) Use of vernacular. Since the use of Latin was universal, when an archivist found himself dealing with a document written in the vulgar, he was obligated to indicate that fact, as: "Unus liber introitus condepnationum Curie ser Scherlacti . . . et est foliorum VIIII in vulgari. Item est cum eo connexus exitus in alio libro qui est foliorum VIIII inceptus in vulgari."[75]

ii) Atypical books. These were documents not easily classified, either because they had an inadequate heading or date or because they did not have a fixed relationship with any office operating in the city or its territory: "Hic sunt certi libri qui non sunt regulati titulo vel nomine alicuius camerarii et qui non sunt formati sub aliquo anno et sunt pro maiore parte pro solutionibus factis pro spiis et nuntiis ut infra continetur, videlicet."[76]

iii) Recovered books. The search for records did not always produce immediate results, and the Inventory indicates that certain books were transferred from the Chancery of the *Anziani* to the *Camera* of the Custody of Books after the Inventory was begun: "infrascripti sunt certi libri transmissi de Cancelleria Dominorum Antianorum ad Camerarium Custodie Librorum suprascriptorum post dictum inventarium inceptum et sunt ipsi libri condictionum et continentium infrasciptarum, sub annis infrasciptis, videlicet . . ." thus justifying the inevitable anomalies and gaps in the course of the organization of the material.[77]

With this notation we reach an element of particular importance, that is, an introduction to a series, defined by the modern term *cappello*. The presence of such an important characteristic in an inventory of the first half of the fourteenth century represents an important step forward in the evolution of the history of archival practice. The presence of *cappelli* is only occasional and the form they take irregular, although they become more frequent and more significant in the latter half of the century. Not to dwell on the question at excessive length, we will here take but a few examples that seem particularly significant.

Ser Giovanni Barellia had found certain *extraordinarii* books in the *Camera*, and when called upon to describe them he felt obligated to detail where and how he had found them and his method of describing them: "Hic sunt libri extraordinarii multarum et diversarum materiarum, qui ordinem noscuntur, reperti in Camera suprascripta lucani Comunis, inter alios libros in ipsa Camera existentes, qui libri extraordiinarii hic scipti sunt in hunc modum videlicet . . . ," almost as if he were justifying his failure to respect an internal order of his adoption of an arrangement that was not entirely appropriate from an archival point of view.[78] Another series heading appears to be in the same vein, given that the compiler indicates that: "hic sunt certi libri qui non sunt regulati titulo vel nomine alicuius Camere et qui non sunt formati sub aliquo anno anno [*sic*] et sunt per maiorem partem pro solutionibus factis pro spiis et nuntiis, ut infra continetur, videlicet . . . ," making it clear that since he was dealing with documents that lacked an organic character of their own and any heading, a short introduction was needed to clarify the situation.[79]

The method adopted for the insertion of a series heading when the archivist had to record that certain books had been sent by the Chancery of the *Anziani* to the *Camera Librorum* is not all that different: "Infrascripti sunt libri transmissi da Cancellaria dominorum Antianorum ad Cameram Custodie Librorum suprasciptam, post dictum inventarium inceptum et sunt ipsi libri condictionum et continentium infrascriptarum, sub annis infrascriptis."[80]

Besides these series headings (*cappelli*) inserted to explain unusual situations that had arisen and were thus in a sense atypical, there are other series headings that we can define without any hesitation as typical, in that they are included solely as an introduction to a series with the aim of describing it and making it easier to consult. The introduction to the "series" of documents stemming from the outlying magistracies already possesses these characteristics despite its brevity: "Hic sunt libri extimationum factarum sub annis infrascriptis infra infracriptis Vicariis et etiam in Sex miliariis, Comitatus, Districtus et Fortie lucani comunis, ut infra continetur, videlicet. . . ."[81] But another conceived along the same lines is yet more informative:

> Hic sunt certe filse, in quibus reperiuntur certe dationes reddituum et affictuum, in quibus homines et persone infracriptorum pleberiorum Sexmiliariorum vel quasi et suburbanorum et aliorum, ut infra notantur et in ipsis filsis continetur, tenentur et debent lucanis civibus et aliis secundum dationes inde factas, sub anno navitatis Domini MCCCVIII et aliis annis, ut infra continetur.[82]

The series heading in this case serves the precise function of illustrating the nature of the documents that were to be described subsequently, and this character represents an element of particular significance.

In this same vein, it is appropriate to quote in full an extended series heading that complements what has been expounded above:

> Hic sunt libri facti, compositi et ordinati pro confessionibus redditarum et affictuum ad quas et quos homines et persone infrascriptorum pleberiorum, Comunium et locorum in dictis Vicariis lucani Comitatus et

Districtus et Fortie tenentur et debent lucanis civibus et aliis ut in ipsis
libris plenius continetur, ac etiam continentes pro parte mensurationum
terrarum factarum in ipsis eisdem locis et partibus et alia secuta ex illis,
que veniunt in favorem civium lucanorum et aliorum habentium ius vel
actionem in terris mensuratis, secundum ea que secuta et facta sunt inde,
unde in ipsis libris ipsarum mensurationum terrarum particulariter est
descriptum; qui libri de predictis infra describuntur et apparent in hunc
modum sub brevitate, videlicet. . . .[83]

This extended description assumes an individuality of its own in
comparison to the entries previously described, since it is not confined merely to categorizing the archival material to which it is attached but extends its scope to go deeply into the contents, so as
to furnish fuller information, which is primarily institutional and
procedural in character.

I believe, on the basis of the above analysis, that it is possible
to argue the thesis that there was a real consciousness of method
in the field of archival technique. This decidedly positive judgement should encourage further research to discover how well developed archival theory was in the medieval period and how it was
applied in practice. This first study, confined strictly to the work
of ser Giovanni Barellia, represents a firm basis on which to proceed to further stages of research. There are two other registers,
also fourteenth century, preserved in the *Archivio di Stato in Lucca*
together with this first Inventory: one bears the date of 12 January
1348 onwards when ser Blasio Mariani of Lucca held the post of
Custos Camere Librorum and was compiled by ser Stefano Bongio-
vanni of Lucca, with, as its subject, certain archival items that had
evaded the earlier search carried out by ser Giovanni Barellia; the
other was begun in 1389 and continued until 1440. It is worth
noting that the archival listings that came into existence in these
three decades were carried out directly by various *Custodes Camere
Librorum* who held office at the times in question without having
recourse to outside appointments, just as happened in the Pisan

period, 1344–48.[84] At the moment the register was begun, ser
Pietro, son of the late ser Michele Bonagiunta, was named in the
first place as *Custos Librorum Camere* in 1389; subsequently in
1400 the entries were made by ser Bartolomeo di Lammari *Custos
Camere Librorum* and his successor in this post, ser Aldibrando
Luporini. From 1428 the additions were made by ser Giovanni Nesi
Custos Camere.[85]

After the destruction suffered in the thirteenth century and even
more in the first three decades of the fourteenth, Lucca was duti-
fully watchful with regard to the preservation of its archival
records, as the richness of the material that has come down to us
bears witness. It is in direct relation to these sources that one can
try out new lines of research aimed at extending our knowledge of
the history of archives and archival studies.

NOTES

1. A. Mancini, *Storia di Lucca* (Florence, 1950), pp. 99–101, 117–46. For the
period of Castruccio, see especially the collective volume *Castruccio Castracani
e il suo tempo*, published as *Actum Luce*, 13–14 (1984–85).

2. S. Bongi, *Inventario del R. Archivio di Stato in Lucca*, 4 vols. (Lucca,
1872–88), 1:xiii. Bongi specifies further that "alquanti documenti che pare fossero
privilegi e carte antiche, affermanti la libertà e i diritti di Lucca, a buon fine e per
amor di patria, erano stati trafugati da que' guelfi che esularono allorché la città
venne in servitù; e dopo essere stati in sicuro a Venezia presso la Scuola del Volto
Santo, furono restituiti, quando riavuta ed assicurata la libertà, la Signoria li
richiese."

3. Bongi, *Inventario*, 1:xi. The archive represented an essential and indispensable
possession "essendovi chi tentava d'usurpare i beni altrui, col pretesto che il
possessore non ne avesse legittimo documento."

4. Series "Anziani avanti la libertà" 7 states "cum propter ignem missum in
Civitate lucana, in anno D. MCCCXXVIIII, die XVIIII martii, multi libri, imo

quasi omnes libri et scripture lucane Camere et lucani Comunis et gabelle, fuerunt combusti et deperditi" (Bongi, *Inventario*, 1:xii). All documents cited are conserved in the *Archivio di Stato in Lucca*.

5. This event had decisive effects on the archival records, which, after the disasters of 1329, had been reconstituted; see Bongi, *Inventario*, 1:xii–xiii.

6. Bongi, *Inventario*, 1:xiii–xiv. Bongi, however adds mischievously that "un Governo malevolo e dispettoso come quello, non é poi a credere fosse molto sollecito nella buona conservazione de' documenti." Recent studies have led to a revision of this judgement (which is also found in many other Lucchese chronicles and historical works). Christine Meek, in her study on *The Commune of Lucca under Pisan Rule, 1342–1369* (Cambridge, Mass., 1980), pp. 120–21, 127, stresses in her conclusion that "it is necessary to look at Pisan rule in context to examine the particular problems that Pisa had to face in trying to rule Lucca and the solutions that it found—before one can see whether its administration was harsher than it need have been" and expresses the considered opinion that "the mere fact that Lucca was ruled by Pisa may have constituted servitude for the Lucchese, but the rule itself does not seem to have been tyrannical." For the most up-to-date bibliography on the period in question, see L. Green, *Castruccio Castracani: A Study on the Origins and Character of a Fourteenth-Century Italian Despotism* (Oxford, 1986).

7. See n. 4 above. The losses caused by these problems are also mentioned in other surviving documents, such as the *Statuto delle Curie* of 1331, where it is stated: "cum tempore combustionis facte in dicta Civitate a.n.D. MCCCXXVIIII, die XIX martii, multi libri et acta Curiarum fuerint combusti et combusta et derobbata" (Bongi, *Inventario*, 1:xii, n. 3).

8. Series *Archivi Pubblici*, I, hereafter cited as *Inventario*. The *Archivi Pubblici* consists of fifty-eight items, made up of inventories, indices, and other manuscripts connected with *Tarpea*, documentation relating to the *Offizio sopra le Scritture*.

9. The civil and criminal courts of the city and its surrounding territory, including those of the Vicariates, occupy the first part of the *Inventario*, to be precise, fols. 2–71. The two volumes for the *Curia del Podestà* are still extant. As far as the *Curia dei Foretani* is concerned we now have volumes for 1312 and 1330 onwards, in contrast to those listed in the fourteenth-century inventory. For the *Curia*

Nova di Giustizia the present situation coincides more closely with that in the *Inventario*.

10. The *Curia dei Treguani* also currently begins in 1328. The *Curia delle Querimonie* shows lacunae beginning in 1333, and the same applies to the *Curia dei Castaldi*, which now has no records earlier than 1331.

11. As far as the *Curia del Maggior Sindaco e Giudice degli Appelli* is concerned the present condition coincides with that of the fourteenth-century inventory, with the first volumes dating back to 1327. The identification of the condition of the *Curia dei Vicari* appears more difficult.

12. The volumes for the *Cancelleria degli Anziani* are listed on fols. 72–77 of the fourteenth-century inventory. From the often very brief descriptions it is not always easy to identify a particular item for comparison with the position described by Bongi.

13. The *Curia de' Ribelli e de' Banditi* begins as a continuous series in 1329, but in Bongi's inventory there are surviving documents dating back to 1296. The *Curia del Fondaco* has suffered major losses, the documents at present extant dating only from 1337. The *Curia della Taglia delle Cinquantasettemila e della Paga de' Pedoni*, with documents as far back as 1329 in the fourteenth-century inventory, now has documents from 1331 onwards.

14. Bongi, *Inventario*, 2:37.

15. For a few outline indications, see nn. 9–13 above. I do not intend to discuss this further at present, although I intend to pursue the subject in a later study.

16. Series *Archivi Pubblici*. As well as these three inventories of the *Camera Librorum*, there are others for the fourteenth century, but they are either fragments (no. 12, fourteenth century), manuscripts made up of different kinds of documents (no. 13, c.1350), *Libri Memoriales* containing, among other things, inventories (no. 14, 1360–86), records of the deposit of documents (no. 15, 1387–1420), or materials connected with notarial activity (no. 30, 1389–1422; no. 31, 1312–61; no. 32, 1361–1446; no. 37, 1388–1422; no. 39, 1361–82).

17. I intend to deal with the whole problem of fourteenth- and fifteenth-century archival practices on another occasion.

18. *Inventario*. The twelve folios at the beginning have the following heading: "Rubrica librorum et scripturarum existentium in presenti libro seu Inventario librorum existentium in Cammera lucani Comunis, sub custodia ser Nicoali Tedaldini de Luca, notarii et dictorum librorum Camere Custodis."

19. Bongi, *Inventario*, 1:xi. Another notary, Conte Clavari, was named along with ser Tedaldino Lazari, as is shown by a reading of the *Statuto del Comune di Lucca dell'anno MCCCVIII*, ed. S. Bongi (Lucca, 1867), *Liber Quartus*, cap. XLI, pp. 269–70: "De officio iudicis Camere et eius notariorum." The two notaries are also mentioned in *Liber Secundus*, cap. LV, p. 110, where they are described as "notarii et custodes librorum lucani Comunis."

20. *Inventario*, fol. 1^r: "scriptus, copiatus et excemplatus ex originali Inventario de dictis libris et scripturis facto, edito et ordinato per discretum virum ser Iohannem Barelie de Luca, notarium ad dictum Inventarium faciendum per dominos Antianos etc. spetialiter deputaum. *Anno n.* D. MCCCXLIIII *et partim anno* MCCCXLV."

21. *Statuto, liber Secundus*, cap. LIIII, p. 108.

22. The events described at the beginning of this essay confirm the unhappy consequences of a method of organization that was extremely correct and of the very greatest importance from an archival point of view.

23. It should be made clear that as happened in other cities—such as the example of Bologna mentioned by G. Cencetti, "Camera Actorum Comunis Bononie," *Archivi*, 2 (1935), 87–120 and by G. Fasoli, "Due inventari degli archivi del Comune di Bologna nel secolo XIII," *Atti delle deputazione di Storia Patria per le Romagne*, ser. 4, 33 (1933), 173–77—the deposit of archival material often took place as a result of the handing over of the office to one's successor, and terms of office were of very limited duration, rarely exceeding a year.

24. The Commune, later the Republic, of Lucca classified the archival records of the outlying bodies, particularly in the vicariates, according to the juridical position of the body that produced them. Those archives of the vicars with a judicial character and, thus, a function that derived strictly by delegation from the central power unconnected with the minor local entities, were deposited periodically in the *Camera Librorum* in Lucca. Those archives with an administrative character

that were produced in cooperation with the local communities remained in the local center of that vicariate. This structural organization has given rise to the present-day archival distribution; the first group are now to be found in the *Archivio di Stato in Lucca*, while the second are in the archives of the local Communes that were the administrative centers of the vicariates in the republican period.

25. For the development of Lucchese offices in the fourteenth century, see A. Romiti, "La Curia del Fondaco ed il commercio minuto lucchese nel secolo decimoquarto," *Actum Luce*, 1 (1972), 59–67.

26. In order to give some idea of the variety of *proventi*, one may cite the titles of the surviving record series now preserved in the Archivio di Stato in Lucca: *Provento del vino venale*; *Provento del macello*; *Provento della farina*; *Provento della mezza oncia del pane*; *Provento dei molini*; and *Provento dei cittadini silvestri* (Bongi, *Inventario*, 2:56–62).

27. The outlying bodies in the vicariates also deposited their archival material very promptly; the vicariate of Camaiore had completed its deposits up to 1343 inclusive, and that of Pietrasanta up to 1342 inclusive, that of Valle Ariana up to 1343 inclusive, and that of Barga up to 1344 inclusive. Only Coreglia was behind schedule, having delivered the documents relative to its judicial activity up to the year 1333.

28. For the *Estimo* it is possible to effect a comparison between the archival material listed in the fourteenth-century inventory and that still extant, on the basis of citations provided by Bongi, *Inventario*, 2:127–67.

29. The methods adopted in compiling the *Inventario* are not entirely uniform, as we shall see. Taken overall, however, they appear to conform to a reasonably consistent general approach, although there are exceptions, which will be made clear later.

30. *Inventario*, fol. 62^r.

31. *Inventario*, fol. 62^r.

32. *Inventario*, fols. 174^v–75^r.

33. *Inventario*, fol. 266^r.

34. *Inventario*, fols. 62^{r-v}, 165^{r-v}, 247^v, 266^r.

35. *Inventario*, fol. 215^r: "Pro registro mesurationum terrarum factarum."

36. *Inventario*, fol. 61^v.

37. *Inventario*, fol. 62^v.

38. *Inventario*, fol. 87^v.

39. *Inventario*, fol. 82^r: "unus liber sive quaternus introitus omnium denariorum habitorum et recollectorum ex officio domini Iohannis Vicarii et Maioris Officialis Viarum et Publicorum lucani Comunis de condepnationibus factis per eum ordinarie et de facto ac etiam per ser Iohannem de Racignano, maiorem officialem dicte Curie, pro ultimis sex mensibus anni MCCCXLIII, exisente Camerario dicte Civitatis ser Iohanne del passo et cetera . . . quaterni unius."

40. *Inventario*, fol. 82^r.

41. *Inventario*, fol. 262^r.

42. *Inventario*, fol. 262^r.

43. *Inventario*, fol. 246^r: "Quaternuli decem in quibus sunt reddite date in scriptis Nove Gabelle, sub anno suprascripto MCCCXVIII et sunt infrascriptorum Comunium plebis masse Pisane."

44. *Inventario*, fol. 61^v, passim.

45. *Inventario*, fol. 240^r, passim.

46. *Inventario*, fol. 62^v: "Una vacchetta in cartis regalibus solucionum factarum certis ultramontanis pro eorum pagis."

47. *Inventario*, fol. 249^v.

48. *Inventario*, fol. 214^v: "Duo quaterni sine cuberta in cartis realibus quorum primus incipit."

49. *Inventario*, fol. 61^v.

50. *Inventario*, fol. 62^v.

51. *Inventario*, fol. 65^r.

52. *Inventario*, fol. 260^r.

53. *Inventario*, fol. 61^v.

54. *Inventario*, fol. 266^r.

55. *Inventario*, fol. 61^v.

56. *Inventario*, fol. 88^r.

57. *Inventario*, fol. 173^r.

58. *Inventario*, fol. 61^v, passim.

59. *Inventario*, fol. 173^r.

60. *Inventario*, fol. 237^r.

61. *Inventario*, fol. 61^v.

62. *Inventario*, fol. 62^r.

63. *Inventario*, fol. 165^r.

64. *Inventario*, fol. 165^r.

65. *Inventario*, fol. 173^r.

66. *Inventario*, fol. 173^r.

67. *Inventario*, fol. 165^r.

68. *Inventario*, fol. 171^v.

69. *Inventario*, fol. 173^r.

70. *Inventario*, fol. 171^v.

71. *Inventario*, fol. 171^v.

72. *Inventario*, fol. 188^r.

73. *Inventario*, fol. 171^v.

74. *Inventario*, fol. 217^v.

75. *Inventario*, fol. 241^r.

76. *Inventario*, fol. 171^v.

77. *Inventario*, fol. 247^r.

78. *Inventario*, fol. 165^r.

79. *Inventario*, fol. 171^v.

80. *Inventario*, fol. 247^r.

81. *Inventario*, fol. 263^r.

82. *Inventario*, fol. 266^r.

83. *Inventario*, fol. 173^r.

84. Series *Archivi Pubblici*, nos. 2 and 3. Bongi, *Inventario*, 1:226–27.

85. The two registers consist of 100 and 248 folios respectively.

Coluccio Salutati, Chancellor of the Republic of Lucca, and the Problem of the *Minute di Riformagioni Pubbliche* (1370–71)

GIORGIO TORI

On 17 July 1370 the *Anziani* of Lucca elected Coluccio Salutati *Cancelliere delle Riformagioni* of the Commune. This appointment came at a particularly critical time in Coluccio's life. In late August 1367 he had left his native Valdinievole to take up the post of Chancellor of the Commune of Todi for a six-month period, but instead of returning to Tuscany when his term of office there came to an end, he decided to transfer to Rome and to the papal court that had recently returned from Avignon.[1] There, in the shelter of the influential friendship of Francesco Bruni, one of the papal secretaries, he served for almost two years in second-rank jobs in the papal chancery, probably in the section directed by Bruni, making various attempts to obtain more important posts. He tried unsuccessfully to obtain the office of Chancellor at Viterbo and at Perugia, and as early as 31 August 1369 he was proposed directly by the pope for the Chancellorship of Lucca. But again, despite the powerful recommendation, another candidate received the appointment.[2]

Coluccio, however, did not give up. His numerous influential friends in Lucca must have duly informed him that the possibility of obtaining the office still existed, for on 9 February 1370 another papal letter was sent to Lucca, this time asking explicitly for the

111

post of Chancellor for Coluccio.[3] A positive decision on the appointment came just in time, on 17 July 1370. A few days later a major political upheaval confirmed the victory of the Lucchese popular party over the aristocratic faction, a turn of events that created considerable difficulties for Coluccio's friends and protectors. Under the leadership of Nino and Giovanni degli Opizi, Niccoloso Bartolomei, and Niccolo Diversi, the aristocrats had turned the political situation to their own advantage in the first few months after Lucca had recovered its independence, and they had succeeded in securing the post of Chancellor for Coluccio in one of the last meetings of the Thirty Six *sapientes et prudentes* held before the political upheaval.[4] Coluccio therefore took up office in mid-August amidst a climate that could not have been particularly favorable to him personally. It was probably only due to the support of the pope and Bruni that his appointment was accepted and confirmed in spite of the changed political situation.

In addition to this difficulty there was added a whole series of troubles and disillusionments that greatly reduced the degree of enthusiasm with which Coluccio bent himself to his important task. The assignment quickly showed itself to be much harder and more tedious than he had expected. The complicated workings of the Lucchese government, divided as it was into a number of councils and commissions, involved Coluccio in periods of heavy and concentrated effort. Indeed, on 24 October 1370, after only a few months in office he wrote to ser Tommaso de' Vergiolesi lamenting the burdens of his duties, which required him to rise at dawn to do the bidding of the *Anziani* and left him little time to do other than eat and sleep.[5] Noting with obvious displeasure the contrast between his humanistic aspirations and the rigidly formalistic tradition inherent in his position as notary and Chancellor, Coluccio looked back nostalgically to the time when he had been free to devote himself to study and to the composition of refined and elegant literary pieces: "I have truly always preferred the studious life with ample free time to be passed, among my books, in reading."[6]

To all this there must have been added an ever-increasing aware-ness of the precariousness of his political position. His hopes of being confirmed in office, if he ever had any, came to a complete end in November 1370, when an unsuccessful attempt by the aris-tocratic party to regain power resulted in accusations of plotting against the Republic implicating Giovanni and Tommaso degli Opizi, and Niccolo Diversi.[7] In fact, on 22 July 1371 the *Anziani* appointed ser Pietro Saraceni as *Cancelliere delle Riformagioni*, in effect dismissing Coluccio.[8]

Coluccio still had powerful friends in the city, however, who were able to render his position a little less difficult, and a few days later he was appointed *Maior Consul* of the Court of Mer-chants, remaining in this office probably until the early months of 1372.[9] But his stay in Lucca was destined to become even more dif-ficult. In the autumn of 1371 his wife, Caterina, pregnant with their second child, died unexpectedly, plunging him into a profound state of depression and dejection from which he only began to re-cover in the early months of 1372.[10] His stay in the city rendered him so miserable that he wrote to his friend Giovanni da Monte-calvo describing his depressed state of mind and requesting assis-tance in finding an honorable way out of his current situation.[11] A few months later, perhaps in February or, at the latest, in March, Coluccio left Lucca permanently for the peace of his native Stignano in the Valdinievole.[12]

There is ample evidence of Coluccio's presence in Lucca as *Can-celliere delle Riformagioni* in the form of a manuscript register, in his hand, containing the official records of the meetings of the com-munal councils and some of the decisions of the *Anziani* of Lucca.[13] In addition to this well-known manuscript, extensively quoted by Armando Petrucci and Ronald Witt, there exists a second register, which Witt also knew and commented upon, containing the *Minute* or notes from which Salutati drew up the official register.[14] In the course of a careful study of the Chancery under Coluccio, connected with the publication in calendar form of his register of *Riformagioni*,[15] I have been able to make a systematic comparison of the official text with that of the *Minute* and to arrive at conclusions of some significant historical and methodological interest.

While the official register covers a year without interruption, that is, from August 1370 to the end of July 1371, the *Minute* survive only for the period 16 April to 27 July 1371. This is a fairly short period, but it is, nevertheless, sufficient to allow us to examine in some detail the workings of the Chancery under Coluccio, which can only be described as puzzling. The differences in form between the two manuscripts are very marked. The *Minute* entries that Coluccio made on the spot during council meetings were hastily written notes in a highly abbreviated form. They were the rough drafts from which the Chancellor later drew up the official council records. They are consequently almost entirely without the usual formulae, reduced to the bare minimum, and written in a chancery hand with the same basic characteristics as that of the official record, but less careful, more cursive, and more abbreviated. The first general point to be made is that there are council records in the *Minute* that were not recorded in the official register. This omission, which might at first glance seem easy to account for, is in fact inexplicable.

Let us examine the cases in question one by one, beginning with the General Council, the most important constitutional body within the Commune. The council deliberations that Coluccio does not include in the official text are seven in all.[16] In some cases his exclusions can be ascribed to the failure to qualify for inclusion for formal reasons, such as not obtaining the majority laid down in the statutes when put to the vote. But in other cases the question is more difficult. This applies to the meeting on 29 April, for example, when two matters were discussed and voted upon: the price to be fixed for the grain belonging to the Commune and the sale of

some of the property of the ex-Doge of Pisa, Giovanni dell'
Agnello. There does not seem to be anything procedural missing:
the discussion and the vote appear to be just as valid as that of
other matters which are recorded.[17] Nevertheless, for reasons that
we are not in a position to explain, Coluccio does not record the
text of this meeting in the official record.

It is also possible to note substantial differences within accounts that are recorded in both volumes. At the meeting of 7 May,
for example, only one proposal was discussed. This dealt with the
imposition of the *gabella terrarum*. The official register records
just one recommendation, attributed to ser Ubaldo Perfettucci,[18] but
the *Minute* record five: the first that of ser Ubaldo, the second that
of Rainerio del Caro, the third that of Bartolomeo Nucci, the fourth
that of ser Jacopo Domaschi, and the fifth that of Donato Panichi.[19]
All five recommendations are joined together in the *Minute* text by
a bracket in the margin to indicate that they were all approved by
137 votes in favor to 37 against. Examining the text of the recommendation recorded by Coluccio in the official register and attributed entirely to ser Ubaldo Perfettucci, it is easy to see that
Coluccio has fused together the recommendations of all the other
speakers. This leads me to make a preliminary observation of a historiographical nature, that is, that one should be extremely cautious
about attributing a certain attitude or a particular opinion to any individual on the basis of the official register alone. This could obviously lead to major distortions in interpreting what actually happened in the council chamber.

The differences between the *Minute* and the final account are
even greater if one passes on to look at the records of the lesser
council, or Council of Thirty-Six. This body, which consisted of
the *Anziani* plus four *Vexilliferi* and eight other councillors for each
of the three *Terzieri* of the city, met far more frequently than the
General Council. It therefore provides us with more material for
comparison.

Between 16 April and 21 July 1371 there were eight meetings of the Council of Thirty-Six that Coluccio did not record in the official text.[20] The most significant case for our purposes is that of the meeting of 22 May, centered on the proposal *de habendo pecuniam*. As many as five councillors spoke on the subject, and the recommendation of Dino di Vanni Malapresa was approved by 46 votes in favor with only 1 vote against, which represents an overwhelming majority.[21] Nevertheless, for reasons that I am unable to explain, Coluccio did not include this meeting in the official record.

Similar observations can be made with regard to the council records of 11, 12, and 21 June, when, in addition to some opinions that were not put to the vote, recommendations were discussed and voted on in the regular way. This is shown by the voting figures written in the margins of the *Minute* that apply to the recommendation of Francesco Dati on 11 June *super factis Tirellii*, which was approved by 52 votes in favor with 8 against,[22] to that of *magister* Federico Trenta on the following day, also approved by the same margin,[23] and finally that of Luigi Boccella on 21 June *super pacta Tirellii tam Comunis quam filiorum domini Francisci*, which was also approved by 62 votes in favor and 5 against.[24] Yet, these too are not to be found in the official account.

If we examine the records of meetings of the Council of Thirty-Six that are included both in the official records and in the *Minute*, we find no cases similar to those in the records for the General Council where opinions are attributed to one councillor when they were in fact expressed by other speakers. But there still remain difficulties and problems of considerable import in dealing with this material. It is obvious that Coluccio recorded in the official register only those recommendations that were put to the vote in the Council, without devoting any space to views that were not approved at the time. This practice is shown in the *Minute* by the fact that there were no voting figures in the margin beside the opinions expressed by councillors. But there are also a number of cases in which the Chancellor failed to record in the official register a recommendation regularly voted and approved. In the meeting of 16 April the Council of Thirty-Six discussed the proposal *statuere super frumento lucani Comunis quod est in quantitate stariorum MCC*. The opinion of Bartolomeo Ronghi has a voting figure in the margin of 49 votes in favor, exactly the same number as Bartolomeo Balbani got on the next proposal, *super ordinamentum ferri sgabellandi in Civitate lucana*, which was included in the official register in the regular way.[25] Yet the opinion of Bartolomeo Ronghi was not recorded in the official register. It is impossible to understand what motive of substance or form could have led to such practices.

A further comparison of the two documents allows us to make some significant comments on the composition of the councils. As is well known, in both the General Council and the Council of Thirty-Six, a number of *invitati*, in addition to those who were members of the council, could take part if the *Anziani* desired and decided to summon them. The number of *invitati* was not fixed but rather tended to vary. This was a system that could hardly fail to have political implications, since it made it possible for the *Anziani* in office to exercise considerable influence on the outcome of votes. The *Minute* make it clear that in some cases, instead of *invitati* being summoned on an individual basis, groups of officials with a specific qualification might also take part in the council. This is especially true for the eighteen *boni homines super regimine*, a kind of constitutional commission created to keep watch on the internal security and order of the Commune. But Coluccio in the official register passes over this fact—although it may be of great significance from a historical point of view—and only indicates in general terms that there were *invitati* present, even when these were, in fact, the members of the Council of Eighteen *super regimine*.

Eight separate meetings of the Council of Eighteen are recorded in the official record, whereas thirteen appear in the *Minute* in the same period. We therefore have the same situation that has already been noted with regard to the records of the General Council and the Council of Thirty-Six. Here, moreover, the voting figures seem satisfactory, and there are no reasons to suggest why it was not thought appropriate to include accounts of these sessions in the official record.

Next let us consider the large number of entries in the *Minute* regarding the activities of the *Anziani*. Not all activities of the *Anziani*, again, were recorded in the official record. In the three months for which we have *Minute* records, ninety-four meetings of the *Anziani* were entered, only forty of which were recorded in the Register of the General Council. There is one example of the opposite happening, that is, of an entry that appears in the official record and not in the *Minute*.[26] This very large discrepancy is again difficult to account for. It should, in any case, be noted that numerous entries are in a hand other than that of Coluccio, which gives one reason to think that two different Chancellors took turns at writing the *Minute* and that, for internal reasons, some entries were regarded as suitable for inclusion in the official record of the deliberations of the *Anziani* and not in that of the *Riformagioni*. This line of reasoning is shown to be unacceptable, however, by a comparison with the register of the *Deliberazioni degli Anziani*, which does not record any of the entries contained in the *Minute* that failed to be included in the official register.

It is not possible at present to give any real answer to all these queries and problems. One can at this point only form hypotheses. The most intriguing possibility would be that there were considerations of a political nature that obliged Coluccio to make a choice as to which entries should be given the official character of law. This is acceptable as a hypothesis, but it is one for which an examination of the substance of the decisions in question does not seem to offer much support. It also may be asked if there were formal reasons beyond a simple count of the votes that decided which entries should be included. If this is the case, one has to admit that at the present stage of research these reasons have not yet been discovered. What is clear is that, considering the characteristics and anomalies we have found, the use of *riformagioni* records, which are among those most frequently cited by historians, presents certain limits and certain risks that should not be underestimated.

Finally, despite the unsolved problems, we find in the register of the *Minute* one curious and pleasant surprise. On some of its folios, perhaps as a result of the boredom that overcame him during the long and inconclusive council discussions, Coluccio amused himself by practicing his Greek. There are just a few lines in which, in an exercise common to almost all students in the early stages of learning a language written in an alphabet different from their own, Coluccio transliterated some Latin phrases into Greek.[27] This curious and moving detail gives us yet further insight into the personality and personal problems of the great humanist who had few, if any, pleasant memories of his stay in Lucca. But from an historical point of view it might also make us think of Coluccio's relations with a hypothetical Lucchese merchant who had perhaps lived for a time in the Eastern Mediterranean or in Sicily and was able to inspire Coluccio with the need to know Greek, a language which, in fact, he never managed to master completely.

NOTES

1. The bibliography on Coluccio is very extensive, and we will cite here only some of the most important works. Fundamental are the studies of F. Novati, *Epistolario di Coluccio Salutati* in *Fonti per la storia d'Italia; Epistolari*, vols. 15–18 (Rome, 1891–1911); and *La Giovinezza di Coluccio Salutati (1331–1353)* (Turin, 1883). The recent studies by Ronald Witt are extremely important: see especially "Coluccio Salutati and the Political Life of the Commune of Buggiano (1351–1374)," *Rinascimento*, 6 (1966), 27–56; "Coluccio Salutati, Chancellor and Citizen of Lucca," *Traditio*, 25 (1969), 191–216; "Toward a Biography of

Coluccio Salutati," *Rinascimento*, 16 (1976), 19–34; and his most recent work, *Hercules at the Crossroads: The Life, Work and Thought of Coluccio Salutati* (Durham, N.C., 1983). Now classics and indispensable are the studies of B. L. Ulmann, *Studies in the Italian Renaissance* (Rome, 1955), pp. 3–26; and *The Humanism of Coluccio Salutati* (Padua, 1963), pp. 3–16. Also of great importance are the works of Armando Petrucci, *Il protocollo notarile di Coluccio Salutati (1372–73)* (Milan, 1963), pp. 1–151; and *Coluccio Salutati* (Rome, 1972). Finally, the following studies of A. de Rosa are useful: "Cenni bibliografici relativi a Coluccio Salutati," in *Atti del Convegno su Coluccio Salutati* (Buggiani Castello, June 1980), pp. 47–62; and *Coluccio Salutati, il Cancelliere e il pensatore politico* (Florence, 1980).

2. Witt, "Coluccio Salutati, Chancellor," pp. 191–96.

3. A. Mancini, *Sulle orme del Salutati* (Lucca, 1920), pp. 6–7.

4. Witt, "Coluccio Salutati, Chancellor," p. 192; A. Romiti, "La classe politica lucchese nei primi anni di libertà," *Atti del III convegno di studi sulla storia dei ceti dirigenti in Toccano* (Florence, 1980), pp. 135–46.

5. Novati, *Epistolario*, 1:133: "cum enim michi et officii huius cura reique familiaris immineat, ego, discendentis aurora in noctis crepuscolo linquente Titonem perfusam conthoralem meam sopore dimitto et ad Antianos, sic enim de istorum more vocantur, matutinus accedo, unde vix pransurus domum rediens usque ad plurimam noctem vigilans sero divellor; illud quod restat crepusculum tum cene, tum prebens domui, tum quieti, vix somnum complevi; ecce et aliud mane, et idem cetus Antianorum per lictorem me revocat, anxiis me laboribus traditurus, si liceret, ponerem tibi ante oculos diem unam; sed sic occupor, ut hec ipsa moleste vix valeam explicare." See also Witt, "Coluccio Salutati, Chancellor," p. 203.

6. Petrucci, *Il protocollo notarile*, p. 18; Novati, *Epistolario*, 1:133: "ego enim semper studiosam optavi vitam et ocio plenam ut inter libellos degens lectione tempus attererem."

7. G. Sercambi, *Le Croniche*, ed. S. Bongi in *Fonti per la storia d'Italia; Scrittori*, vol. 1 (Rome, 1892), pp. 204–06. There is an error of dating in Chapter CCXXXVIII of the *Cronaca* that needs to be corrected in order to avoid a mistaken interpretation of subsequent events. Sercambi ascribes to the year 1371 the

events that culminated in the revolution of 31 July 1370. The error is made clear by the fact that Ugolino dei Galluzzi, whom Sercambi names as *Podestà* of Lucca during these events, in fact left office in November 1370. It is thus evident that Sercambi simply made a mistake through a slip of the pen when writing up his chronicle. From this mistake, which Witt failed to recognize as such, there has followed an erroneous interpretation of subsequent events. Witt, in fact, writes: "then in February 1371 the aristocratic faction tried to overthrow the regime of July 31 by an overt act of revolution. Giovanni degli Opizzi was subsequently accused of treason and Niccolò Diversi and Tommaso degli Opizzi were forced to go surety for him" ("Coluccio Salutati, Chancellor," p. 200). In reality these events happened in November 1370, as the *Riformagioni* clearly show (fols. 74^r–^{v}). A final proof of this is Chapter CCXXXIX of the *Cronaca*, where Sercambi, quoted by Witt ("Coluccio Salutati, Chancellor," p. 205), names as *Gonfaloniere di Giustizia*, *magister* Federigo Trenta, who did indeed hold this office in November and December 1370 (*Consiglio Generale* 2, fol. 64^r, hereafter cited as *Cons. Gen.*). All documents cited in this study are preserved in the *Archivio di Stato in Lucca*.

8. *Cons. Gen.* 1, fol. 241^r; A. Romiti, *Riformagioni della Repubblica di Lucca, (1369–1400), Volume primo, 1369–1370*, in *Accademia Nazionale dei Lincei, Commissione per gli Atti delle Assemblee Costituzionali Italiane* (Rome, 1985).

9. Witt, "Coluccio Salutati, Chancellor," pp. 201–02.

10. Witt, "Coluccio Salutati, Chancellor," pp. 208–09.

11. Novati, *Epistolario*, 1:159: "quod hic mestissimus sum et, si fiat hec mora diuturnior, forte, quamvis libenter, coniugis mee funera comitabor, provide tu, si qua via est, ut hic me coneris honoranter evellere."

12. Witt, "Coluccio Salutati, Chancellor," pp. 209–10.

13. *Cons. Gen.* 2.

14. Series *Anziani al tempo della libertà* 2, hereafter cited as *Anz. temp. lib.*

15. A. Romiti, *Riformagioni della Repubblica di Lucca (1369–1400), Volume secondo, Agosto 1370–Luglio 1371 e Appendice, per cura di Giorgio Tori, Accademia Nazionale dei Lincei: Commissione per gli Atti delle Assemblee*

Costituzionali Italiane (Rome, 1985).

16. These are 23 and 29 April, 4 and 7 May, 18 June, and 4 and 16 July 1371.

17. *Anz. temp. lib.* 2, fol. 19^r.

18. *Cons. Gen.* 2, fol, 150^v.

19. *Anz. temp. lib.* 2, fol. 23^v.

20. They are the meetings of 27 April, 22 May, 11, 12, and 21 June, and 3 July; there are some doubts about the meetings of 18 and 29 May, because it is not specified which council it was. But the type of decision taken makes it very probable that the meetings in question were those of the Council of Thirty-Six rather than the General Council.

21. *Anz. temp. lib.* 2, fols. 30^{r-v}.

22. *Anz. temp. lib.* 2, fol. 39^v.

23. *Anz. temp. lib.* 2, fol. 40^r.

24. *Anz. temp. lib.* 2, fols. 47^{r-v}.

25. *Anz. temp. lib.* 2, fol. 1^r; *Cons. Gen.* 2, fol. 136^r.

26. This was the meeting of 7 May, where the *Anziani* took the decision to summon the General Council; *Cons. Gen.* 2, fol. 150^r.

27. *Anz. temp. lib.* 2, fols. 39^r, 44^v.

Pisan Consular Families in the Communal Age: The Anfossi and the Ebriaci (or Verchionesi or da Parlascio) in the Eleventh to Thirteenth Centuries

MARIA LUISA CECCARELLI-LEMUT

It is my purpose in this paper to inquire into two Pisan consular families that may be considered in some respects representative: the descendants of Alkerio, called Anfossi for convenience, and the Ebriaci, also called Verchionesi or da Parlascio. These little-known families have not been extensively studied. Nonetheless they throw light on aspects of city life that are rarely mentioned in contemporary documents: seafaring activities, connections with Sardinia and Byzantium, and the Crusades in particular.

As is widely known through the studies of scholars from Gioacchino Volpe to Emilio Cristiani and Marco Tangheroni, the consular class in Pisa was drawn from families connected both to the city and its territory. These families owned properties in Pisa and in the old county, an area much smaller than the thirteenth-century *contado* and that extended for a distance of roughly ten kilometers to the north and east of the town and thirty kilometers to the south along the Serchio, Arno, and Tora valleys.[1] While these families' possessions were primarily allodial, they also controlled the property of archbishoprics held under long-term leases

known as feuds, or emphyteusis, but without the exercise of jurisdiction. Here too, as Chris Wickham has shown for land close to
Lucca, early communal development prevented the rise of true territorial seignories, although they were present in areas farther away
from the city that were conquered later.[2]

Land and town interests were closely connected to seafaring
and commercial ventures overseas, which in turn involved shipping,
mercantile, and financial activities. Often the legal profession
(judges and lawyers) was involved too, a manifestation of renewed
interest in law in the twelfth century. Unfortunately, the extant
documents, until the mid-twelfth century chiefly of ecclesiastical
origin, reveal little or nothing about the affairs of the Anfossi and
Ebriaci apart from land and its possession.

The first family to be considered here is that conventionally
known as the Anfossi. They were descended from Alkerio, who died
some time before 1142; the line can be traced up to 1233 (see Table
1). The founder of the family, Alkerio, may perhaps be identified
with Alkerio, son of the late Hildeprand who, on 9 November 1101,
was the owner of land in Pisa near the church of St. Bartholomew
of the Erizi, where later the Anfossi lived.[3] The same person, together with other Pisans in Sardinia, witnessed the donations of
Turbino, king (*iudex*) of Cagliari, to the Pisans and to the *opera* of
the Cathedral in May 1103.[4] He also witnessed the renewal in 1128
by Archbishop Roger of a pledge for the artisans working on the
Cathedral.[5] The first definite member of this family was Anfosso,
Jurisconsul and son of the late Alkerio, Consul in Pisa in 1139 and
1142.[6] He was present in southern France on 13 September 1143
when the peace treaty between Count Alphonse of Toulouse and the
consuls and the Abbot of St. Gilles was signed with the Communes
of Pisa and Genoa.[7] He appears for the last time with his brother
Hermann as a witness to a sale between private citizens dated 5
December 1147 in Pisa in the Saracen tower of the late Carletto by

the church of St. Margaret, not far from his residence.[8] His brother Hermann appears some years later in the oldest known money-lending transaction for the Pisan commune. In early 1160, together with four others from the consular class, he repaid £62 lent to the Pisan Commune by Ursico, son of the late Alkerio *de Intadi*.[9]

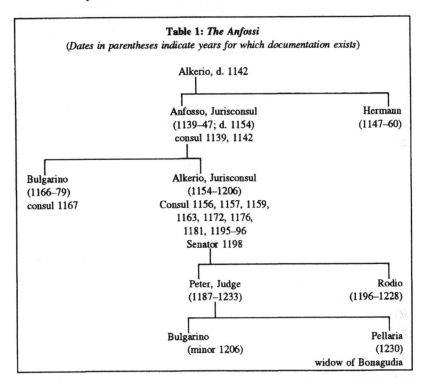

Table 1: *The Anfossi*
(Dates in parentheses indicate years for which documentation exists)

Alkerio, d. 1142

Anfosso, Jurisconsul
(1139–47; d. 1154)
consul 1139, 1142

Hermann
(1147–60)

Bulgarino
(1166–79)
consul 1167

Alkerio, Jurisconsul
(1154–1206)
Consul 1156, 1157, 1159,
1163, 1172, 1176,
1181, 1195–96
Senator 1198

Peter, Judge
(1187–1233)

Rodio
(1196–1228)

Bulgarino
(minor 1206)

Pellaria
(1230)
widow of Bonagudia

The sons of Anfosso, Bulgarino and Alkerio, were important figures in city politics during the second half of the twelfth century. Bulgarino Anfossi was a member of the body of Consuls that elected the anti-archbishop Benincasa in 1167. He also took part in three embassies: one in May to the court of the Emperor Frederick I at Ancona; one to Rome in the summer; and one at the court of King William of Sicily in November.[10] Of particular interest are his shipping activities, especially in view of the rarity of such notices on the commercial transactions of the Anfossi.

According to the contemporary chronicler Bernard Maragone, in July 1166, Bulgarino and Guy, son of the late Fornario, outfitted two war galleys that captured a Genoese vessel at Cape Corse. Then, while proceeding towards Provence, the Pisans captured another two vessels and, off Albenga, a merchant ship sailing from Spain, for a total prize of £5,000. Two years later, in the spring of 1168, Bulgarino sailed with nine galleys to Spain to harass the Genoese, but he did not come across enemy ships. In June 1170, in the company of Guy Fornario, Morello, and Hugh Laggio, he sailed again with four galleys against the Genoese in Sardinia and captured ten enemy vessels, five of which were burned; the remaining ships, loaded with merchandise, were towed to Pisa and sold there.[11] All the participants who had put their personal fortunes into the war were amply rewarded with the booty from the capture of these enemy ships and goods.

In 1175 Bulgarino was invited to Venice as ambassador. There he concluded a treaty with the Doge Sebastian Ziani;[12] a year later he was a member of the commission (the *cognitores guarigangorum et debiti et crediti communis*) appointed to administer the public debt.[13] Finally, during the summer of 1179, he was ambassador to Egypt at the court of Sultan Saladin, with whom he renewed the peace and obtained the liberation of twenty prisoners. From there he travelled to Constantinople to the Emperor's court, and this is the last we hear of him. Maragone describes him as "homo savio et forte et di bona progenie."[14] We also know of two pieces of land that he owned: one near the Church of St. Apollinare in Barbaricina—a village lying west of the city—near the river Arno,[15] and the other "ad Ponticellum usque ad Musileos" to the north.[16]

Alkerio, the brother of Bulgarino, was a Jurisconsul like his father, Anfosso. He was Consul eight times—in the years 1156, 1157, 1159, 1163, 1172, 1176,[17] 1181[18] and between 29 March 1195 and 22 September 1196.[19] In 1183 he was a member of the committee of arbitrators elected to settle the differences between the Pisans and the Lucchese.[20] Like his brother, he was charged with embassies to the court of Frederick I, the first in the spring of 1165, when the Emperor gave Sardinia as a fief to Pisa and again in 1175, when the Tuscan communes concluded a general peace with the Emperor.[21] Later, from 1184 to 1185, Alkerio was one of the ten *capitanei et cognitores guarigangorum*, a body charged with repaying the Commune's creditors by awarding portions of uncultivated or marshy land known as *guarigangi*.[22] Finally, on 19 July 1198, he became a senator.[23] He also witnessed documents redacted by the archbishop on 13 November 1154 and 7 May 1178,[24] and two sentences passed by the judges of the arbiters' tribunal on 23 August 1175 and 16 June 1180.[25] On 30 April 1162 he was present as a witness at the Sienese consular arbitration between the Bishop of Volterra and Count Hildeprand Aldobrandeschi.[26] Alkerio is mentioned for the last time in Pisa on 15 March 1206, when the nuncio from the *curia usus* executed a sentence passed against Alkerio and his son Peter, administrators for Peter's son Bulgarino, a minor, in favor of Mulinaria, widow of one Marignano, concerning two plots of land with buildings located in Pisa by the church of St. Felix and five plots at Orzignano in the Serchio valley.[27] We also know that Alkerio owned property along the Serchio valley at Arena.[28]

Peter and Rodio, Alkerio's sons, were unable to maintain their father's, and above all their uncle's, high position and prestige. They never reached the higher consular offices. We possess very little information about Rodio. On 22 September 1196, acting on behalf of the Consul Tregano, son of the late Tedesco from St. Clement, he recognized Communal debts incurred by Count Tedice Della Gherardesca, recently elected *Podestà*.[29] Rodio is further mentioned among the more than four thousand Pisan citizens who, in July 1228, swore to the league between the cities of Siena, Pistoia, and Poggibonsi. This document tells us that the family resided by the chapel of St. Bartholomew of the Erizi, inside the ancient and early medieval *civitas*. Rodio's brother, Peter, also appears in the same document among the *capitanei ecclesiarum*, in other words among the leaders of the armed associations organized by parishioners.[30]

Peter followed the family's legal tradition and is mentioned as a judge in several city tribunals: the foreigners' court in 1187;[31] the appeals court in 1191, 1210, and 1227;[32] the law tribunal before 1225;[33] and, finally, the wards' court (*curia nova*) in 1223, 1225, and 1233.[34] Peter had two children, Bulgarino, who was still a minor in 1206,[35] and Pellaria, widow of Bonaguida who, with the consent of her uncle Rodio, sold a plot of land to the Prior of the Preaching Friars in Pisa, by their church, St. Catherine's, on 31 July 1230.[36]

The Anfossi can be seen as representative of that middle consular class, dedicated to seafaring and the law with solid family fortunes, which prospered during the second half of the twelfth century. They were, however, unable to maintain their position in the decades around the turn of the century when there were crucial changes in Pisan history, during which the consular regime gave way to one organized around the *Podestà*, when popular bodies arose and when the social base of the commune was widened.

The two brothers, Bulgarino and Alkerio, were typical exponents of the consular class in the Frederician period. They were loyal to the Commune, and its interests guided their politics, which meant being, at turns, in favor of the Empire or cautiously and even openly cold towards Frederick I. They were ambassadors in times of trouble or when it was necessary to strengthen old alliances and create new ones, as in the case of Venice. Alkerio's sons did not take much part in politics and their presence at the swearing in of 1228 is in itself insufficient evidence for their alignment with the Visconti.[37]

The second family to be discussed here was definitely of a higher rank than the Anfossi and has already been identified and partly studied for the thirteenth and fourteenth centuries by Mauro

Ronzani.[38] Already belonging to the Consular class in the late eleventh century, it became extinct in the early fifteenth; it was known by several surnames: "da Parlascio" from its place of residence (a surname common to other individuals who do not, however, seem to have belonged to this family); "Ebriaci" and "Verchionesi" from nicknames given to two of its members, namely, Hugh Ebriaco who lived in the early twelfth century and Gerard Verchione who lived in the early thirteenth. The first known member was Hugh, son of Pagano, who appears together with representatives of the Visconti, Orlandi, Gualandi, Lanfranchi da San Casciano, Matti, and da Caprona families in the circle of eminent citizens known as *Longubardi Pisani* (See Tables 2–4). These individuals owned property in the Valdiserchio and in 1091–92 were obliged by the Consuls to reach a compromise with the inhabitants of that area whom they were unjustly taxing.[39]

We know Hugh had two sons, Peter and Hugh Ebriaco, who took part in the victorious Pisan-Genoese expedition against the

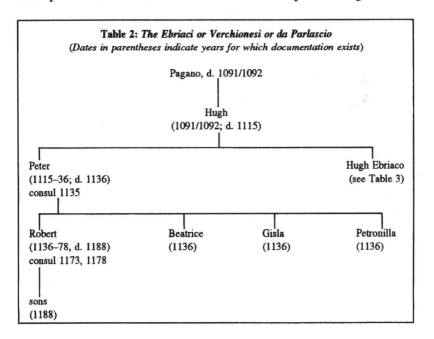

Table 2: *The Ebriaci or Verchionesi or da Parlascio*
(Dates in parentheses indicate years for which documentation exists)

Pagano, d. 1091/1092

Hugh
(1091/1092; d. 1115)

Peter
(1115–36; d. 1136)
consul 1135

Hugh Ebriaco
(see Table 3)

Robert
(1136–78, d. 1188)
consul 1173, 1178

Beatrice
(1136)

Gisla
(1136)

Petronilla
(1136)

sons
(1188)

Saracens in the Balearic Isles in 1113–15.[40] Peter subsequently played a prominent role in the city's public life as evidenced by the presence of his name in several important documents. On 26 September 1115 he witnessed the agreement between the Abbot of the Monastery of St. Justinian of Falesia, near Piombino, and the Procurator of the *opera* of the Pisan Cathedral, while on 20 November 1130 he witnessed a donation made by Count Arduin to the Pisan Archbishopric.[41] He was a Consul in January 1135[42] but died a year later.

Peter's testament, dictated on 30 May 1136, has come down to us. He named as his heir his only son Robert and bequeathed dowries to Beatrice, Gisla, and Petronilla, his three daughters. He also left a *mansia* at *Selvalonga* in the Valdarno to Petronilla and legacies to the chapel of St. Simon in Parlascio (near his residence), the parish church of Camaiano in Val di Fine, and the churches of Vada and St. Mary's at Vecchiano, all places where he held property. He left his white palfrey and the castle of Cugnano in Val di Tora to Archbishop Hubert. To the sons of his dead brother, Hugh Ebriaco, he left the rightful portion of the division of the castle of Muterno.[43] This document is interesting for many reasons. First, it provides a clear picture of the family possessions in localities where the family continued to own property in later centuries; for example, in Pisa by the church of St. Simon in Parlascio, in the ancient County along the Serchio, Arno, and Tora valleys, and at Vada on the sea. Second, it reveals ties that existed between the Ebriaci family and other families and the strong institutional ties that lasted throughout the following centuries. The Archbishop, for instance, was named both as the beneficiary of a legacy and as an executor of the will. The churches of St. Simon in Parlascio and St. Mary in Vecchiano were still under the patronage of the family during the thirteenth and fourteenth centuries, and one member of the Orlandi family, Hildeprand, son of Roland and Lambert's nephew, was another executor.[44]

We know little of Peter's son, Robert. He was involved, together with his cousins, in a quarrel (resolved in 1159) with the Archbishop of Pisa over the Vecchiano marshes;[45] he was a consul in 1173 and 1178.[46] He owned property at Macadio in the Serchio Valley[47] and by 23 July 1188, when some land in Val di Tora belonging to his cousins was recorded as bordering on others belonging to his sons, he was dead.[48] We know nothing more about his descendants.

Hugh Ebriaco, Peter's brother, was active in Sardinia, where the Pisans had already been present for some time. A group of prominent citizens, including Hugh, had helped Mariano Torkitorio, king of Cagliari, regain his kingdom by providing three galleys for his use. For this reason, in 1108, Mariano made several concessions to the Archbishop and citizens of Pisa.[49] A few years later, when the young king of Torres, Gonnario II, was forced by relatives to leave his kingdom, he went to Pisa, where he was certain to find help thanks to the bonds between the city and his father and grandfather. When in 1130 he regained possession of his kingdom, he was accompanied by his Pisan wife Mary and his father-in-law Hugh Ebriaco.[50] This was the earliest known marriage between a Pisan citizen and a member of a Sardinian royal family. Hugh Ebriaco was, in a certain sense, the initiator of a policy that was to be followed by the most important Pisan families (the Visconti and the Counts Della Gherardesca) from the end of the twelfth century on. Gonnario was a prominent figure in Sardinian history. He visited the Holy Land in 1147; in 1153 he became a monk at Clairvaux. His marriage to Mary certainly conferred a particularly high rank on her family within his kingdom but the dearth of Sardinian documents prevents us from giving any concrete information.[51] A Pisan document dated 31 July 1144 tells us of one of Hugh Ebriaco's sons, Ganis, who married a Sardinian, one Susan, daughter to Constantine of Athens, a member of one of the greatest families in the Torres kingdom and related to the royal family.[52]

Close relations between the Ebriaci and their Sardinian relatives

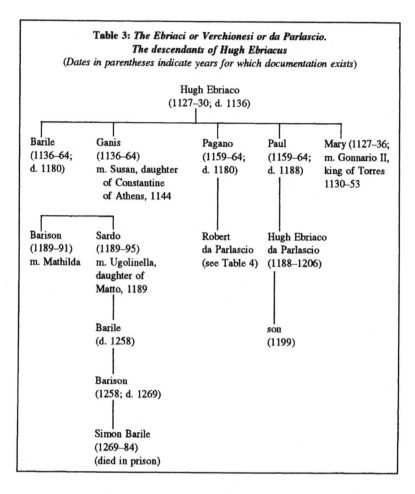

Table 3: *The Ebriaci or Verchionesi or da Parlascio.*
The descendants of Hugh Ebriacus
(*Dates in parentheses indicate years for which documentation exists*)

Hugh Ebriaco
(1127–30; d. 1136)

Barile	Ganis	Pagano	Paul	Mary (1127–36;
(1136–64;	(1136–64)	(1159–64;	(1159–64;	m. Gonnario II,
d. 1180)	m. Susan, daughter	d. 1180)	d. 1188)	king of Torres
	of Constantine			1130–53
	of Athens, 1144			

Barison	Sardo	Robert	Hugh Ebriaco
(1189–91)	(1189–95)	da Parlascio	da Parlascio
m. Mathilda	m. Ugolinella,	(see Table 4)	(1188–1206)
	daughter of		
	Matto, 1189		

Barile
(d. 1258)

son
(1199)

Barison
(1258; d. 1269)

Simon Barile
(1269–84)
(died in prison)

were maintained throughout the twelfth century. In April 1164 Barison, king of Torres, and Peter Torkitorio V, king of Cagliari, the sons of Gonnario, were aided in the war against Barison, king of Arborea, an ally of the Genoese, by their uncles Barile, Ganis, Pagano, and Paul Ebriaco.[53] The situation in Sardinia changed radically, however, near the end of the century. Both Barison II of Torres and his brother Peter of Cagliari broke their treaty with Pisa and allied themselves with Genoa. Pisa invaded the kingdom of

Cagliari in 1187 replacing Peter with his brother-in-law, Hubert, Marquis of Massa. Some years later, Hubert's son William, king of Cagliari, attacked the kingdom of Torres, but King Constantine managed to reach an agreement with the Pisan Consuls on 29 March 1195. It was still one of his Pisan relatives, one Sardo, son of the late Barile, who acted in the name of the king in this Pisan document.[54] This is the last reference to relations between the Ebriaci and the Torres royal family. Comita, brother and successor to Constantine, politically favored the Genoese more than the Pisans, a policy that culminated in open opposition to Pisa in 1206.[55]

The direct intervention by Pisans in Sardinian affairs in 1187 initiated a competitive race among families for possession of the Sardinian kingdoms. During the fifty years from 1187 to 1237 there took place a complicated and confused series of struggles for supremacy in Sardinia, of which the repercussions were felt even in Pisa. However, the Ebriaci were not active in these thirteenth-century struggles. Following the dethronement of Peter Torkitorio V, king of Cagliari, and Comita di Torres' anti-Pisan politics, they were unable to take a leading part in the ensuing complex political game, the prize for which was not only supremacy over Sardinia but also hegemony over the Pisan Commune.[56]

Instead, by the end of the twelfth century, the Ebriaci had turned their attention to the Orient. Sardo and Barison, sons of Barile, took part in the Pisan contingent that left for the Third Crusade under the leadership of Archbishop Hubald.[57] Barison may perhaps be the same person as that *Parason* who at Tyre in 1191 witnessed, with three fellow citizens, the charter granted to the Pisans by Conrad of Monferrato.[58] Nothing more is known of Barison although Sardo subsequently returned to Pisa.[59] Their cousin, Hugh Ebriaco, went to Constantinople where he appeared in 1199 with his son as a member of the flourishing Pisan colony there.[60]

Despite their strong interest in the Orient and Sardinia, the Ebriaci did not play a particularly prominent role in Pisan politics.

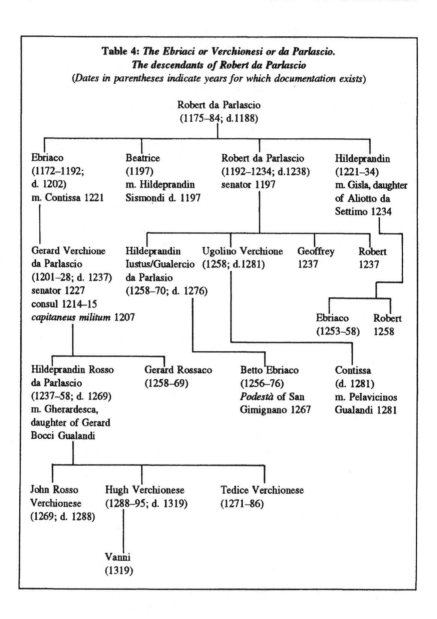

Table 4: *The Ebriaci or Verchionesi or da Parlascio.*
The descendants of Robert da Parlascio
(Dates in parentheses indicate years for which documentation exists)

Robert da Parlascio
(1175–84; d.1188)

Ebriaco	Beatrice	Robert da Parlascio	Hildeprandin
(1172–1192;	(1197)	(1192–1234; d.1238)	(1221–34)
d. 1202)	m. Hildeprandin	senator 1197	m. Gisla, daughter
m. Contissa 1221	Sismondi d. 1197		of Aliotto da
			Settimo 1234

Gerard Verchione da Parlascio (1201–28; d. 1237) senator 1227 consul 1214–15 *capitaneus militum* 1207

Hildeprandin Iustus/Gualercio da Parlasio (1258–70; d. 1276)

Ugolino Verchione (1258; d.1281)

Geoffrey 1237

Robert 1237

Ebriaco (1253–58)

Robert 1258

Hildeprandin Rosso da Parlascio (1237–58; d. 1269) m. Gherardesca, daughter of Gerard Bocci Gualandi

Gerard Rossaco (1258–69)

Betto Ebriaco (1256–76) *Podestà* of San Gimignano 1267

Contissa (d. 1281) m. Pelavicinos Gualandi 1281

John Rosso Verchionese (1269; d. 1288)

Hugh Verchionese (1288–95; d. 1319)

Tedice Verchionese (1271–86)

Vanni (1319)

They maintained and strengthened their relations with the city's chief institutions and families. Barile and Ganis had connections with the cathedral chapter,[61] and their nephew Robert da Parlascio—son of their brother Pagano—is named among the *fideles* of Archbishop Hubald on 24 October 1180, together with the Visconti, Lanfranchi da San Casciano, and the Matti.[62] Robert also acted as arbitrator in a dispute between the archbishop and the children of a certain Lambert over an inheritance.[63] His daughter Beatrice was wed to Hildeprandin, a Sismondi, one of the more important consular families.[64]

Especially interesting are the continuing connections with those families which, together with the Ebriaci, constituted the *Longubardi Pisani*, property owners between Valdiserchio in 1091 and 1092. For instance, on 6 August 1130, Hugh Ebriaco witnessed an agreement among the members of the da Caprona family;[65] an Orlandi was named as executor of Peter's will in 1136;[66] on 22 December 1159 the Pisan *publici judices* issued a sentence against the Ebriaci (represented by Peter's son and his cousins Barile, Pagano, and Paul), and against the Visconti, Lanfranchi da San Casiano, Orlandi-Pellai, and da Caprona, who were in contention with Villano, Archbishop of Pisa, regarding the ownership of the Vecchiano marshes in Valdiserchio.[67] Some of these families were united once again in 1180, as we have just noted, among Archbishop Hubald's *fideles*. It will shortly be seen that the Ebriaci were politically linked to the Visconti during the second and third decades of the thirteenth century, when the Visconti effectively held the hegemony of the Pisan Commune.

The Ebriaci returned to public office at the end of the twelfth century. Robert da Parlascio became Senator in September/October 1197,[68] but the most important political figure in the family at the beginning of the thirteenth century was his nephew Gerard Verchione, son of Robert's brother Ebriaco. On 28 February 1207 Gerard, in the role of *capitaneus militum* of the association of knights or noblemen,[69] swore peace with Volterra; he was Consul from 30 May 1214 to 29 March 1215[70] and was present at the submission of the bishop of Massa Marittima to the Pisan Commune on 23 April 1215.[71] A senator in April 1227,[72] he witnessed the league formed between Pisa, Siena, Pistoia, and Poggibonsi on 7 June 1228 and is mentioned, together with members of some of the more important families (Visconti, Orlandi-Pellai, Casalei, Gualandi, da Caprona, and Gaetani) among the twenty-seven *maiores civitatis* present during the swearing of allegiance to the league by more than four thousand Pisan citizens.[73]

The presence of Gerard Verchione in important public acts when Hubald Visconti was *Podestà* (1215–18 and 1227–28) suggests political connections with the Visconti branch of Albert *Viscomes maior*, a branch that, through this office, was able to control the Pisan commune.[74] But when the Visconti predominance ended in 1229, the Ebriaci were absent from public affairs for more than twenty years, until 4 December 1253, when Hildeprandin Rosso, son of Gerard Verchione, and Ebriaco, Gerard's cousin, were among the Pisan citizens who acted as guarantors for the pact between the Pisan Commune and the Da Corvaia and Vallecchia families.[75] Ebriaco and Betto (a son of Ebriaco's cousin, Hildeprandin Gualercio) were again among the counsellors of the Commune, who on 1 October 1256, approved the peace agreement with Florence.[76] A few months later, on 29 March 1257, Betto was one of the Counsellors to the Elders in agreements with the Archbishop of Lucca.[77] Betto was the most important person in the family during the second half of the thirteenth century. He was also the only one to hold public office outside Pisa. He was *Podestà* of San Gimignano in 1267 but was obliged to leave the post when the town submitted to Charles of Anjou in May thus joining the Guelph party.[78] Finally we should mention Simon Barile who, taken prisoner probably during the unlucky battle of Meloria on 6 August 1284, died in prison at Genoa.[79]

We do not know the precise size of the family's fortune since our information is derived chiefly from the naming of the Ebriaci as neighbors in land transactions and descriptions of their actual possessions are rare. However, their patrimony was, in all probability, considerable. It was located mostly in the Valdiserchio, Valdarno around Selvalonga, in the Pisan hills, and at Vada, as Peter's will of 1136 indicates. Documents from the late twelfth and the thirteenth centuries also mention lands in the Pian di Porto, that is, the area east and south of Porto Pisano near Leghorn.

Most of their property was probably situated in the Valdiserchio, where they were already present in 1091–92 and where in 1159 they disputed the ownership of the Vecchiano marshes with the archbishop.[80] We know of property in this area at Patrignone and at Lugnano in the parish of Pugnano[81] and at Vecchiano and the nearby S. Andrea in Pescaiola.[82] Closer to Pisa they held property at Cornazzano, Bottano, and Macadio.[83] Three *panoyes* of land at Rigoli were sold for £4½ on 16 October 1221 by Hildeprandin, son of the late Robert, and his nephew Gerard Verchione together with his mother Contissa.[84]

The Ebriaci also figure in this area as patrons of two churches, S. Andrea in Pescaiola and St. Mary in Castello. According to a document dated 11 March 1258, the patrons of S. Andrea's in Pescaiola were Hildeprandin Rosso, son of Gerard Verchione, Gerard Rossaco, Hildeprandin's brother, Ebriaco and Robert, sons of Hildeprandin, and the cousins of the latter, Hildeprandin and Ugolino, sons of Robert da Parlascio, and Barison, son of the late Barile, together with several da Capronas (John and his brother Ugolino, William and his brothers Conrad and Henry, and Guy, son of Uguccione) as well as James, son of Guy Orlandi.[85] On 8 September 1319 Vanni, the son of the late Hugh Verchionese, whose father was the above-mentioned Hildeprandin Rosso, was mentioned in the long list of patrons of St. Mary in Castello near Vecchiano, with all the branches of the Orlandi and the Visconti, and with Vanni, son of the late Bacciameo da Caprona and several Lanfranchi.[86] Here too we see the long-lasting connections and common interests between the Ebriaci and other prominent families with property in the Valdiserchio—the so-called *Longubardi Pisani* of 1091–92 noted above.

The Ebriaci also owned property nearer town, north of the river Arno at Cisanello[87] and south at Oratoio, where the plot of three staria was sold by Hildeprandin, son of the late Robert da Parlascio, on 6 February 1234 for £32 to a priest, Homodeo, chaplain to the church of St. Thomas à Becket in Parlascio. Consenting to this sale was Hildeprandin's wife Gisla, daughter of the late Aliotto da Settimo, a family from Settimo in the Pisan Valdarno.[88] The Ebriaci had property in the Valdarno, too, chiefly at S. Pietro's in Pagnatico[89] and Visignano, where Hildeprandin Rosso, son of the late Gerard Verchione, sold one staioro of land on 1 May 1237 to Bonaventura da Arquata for £7. This sale also had the consent of the seller's wife, Gherardesca, daughter of the late Gerard Bocci, a member of one of the most prominent urban families, the Gualandi.[90]

The Ebriaci are documented as owning property in Pian di Porto from the end of the twelfth century: these possessions were chiefly at Oliveto, at nearby Saliano and Collinaia, and near Leghorn.[91] Further east, in Val di Tora, they were long the owners of property at Cugnano.[92] The patrons of St. Cassian's church in Cugnano, on 8 February 1295, were the heirs of Simon Barile together with Hugh, son of Hildeprandin Rosso, his nephews (the sons of his brother John Rosso), and Vanni Mannaria, as well as the sons of Tedice del Cane, a Sismondi.[93] Further south the Ebriaci owned property near Vada.[94] The family lived, as we have seen, in a house with a colonnade near the church of St. Simon in Parlascio,[95] of which the Ebriaci were patrons.[96] Little is known of other property in the town. Hugh Pagani's sons owned a plot at Petricio near the St. Zeno monastery on 21 April 1129,[97] and Hugh Ebriaco had land by the church of St. Leonard in Pratuscello on 1 December 1204.[98]

The Ebriaci were certainly one of the most prominent families in twelfth-century Pisa: they had important connections with the archbishop and the cathedral chapter as well as the chief families in the consular class; they were among the very first to marry into the king of Torres's family in Sardinia for political reasons, and they were involved in ventures in Constantinople and the Orient, probably for commercial reasons, of which, however, we know nothing. They also possessed an enormous amount of landed property in and around the town, as well as in the valleys of the rivers Serchio, Arno, and Tora, in the Pisan Hills, and at Vada, within the boundaries, that is, of the ancient county of Pisa. They were a close-knit family bound by the patronage of churches—four in all in town and in the country—held undivided by members of the family. But during the political and institutional changes of the thirteenth century, the Ebriaci were unable to maintain their prominent position. After flanking the Visconti during the first three decades of the century, they were temporarily eclipsed, but definitely not because of financial difficulties. Unfortunately, the extant documentation from the period does not permit a determination of the relative importance of the family's financial and commercial fortune as compared to the revenues they derived from landholding.

This paper is a sample of the studies on Pisan consular families, which have been the subject of many papers and M.A. dissertations at the University of Pisa, first by Professor Cinzio Violante, next by Professor Gabriella Rossetti, and then by their students.[99] Nevertheless, many other families, some very prominent in the political, economic, and social life of the twelfth and thirteenth centuries, are very little known.[100] But for a better knowledge of Pisan society and history it is necessary to study not only the most important families but also the minor ones, in order to throw new light on aspects of city life, such as we have seen in this paper on the Anfossi and the Ebriaci. Thus we have been able to inquire into a consular class connected not only to the city and its territory but also to the

seafaring activitites (the basis of the fortune of Pisa) and thus to
the isles and the coasts of the Mediterranean Sea—from Sardinia
and Corsica to Tunisia and Egypt, from Constantinople to Pales-
tine. We also have observed members of this class involved in
moneylending and the law. It is interesting to see how this class
was affected in the crucial years of the turn of the twelfth century,
when there were important changes, both institutional and social,
and when popular bodies arose and the social base of the Commune was widened. For that reason it would be signficant to inquire further into the "popular" families, of which we are able to
say so little. The study of the "popular" milieu of merchants, ship-
owners, and moneylenders who formed the Three Orders can provide us with a better understanding of Pisan history in the thirteenth century and of the complex changes in the city's social, political, and economic life.

NOTES

1. See G. Volpe, *Studi sulle istituzioni comunali a Pisa*, 2nd ed. (Florence, 1970);
E. Cristiani, *Nobiltà e popolo nel Comune di Pisa. Dalle origini del podestarriato
alla signoria dei Donoratico* (Naples, 1962); and M. Tangheroni, *Politica,
commercio, agricoltura a Pisa nel Trecento* (Pisa, 1973).

2. C. Wickham, "Economia e società rurale nel territorio lucchese durante la
seconda metà del secolo XI," *Atti del convegno internazionale "S. Anselmo
vescovo di Lucca (1073–1086) nel quadro delle trasformazioni sociali e della
riforma ecclesiastica,"* in press. See also, for the Arno valley east of Pisa, G.
Garzella, "Cascina. L'organizzazione civile ed ecclesiastica e l'insediamento," in
M. Pasquinucci, G. Garzella, M. L. Ceccarelli-Lemut, *Cascina. Dall'Antichità al
Medioevo* (Pisa, 1986), pp. 72–83.

3. *Archivio di Stato di Pisa* (henceforth *ASP*), *Diplomatico* (henceforth *Dipl.*), *R.
Acquisto Roncioni*, ed. M. Guastini, "Le pergamene dell'Archivio di Stato di Pisa
dal 1100 al 1115" (M.A. diss., University of Pisa, 1964–65), no. 5. The church of

St. Bartholomew of the Erizi was destroyed in the sixteenth century to build the Piazza delle Vettovaglie; see E. Tolaini, *Forma Pisarum. Storia urbanistica della città di Pisa. Problemi e ricereche*, 2nd ed. (Pisa, 1979), p. 25.

4. *Codice diplomatico di Sardegna*, ed. P. Tola (henceforth *CDS*), vols. 10 and 12 of *Historiae Patriae Monumenta* (Turin, 1861–68), 1: nos. 1–2, pp. 177–78; also *Carte dell'Archivio Capitolare di Pisa*, 4 (1101–20), ed. M. Tirelli Carli, in *Thesaurus Ecclesiarum Italiae* 7, 4 (Rome, 1969), no. 15, pp. 31–32.

5. *Statuti inediti della città di Pisa dal XII al XIV secolo*, ed. F. Bonaini, 3 vols. (Florence, 1854–57), 3:891.

6. 25 July 1139: *Zur Geschichte des XII. und XIII. Jahrhunderts. Diplomatische Forschungen*, ed. P. Scheffer-Boichorst, *Historische Studien Ebering* 8 (Berlin, 1897), pp. 403–04; 27 April 1142: A. D'Amia, *Le sentenze pisane dal 1139 al 1200: contributo allo studio della diplomatica giuridica e della cultura giuridica in Pisa, con la trascrizione di alcune pergamene dell'Archivio di Stato* (Pisa, 1922), repr. in D'Amia, *Diritto e sentenze di Pisa ai primordi del rinascimento giuridico* (Milan, 1962), no. 2, pp. 221–22.

7. *Codice diplomatico della Repubblica di Genova*, ed. C. Imperiale di S. Angelo, 3 vols., in *Fonti per la storia d'Italia*, vols. 77, 79, 89 (Rome, 1936–42), 1:no. 126, pp. 149–52.

8. *ASP, Dipl., S. Michele in Borgo*, ed. S. Caroti, "Le pergamene dell'Archivio di Stato di Pisa dal 1145 al 1155/1158," (M.A. diss., University of Pisa, 1965–66), no. 17. The church of St. Margaret, on the present Piazza D. Cavalca, was destroyed in 1753; see E. Tolaini, *Forma Pisarum* (Pisa, 1967), p. 132. It was not far from the church of St. Bartholomew, see n. 3 above. On the Carletti family, see Cristiani, *Nobiltà e popolo*, p. 379.

9. G. Garzella, "Proposta di datazione e di interpretazione di una pergamena proveniente dal monastero pisano di S. Michele in Borgo," *Bollettino Storico Pisano*, 53 (1984), 261–74, with some information on Anfosso and his sons on pp. 266–67; and S. P. P. Scalfati, "Edizione e nota diplomatistica," *Bollettino Storico Pisano*, 53 (1984), 275–78. The document dates from 1 January–24 March 1160, because consul Boccio was in office in the year 1160; see Bernardo Maragone, *Annales Pisani*, ed. M. Lupo Gentile, *Rerum Italicarum Scriptores*, 2nd

ed., 6/1 (Bologna, 1936), p. 20 n. 5 for 18 March 1160. See also *Documenti sulle relazioni delle città toscane coll'Oriente cristiano e coi Turchi fino all'anno 1531*, ed. G. Müller (Florence, 1879), no. 7, pp. 8–9.

10. Maragone, *Annales Pisani*, pp. 41–42, 44. On Bulgarino, see also S. P. P. Scalfati, "Bulgarino di Anfosso," *Dizionario biografico degli Italiani*, 15 (Rome, 1972), pp. 46–47.

11. Maragone, *Annales Pisani*, pp. 39, 45, 49.

12. The peace of 1175 is mentioned in the treaty of 13 October 1180, between Doge Aureus Mastropetrus and the Pisan ambassador, Hildeprand Familiati; see Müller, *Documenti sulle relazioni*, no. 18, pp. 20–23.

13. 30 April 1176: *ASP, Carte Lupi, Fonti* I.1, pp. 658–59; 26 May, 8 June, and 25 March/24 September: *Regesto della Chiesa di Pisa*, ed. N. Caturegli (henceforth *RP*), *Regesta Chartarum Italiae*, 24 (Rome, 1939), nos. 518, 519, 521; 18 September: "Le 'guariganga'," ed. C. Giardina, *Atti della R. Accademia di Scienze e Lettere di Palermo*, 23 (1934), repr. in Giardina, *Storia del diritto*, vol. 1 (Palermo, 1965), no. 5, pp. 174–75.

14. Maragone, *Annales Pisani*, p. 69.

15. 8 August 1173: *ASP, Dipl., S. Michele in Borgo*, ed. B. Carmignani, "Le pergamene dell'Archivio di Stato di Pisa dal 3 maggio 1172 al 18 marzo 1175" (M.A. diss., University of Pisa, 1965–66), no. 29.

16. 11 August 1180: D'Amia, *Le sentenze*, no. 20, pp. 251–52.

17. Maragone, *Annales Pisani*, p. 17 (1156). 28 November 1157: *ASP, Carte Lupi, Fonti* I.1, p. 522; 16 December 1159: *Archivio Capitolare di Pisa* (henceforth *ACP*), *Diplomatico*, no. 527, ed. R. Sgherri, "I documenti dell'Archivio Capitolare di Pisa dall'agosto 1155 al 18 febbraio 1176" (M.A. diss., University of Pisa, 1963–64), no. 30; 27 November 1163: *RP*, no. 477; 23 May, 1172: D. Hägermann, "Die Urkunden Christians I. von Mainz als Reichslegat Friedrich Barbarossas in Italien," *Archiv für Diplomatik*, 14 (1968), no. 15, pp. 250–52.

18. 16 and 29 June, 4 September, 19 October: M. L. Ceccarelli-Lemut, "L'uso

della moneta nei documenti pisani dei secoli XI e XII," in G. Garzella, M. L. Ceccarelli-Lemut, B. Casini, *Studi sugli strumenti di scambio a Pisa nel Medioevo* (Pisa, 1979), pp. 95–120; and 23 November: Müller, *Documenti sulle relazioni*, no. 18, pp. 20–23.

19. Alkerio was expressly mentioned on 29 March 1195: *Documenti inediti relativi ai rapporti economici tra la Sardegna e Pisa nel Medioevo*, ed. F. Artizzu, 2 vols. (Padova, 1961–62), vol. 1, no. 3, pp. 5–8 (see also n. 54 below and text); and on 13 July 1195; *ACP, Diplomatico*, no. 717. The body of consuls, however, was in office until 22 September 1196: *ASP, Dipl., Atti Pubblici*, ed. M. T. Alampi, "Le pergamene dell'Archivio di Stato di Pisa dal 1195 al 1198" (M.A. diss., University of Pisa, 1967–68), nos. 24–27. The third example is edited by M. L. Ceccarelli-Lemut in the appendix to C. Violante, "Le origini del debito pubblico e lo sviluppo costituzionale del Comune," in *Studi per Enrico Fiumi* (Pisa, 1979), repr. in Violante, *Economia società istituzioni a Pisa nel Medioevo* (Bari, 1980), no. 4, pp. 95–100.

20. 20 October: D'Amia, *Le sentenze*, no. 22, p. 263.

21. Maragone, *Annales Pisani*, pp. 34–35, 61–62.

22. 31 December 1184: Giardina, "Le 'guariganga'," no. 7, p. 176 (incorrectly dated from 1179); and 29 January 1185: *ASP, Dipl., R. Acquisto Roncioni*, ed. M. L. Blanda, "Le pergamene dell'Archivio di Stato di Pisa dal 1184 al 1188" (M.A. diss., University of Pisa, 1966–67), no. 12. He is also mentioned as a member of that committee on 1 April 1199; see *ASP, Carte Lupi, Fonti* I.1, p. 894.

23. Müller, *Documenti sulle relazioni*, no. 44, pp. 71–73.

24. Bonaini, *Statuti inediti*, 1:319–20; *RP*, no. 529.

25. Giardina, "Le 'guariganga'," no. 4, pp. 174–75; F. Natale, "Documenti pisani inediti in una collezione americana," *Bollettino Storico Pisano*, 26–27 (1957–58), 109–12.

26. *Regestum Volaterranum*, ed. F. Schneider, *Regesta Chartarum Italiae* 1 (Rome, 1908), nos. 191–92.

27. *ASP, Dipl., Primaziale*, ed. A. Pirrone, "Le pergamene dell'Archivio di Stato di Pisa dal 1204 al 1208" (M.A. diss., University of Pisa, 1965–66), no. 38. The church of St. Felix, now a bank, is on the present Via U. Dini; see Tolaini, *Forma Pisarum*, p. 27. Orzignano is 7 km north-northeast of Pisa; see E. Repetti, *Dizionario geografico, fisico, storico della Toscana*, 6 vols. (Florence, 1833–46), 3:689–90.

28. 12 December 1169, 9 June 1172, [20 February 1182?]: *ACP, Diplomatico*, nos. 552, 570, 576, ed. Sgherri, "I documenti," nos. 55, 73, 79. Arena is 8 km north-northwest of Pisa; see Repetti, *Dizionario*, 1:111–12.

29. *ASP, Dipl., Atti Pubblici*, ed. Alampi, no. 24.

30. *Il Caleffo Vecchio del Comune di Siena*, ed. G. Cecchini, 4 vols. (Siena, 1931–84), 1:378, 388.

31. 29 December: Caturegli, *RP*, no. 585.

32. 14 January 1191: D'Amia, *Le sentenze*, no. 26, pp. 269–70; 21 May 1210: *Le carte arcivescovili pisane del secolo XIII*, ed. N. Caturegli, vol. 1 (1201–38), *Regesta Chartarum Italiae* 37 (Rome, 1974), no. 51, pp. 92–101; 22 December 1227: *ASP, Dipl., R. Acquisto Cappelli*.

33. 30 November 1225: execution of a decision of Peter Alkerii and his colleague, *publici Pisanorum iudices*, in Caturegli, *Le carte arcivescovili*, 1, no. 111, pp. 259–61.

34. 12 January 1223: Caturegli, *Le carte arcivescovili*, 1, no. 96, pp. 220–22; 22 February and 15 March 1225: Caturegli, *Le carte arcivescovili*, 1, no. 106, pp. 247–50; 12 January 1233: *ASP, Dipl., R. Acquisto Roncioni*.

35. See n. 27 above.

36. *Biblioteca del Seminario Arcivescovile di Pisa, Diplomatico*, C. 7, ed. R. Paesani, "Codice diplomatico del convento di S. Caterina in Pisa (3 dicembre 1211–27 ottobre 1286)" (M.A. diss., University of Pisa, 1970–71), no. 11. On the Dominicans in Pisa and their church, see M. Ronzani, "Per la storia degli ordini mendicanti a Pisa: Francescani e Domenicani fino ai primi decenni del Trecento,"

(M.A. diss., University of Pisa, 1975–76).

37. On Pisan politics during the reign of Frederick I, see Volpe, *Studi sulle istituzioni*, pp. 167–230; and G. Rossi Sabatini, "Pisa e lo scisma del 1159," *Bollettino Storico Pisano*, 2/2 (1933), 7–28; 2/3 (1933), 7–31. On Visconti hegemony, see M. Ronzani, "Pisa nell'età di Federico II," *Atti del Centro di studi sulla civiltà del tardo medioevo: Politica e cultura nell'Italia di Federico II* (Pisa, 1986), pp. 134–59.

38. M. Ronzani, "Un aspetto della 'Chiesa di Città' a Pisa nel Due e Trecento: ecclesiastici e laici nela scelta del clero parrocchiale," in *Spazio, società, potere nell'Italia dei Comuni*, ed. G. Rossetti (Naples, 1986), pp. 176–79.

39. R. D'Amico, "Note su alcuni rapporti tra città e campagna nel contado di Pisa tra XI e XII secolo: uno sconosciuto statuto rurale del Valdiserchio del 1091–92," *Bollettino Storico Pisano*, 39 (1970), 15–28; but the document is better explained by G. Rossetti, "Società e istituzioni nei secoli IX e X: Pisa, Volterra, Populonia," *Atti del V Congresso internazionale di studi sull'alto medioeveo "Lucca e la Tuscia nell'alto medioevo"* (Spoleto, 1973), pp. 321–92. Concerning the families cited in the text, see M. C. Pratesi, "I Visconti" and G. Lugliè, "I Da Caprona," both in *Pisa nei secoli XI e XII: formazione e caratteri di una classe di governo*, ed. G. Rossetti (Pisa, 1979), pp. 3–61 and 171–221; and the M.A. dissertations, University of Pisa: M. Rosellini, "Ricerche sulla consorteria degli Orlandi Pellai (secoli XI–XIII)" (1970–71); G. C. Virdis, "Per la storia della classe dirigente del Comune di Pisa: i Gualandi" (1968–69); and M. Soldaini, "Per la storia della classe dirigente del Comune di Pisa: i da Sancasciano-Lanfranchi (secoli XI–XII)" (1972–73). On the Ebriaci property in the Serchio Valley, see notes 43, 44, 47, 67, and 80–86 below, and texts.

40. *Liber Maiolichinus de gestis Pisanorum illustribus*, ed. C. Calisse, *Fonti per la storia d'Italia*, 29 (Rome, 1904), vv. 742, 1327, 1713–21, 1901–03, 2842. Professor Giuseppe Scalia of the University of Rome, La Sapienza, is now more carefully editing the poem.

41. L. A. Muratori, *Antiquitates Italicae Medii Aevi* (henceforth *AIMA*), 6 vols. (Milan, 1738–42), 3:1117–18, 1147–48; *RP*, nos. 259, 314–15.

42. *RP*, no. 336.

43. *RP*, no. 346. St. Simon in Parlascio, destroyed before 1777, was between the present churches of St. Joseph and St. Anne in the northern part of the town: Tolaini, *Forma Pisarum*, p. 23 and tab. 6, p. 20. The old baptismal church of St. Jerusalem of Camaiano was near present Castelnuovo della Misericordia, 30 km south of Pisa; Vada, 40 km south of Pisa, was in the Middle Ages an important seaport; Vecchiano is in the Serchio Valley, 8 km north of Pisa; Cugnano was not far from Nugola, 15 km south of Pisa. On these places, see, repectively, Repetti, *Dizionario* 1:398, 573–74; 5:616–18, 680–86; 6:84; 3:651–52. I have not been able to locate *Muterno*. In the Middle Ages Selvalonga was the name of the area around S. Lorenzo a Pagnatico, 9 km southeast of Pisa; see M. L. Ceccarelli-Lemut, "Cascina. Economia e società," in Pasquinucci, Garzella, Ceccarelli-Lemut, *Cascina. Dall'Antichità al Medioevo*, pp. 114–15.

44. On the relationship with the archbishopric, see notes 62–63 below; with the Orlandi, see notes 67, 85, 86; and on the patronage of the two churches, see notes 87, 96.

45. See note 67 below.

46. Maragone, *Annales Pisani*, pp. 58, 67.

47. *Carte dell'Archivio della Certosa di Calci* 2 (1100–50), ed. Scalfati, *Thesaurus Ecclesiarum Italiae*, 7, 18 (Rome, 1971), no. 85, pp. 202–07. Macadio, in the parish of the cathedral, was north of the Maltraverso ditch, 3 km north of the town; see Repetti, *Dizionario* 3:5.

48. *ASP, Dipl., S. Lorenzo alla Rivolta*, ed. M. D. Casalini, "Le pergamene dell'Archivio di Stato di Pisa dal 1188 al 1192" (M.A. diss., University of Pisa, 1966–76), no. 2.

49. *CDS*, 1, no. 6, pp. 181–82.

50. E. Besta, *La Sardegna medievale; le vicende politiche dal 450 al 1326* (Palermo, 1908), pp. 101–03.

51. Besta, *La Sardegna medievale*, pp. 108–11. See also *CDS* 1:215.

52. *ASP, Dipl., Primaziale*, ed. G. Viviani, "Le pergamene dell'Archivio di Stato

di Pisa dal 19 giugno 1129 al 9 febbraio 1145" (M.A. diss., University of Pisa, 1964–65), no. 62. About the Athen family, see Besta, *La Sardegna medievale*, pp. 79, 92, 101–02, 107. Susan's mother was Pretiosa de Lacon (*CDS* 1: no. 45, p. 210, 20 May 1136), very likely of the royal family of Lacon, but it is impossible that she was a sister to Marianus, king in the years 1065–82, as G. Bonazzi, ed., *Il condaghe di S. Pietro di Silki* (Sassari, 1900), pp. xxi–xxii and genealogical table, argues. Perhaps she was King Gonnarius's sister or cousin.

53. Maragone, *Annales Pisani*, p. 32; Besta, *La Sardegna medievale*, pp. 122–23. Peter married the first-born daughter of Constantine (Salusius IV), king of Cagliari, and, when he became king, he took the dynastic name of Torkitorius. The kings of Cagliari were called, alternatively, Salusius and Torkitorius; see A. Solmi, "Carte volgari dell'Archivio Arcivescovile di Cagliari," *Archivio Storico Italiano*, 5th ser., 36 (1905), 3–65.

54. Artizzu, *Documenti inediti* 1, no. 3, pp. 5–8; see also Besta, *La Sardegna medievale*, pp. 153–60.

55. Besta, *La Sardegna medievale*, pp. 168–77.

56. On that period of internal and external war and confusion, see Besta, *La Sardegna medievale*, chapters 10 and 11; and M. Ronzani, "Pisa nell'età di Federico II," pp. 128–78.

57. Before they left, the two brothers made their wives their proxies: 21 and 22 August 1189: *Documenti sulle relazioni*, ed. Müller, nos. 29–30, pp. 35–36. On the role of the Pisans and their archbishop in the Third Crusade, see S. Runciman, *A History of the Crusades*, 3 vols. (Cambridge, 1951–54), 3:3–104.

58. *Documenti sulle relazioni*, ed. Müller, no. 33, pp. 39–40.

59. See n. 5 above.

60. *Documenti sulle relazioni*, ed. Müller, nos. 46–47, pp. 74–75.

61. *ACP, Diplomatico*, nos. 467, 471–72, ed. I. Baldi, "Le pergamene dell'Archivio Capitolare di Pisa dall'8 febbraio 1120 al 9 giugno 1156" (M.A. diss., University of Pisa, 1962–63), no. 85 (25 January 1146), and no. 89 (22

September 1147). Also, Robert da Parlascio, Paganus' son, was a witness with some other important citizens at a document of the Pisan canons on February 5, 1175: *ACP, Diplomatico*, no. 591, ed. Sgherri, no. 94.

62. *RP*, no. 545.

63. The arbitration is mentioned on 24 July 1181, see *RP*, no. 554.

64. *ASP, Dipl., Primaziale*, ed. Alampi, no. 41, 19 February 1197. On the Sismondi, see I. Farina, "Per la storia della classe dirigente del Comune di Pisa: I Sismondi" (M.A. diss., University of Pisa, 1969–70).

65. *ASP, Dipl., Primaziale*, ed. Viviani, no. 4. On the document of 1091–92, see note 39 above.

66. See note 44 above and text.

67. *RP*, no. 463.

68. *Documenti sulle relazioni*, ed. Müller, no. 44, pp. 71–73.

69. *Archivio di Stato di Firenze, Dipl. Comunità di Volterra*, partially and incorrectly ed. by L. A. Cecina, in *Memorie istoriche della città di Volterra*, ed. F. Dal Borgo (Pisa, 1758), pp. 23–24.

70. The first document is edited by P. Santini in *Documenti dell'antica costituzione del Comune di Firenze* (Florence, 1895), no. 62, pp. 177–19; the last in *Diplomi arabi del R. Archivo di Stato fiorentino*, ed. M. Amari, 2 vols. (Florence, 1863–67), 1, no. 27, pp. 81–82 (Arabic), no. 23, p. 284 (Latin).

71. Ed. G. Volpe, "Vescovi e comune di Massa Marittima," in *Studi Storici*, ed. A. Crivellucci, 19 (1910), no. 3, pp. 271–75.

72. Ed. E. Baratier, "Un épisode des relations entre Marseille, Pise et Oristano en 1227," in *Studi storici e giuridici in onore di A. Era* (Padova, 1963), no. 2, pp. 27–28.

73. *Il Caleffo Vecchio*, ed. Cecchini, 1, nos. 354–55, pp. 360–88.

74. About the policy of Hubald and his brothers and cousins in Pisa and in Sardinia (where Lambert, Hubald's brother, became in 1206 king of Gallura), see Ronzani, "Pisa nell'età di Federico II," pp. 134–40, 153–58; and Besta, *La Sardegna medievale*, pp. 174, 182–94.

75. *ASP, Miscellanea Manoscritti Proprietà Libera*, fasc. 84, fols. 8^r–11^v.

76. *Documenti dell'antica costituzione del Comune di Firenze*, ed. P. Santini, *Appendice* (Florence, 1952), no. 67, pp. 204–09.

77. ASP, *Dipl.*, *Atti Pubblici*, *sub anno*.

78. R. Davidsohn, *Forschungen zur Geschichte von Florenz*, 2: *Aus den Stadtbüchern und -Urkunden von San Gimignano* (Berlin, 1906), nos., 936, 940–41, 948, 952, 956–57, 959, 1004.

79. E. Cristiani, "I combattenti della battaglia della Meloria e la tradizione cronistica," *Bullettino Storico Livornese*, n.s., 2/1 (1952), 21; see also M. L. Ceccarelli-Lemut, "I Pisani prigionieri a Genova dopo la battaglia della Meloria: la tradizione cronistica e le fonti documentarie," *L'anno della Meloria* (Pisa, 1984), p. 80.

80. See nn. 39 and 67 above.

81. At Patrignone, the sons of Robert da Parlascio, on 11 June 1211: *ASP, Carte Lupi, Fonti* I.1, pp. 1054–56; at Lugnano, Hildeprandin Rosso, Gerard Verchione's son, on 23 August 1243: *Archivio della Mensa Arcivescovile di Pisa* (henceforth *AMAP*), *Contratti*, no. 1, fol. 81^r–^{v}, ed. F. Famoos-Paolini, "Atti della Mensa Arcivescovile di Pisa negli anni 1204–45, al tempo degli arcivesovi Ubaldo Lanfranchi e Vitale" (M.A. diss., University of Pisa, 1977–78), no. 164. Patrignone is 10 km north of Pisa, Lugnano was near Molina di Quosa, 9 km north-northeast of Pisa; see Repetti, *Dizionario*, 2:931–32; 4:73.

82. At Vecchiano, the sons of Robert da Parlascio, at the end of the twelfth century (*ASP, Carte Lupi, Fonti* I.1, pp. 878–79), and Hugh Ebriacus on 7 January 1258 (*AMAP, Contratti*, no. 3, fols. 161^r–62^r, ed. S. Giancoli, "Atti di ser Leopardo del Fornaio dal registro n. 3 della serie Contratti dell'Archivio della Mensa Arcivescovile di Pisa" [M.A. diss., University of Pisa, 1975–76], no. 25);

at S. Andrea in Pescaiola, Robert da Parlascio, on 25 March 1196 (*ASP, Carte Lupi, Fonti* I.1, pp. 826–27).

83. At Cornazzano, the sons of (Hugh) Ebriacus, on 3 June 1193: *ASP, Dipl., S. Michele in Borgo*, ed. G. M. Dolo, "Le pergamene dell' Archivio di Stato di Pisa dal 1192 al 1195" (M.A. diss., University of Pisa, 1967–68), no. 18; at Bottano, the sons of Robert da Parlascio, on 8 May 1223: *ASP, Carte Lupi, Fonti* I.1, pp. 1218–21; at Macadio, Robert, Peter's son (see n. 47 above), and Robert da Parlascio on 10 January 1185 (*ASP, Carte Lupi, Fonti* I.1, pp. 732–33), and—after his death—his sons Robert on 5 August 1192 and 18 September 1194, and Ebriacus on 28 April and 16 May 1192: *ASP, Carte Lupi, Fonti* I.1, pp. 782–83, 786–87, 792–93, 801–11; Robert again and his grandson Gerard Verchione (Ebriacus' son) on 30 July 1202: *ASP, Carte Lupi, Fonti* I.1, pp. 948–49. On Bottano, see Repetti, *Dizionario*, 1:357.

84. *ASP, Dipl., R. Acquisto Roncioni, sub anno*. I thank my friend and colleague Mauro Ronzani, researcher at the *Scuola Normale Superiore* of Pisa, who very kindly communicated to me this document and several others of the thirteenth century.

85. *AMAP, Contratti*, no. 3, fols. 200ᵛ–01ʳ, ed. Giancoli, no. 121.

86. *Archivio Agostini Venerosi della Seta*, ed. C. Gambini, "Le pergamene dell'Archivio pisano dei conti Agostini Venerosi della Seta dal 1043 al 1330" (M.A. diss., University of Pisa, 1968–69), no. 44. See also Ronzani, "Un aspetto della 'Chiesa di Città'," p. 179, n. 114.

87. Near the church of St. Blasius (now in the eastern suburbs of the town) on 23 December 1193: *ASP, Dipl., Ospedali Diversi*, ed. Dolo, "Le pergamene," no. 27.

88. Caturegli, *Le carte arcivescovili*, 1, no. 179, pp. 412–14. Oratoio is 3 km southeast of the town, nearly in front of Cisanello. The church of St. Thomas à Becket, destroyed between 1782 and 1789, was on Via S. Apollonia, not far from the church of St. Simon in Parlascio; see Tolaini, *Forma Pisarum*, map on p. 21. Settimo, now S. Benedetto a Settimo, lies 10 km east-southeast of Pisa; see Garzella, "Cascina. L'organizzazione," pp. 77–78, and Ceccarelli-Lemut, "Cascina. Economia," pp. 137–41, 151.

89. Robert da Parlascio, on 28 January 1182: *RP*, no. 545 and 17 February 1182: *ASP*, *Dipl.*, *S. Lorenzo alla Rivolta*, ed. B. Pellegrini, "Le pergamene dell'Archivio di Stato di Pisa dal 1179 al 1185" (M.A. diss., University of Pisa, 1965–66), no. 40. S. Pietro a Pagnatico was about 9 km southeast of Pisa.

90. *ASP*, *Dipl.*, *Olivetani*, *sub anno*. Visignano is 7 km southeast of Pisa; see Garzella, "Cascina. L'organizzazione," pp. 94–96, 98. About the Gualandi, see L. Martini, "Per la storia della classe dirigente del Comune di Pisa. La 'domus Gualandorum'" (M.A. diss., University of Pisa, 1975–76), but she does not identify exactly the Bocci branch.

91. Ebriaco at Oliveto on 7 August 1189, *ASP*, *Dipl.*, *S. Lorenzo alla Rivolta*, ed. Casalini, no. 14; his son owned a wood near Salviano on 16 August 1206: *ASP*, *Corporazioni Religiose Soppresse*, no. 1182, fol. 19^r, ed. V. M. Trombi, "Ricerche sulle proprietà fondiarie dell'Ospedale di S. Leonardo di Stagno e del monastero di Ognissanti (1200–1367)" (M.A. diss., University of Pisa, 1969–70), no. 21; *terra de Ebriacis* at Collinaia on 15 August 1208: *ASP*, *Dipl.*, *Coletti*, ed. M. L. Ricci, "Le pergamene dell' Archivio di Stato di Pisa dal 1208 al 1213" (M.A. diss., University of Pisa, 1980–81), no. 11; and near Leghorn on 9 April 1233: *ASP*, *Dipl.*, *Primaziale*, *sub anno*. Oliveto is about 5 km east of Leghorn, Salviano and Collinaia are nearly in the southeastern suburbs of the town; see Repetti, *Dizionario* 3:655; 5:12–13. The commercial port of Pisa, *Portus Pisanus*, was from the third century A.D. north of Leghorn, between the present mouth of the Calambrone canal, S. Stefano ai Lupi, and the Leghorn headland; see *Terre e paduli. Reperti documenti immagini per la storia di Coltano* (Pontedera, 1986), p. 124.

92. Robert da Parlascio, Pagano's son, on 10 June 1184: *ASP*, *Dipl.*, *S. Lorenzo alla Rivolta*, ed. Blanda, no. 4; Sardo and Barison, Barile's sons, their cousin Hugh Ebriaco, and the sons of Robert—Peter's son—on 23 July 1188: *ASP*, *Dipl.*, *S. Lorenzo alla Rivolta*, ed. Casalini, no. 2; *terra filiorum Ebriaci* on 27 September 1209 and 11 October 1240: *ASP*, *Corporazioni Religiose Soppresse*, no. 1182, fols. 26^r–27^v, 24^r–25^v, ed. Trombi, nos. 34 and 82; *terra Ebriacorum* on 15 June 1246: *ASP*, *Dipl.*, *R. Acquisto Roncioni*, *sub anno*; and on 15 May 1262: *AMAP*, *Contratti*, no. 5, fols. 268^v–69^v, ed. F. Innocenzi, "Atti della Mensa Arcivescovile di Pisa al tempo dell'arcivescovo Federico Visconti (1261–64)" (M.A. diss., University of Pisa, 1973–74), no. 35; and Vanne Barile, Simon Barile's son, on 2 August 1312: *Archivio Arcivescovile di Pisa, Acta Extraordinaria* (1311–12), fol. 55. On Cugnano, see n. 43 above.

93. *ACP*, A/3, fols. 11ʳ, 13ʳ–14ʳ.

94. *Terra Ebriacorum* on 27 January 1237, 11 April 1258, and 14 June 1300: *ASP, Dipl., S. Paolo all'Orto, sub anno*. On Vada, see n. 43 above.

95. "Pisis in porticu domus ipsius Sardi [Barile's son] et consortum prope ecclesiam s. Symonis de Parlascio on August 22, 1189: *Documenti sulle relazioni*, ed. Müller, no. 30 pp. 35–36."

96. See Ronzani, "Un aspetto della 'Chiesa di Città'," pp. 178–79.

97. *ASP, Dipl., S. Lorenzo alla Rivolta*, ed. R. Nardi, "Le pergamene dell'Archivio di Stato di Pisa dall'8 novembre 1115 al 13 febbraio 1130" (M.A. diss., University of Pisa, 1964–65), no. 53. The church of St. Zeno is in the northeastern corner of the city walls built after 1155.

98. *ASP, Dipl., Coletti*, ed. Pirrone, no. 17. The remains of the front of the church of St. Leonard in Pratuscello are on present day Via Roma that extends from the Arno river to the cathedral; see Tolaini, *Forma Pisarum*, pp. 24, 212.

99. See nn. 38, 39, 64, 90 above; and C. Violante, "Nobiltà e chiese in Pisa durante i secoli XI e XII: il monastero di S. Matteo (prime ricerche)," now in Violante, ed., *Economia società istituzioni a Pisa nel medioevo. Saggi e ricerche* (Bari, 1980), pp. 25–65; see also, in G. Rosetti, ed., *Pisa nei secoli XI e XII*: Rosetti, "Ceti dirigenti e classe politica," pp. xxv–xli; G. Garzella, "Marignani, Azzi, Alabarba," pp. 65–124; M. B. Guzzardi, "Erizi," pp. 127–68; and C. Sturmann, "La 'domus' dei Dodi, Gaetani e Gusmari," pp. 225–336. See also M. A. Delfino, "Per la storia della classe dirigente del Comune di Pisa: i da Ripafratta" (M. A. diss., University of Pisa, 1971–72); and L. Ticciati, "Da S. Casciano-Lanfranchi: una dinastia e una denominazione di origine" (M.A. diss., Univerisity of Pisa, 1981–82).

100. L. Ticciati is now finishing her doctoral dissertation on the Casapieri. Under my guidance L. Rege Cambrin wrote her M.A. diss. "La famiglia Casalei dalle origini alla metà del XIII secolo" (1989–90), and I have charged another student with the study of the Ricucchi.

The Political and Economic Relations of Pisa and the Guelf League in the Late Thirteenth and Early Fourteenth Centuries

EMILIO CRISTIANI

This study will concentrate on a particularly significant moment in the history of Pisa and its commercial and maritime traffic, when the influence of Genoa, the Angevins, and the Aragonese brought substantial changes in the relations among the Tuscan cities, Sardinia, Corsica, and southern Italy. A volume of studies was published recently on the occasion of the seventh centenary of the battle of Meloria (1284–1984).[1] The articles contained therein deal not only with the direct consequences of the battle but also with the possibility of discerning in the years surrounding it a change in direction in political and economic affairs, especially in the field of commerce and banking, a change in direction that was greatly influenced by the new policies of Boniface VIII with regard to Sardinia and by the entry of the Aragonese into Mediterranean and Italian affairs.

Pisa shared in the historical vicissitudes of those maritime republics that, like Venice, showed an ever-increasing involvement in *terraferma* politics in the course of the thirteenth and fourteenth centuries. Genoa had already established an ever more marked naval predominance in the Tyrrhenian Sea and the Mediterranean in the last decades of the thirteenth century. For Pisa this meant a gradual restriction of her markets to the zone within the Tyrrhenian area, while year by year the pressure from the Guelf cities increased, above all from Florence and Lucca, who sought to occupy the port of Pisa and completely overcome her military resistance.

By the end of the thirteenth and the beginning of the fourteenth century Pisa was receiving very limited support from the Empire, its Ghibelline allies, or the White Guelfs, except for the moment of the great but illusory hopes placed in Henry VII of Luxembourg between 1310 and 1313. The actual political situation was in a continuous state of evolution, despite the fact that, following the victory won at Meloria, the commune of Genoa believed that it could establish its predominance once and for all by means of two peace treaties imposed on Pisa in 1288 and 1299. The text of these treaties reveals an extraordinary situation not only in terms of the difficulties faced by Pisa, which found itself besieged by land and by sea, but also with regard to the peculiar harshness and intransigence of the conditions they contained. In fact, the negotiations between Pisa and Genoa were conducted in a highly unusual way. It is clear from the context of the settlement that there was no form of preliminary arbitration or agreement. There was only the imposition of what amounted to an unconditional surrender that resulted in an impressive series of territorial concessions.

The whole area of the port of Cagliari, with the city itself and the territory surrounding it, was to pass to the Genoese together with the castles of Logudoro, situated in the north of the island; in practice the Pisans were to hand over the whole of Sardinia to Genoa, since the territories of the interior were to be cut off, with the prohibition of all access to them from the sea. The same applied to Corsica, where both commercial and naval enterprise by individuals were prohibited. Equally drastic was the provision whereby the Pisans were to give up their colonies and trading stations at Acre, which was their last bridgehead in the Middle East. The territorial limits to which Pisan ships might sail were strictly laid down: to the south no further than Sardinia and Naples, to the north not beyond Aigues Mortes and the Rhone delta. The delivery of the island of Elba to the Genoese was also envisaged, by means of Genoese garrisons in the castles and fortifications there.

As Professor Ottavio Banti has shown,[2] the treaty of 1288 used formulae characteristic of private documents, and this not by chance but for a particular reason. The form of the document was in fact a legal fiction by means of which it was possible to dictate more onerous conditions to the Pisans, since in the guise of a private act it was possible to ignore the rights of the Papacy and the Empire over Sardinia and Corsica. In addition, the Genoese selected some of the most prominent individuals from among the Pisan prisoners in Genoa to serve as guarantors for the treaty. At the same time, the Pisans were required to hand over their oldest documents regarding the sovereign rights of the Papacy and the Empire, which had been cited in the privileges granted to Pisa. Furthermore, a deposit of £50,000 Genoese was provided for, to be distributed among seven different Italian cities (Genoa, Asti, Piacenza, etc.).

Despite, or perhaps because of, its severity the treaty of 1288 was never fully enforced.[3] The commune of Pisa took advantage of every opportunity to recover its losses. One demonstration of this resistance is the fact that when, in 1290, Elba was occupied by the Genoese for fear of some Pisan ships that were still in Piombino, the Pisans immediately and definitively reconquered the island. The action of the Pisans can be explained by the fact that the production of iron was still important on Elba, with wage laborers recruited from as far away as Lombardy.[4] In 1299, therefore, the Genoese demanded another treaty, which took the form of a new truce to last for twenty-five years, with a provision for the enforcement of the terms already imposed in 1288. Pisa was obliged to pay a penalty of £160,000 Genoese for its failure to observe some of the stipulated terms of the earlier accord and for not having ceded the castles of Logudoro. In the meantime, while the descen-

dants of Count Ugolino della Gherardesca, that is, the Counts of
Donoratico of the Guelf branch, had transferred themselves partly
to Sardinia and partly to Genoa itself, most Pisan exiles tended to
ally themselves with the Guelf league and with the Florentines.

The most recent research on the relations among Pisa, Genoa,
and the cities of their hinterlands has examined the activities of
some of the most important noble families of Guelf leanings—such
as the Gaetani, the Duodi, the Visconti, and some *popolano* families that were associated with the Gaetani—in forming a banking
company entitled the *Societas Benedicta*, inspired and guided by
Cardinal Benedetto Gaetani (from whom it took its name) before
he became pope as Boniface VIII. Recent articles by two young
scholars, Gaetano Ciccone and Salvatore Polizzi,[5] have dealt with
this very question, and I will discuss it now because of its relevance to political affairs. For as long as it was possible, these
families of noble origin took part in the official politics of the
commune, and then they left to join the Guelf exiles.[6] The information regarding this *Societas* is of obvious interest, given the
scarcity of material on banking companies in this period.

In 1276 Oddo Gaetani, a leading member of the *Societas*, was
the leader of initiatives within the commune in favor of the pardon
of Ugolino and the rebel exiles.[7] After the peace of 1275 with the
Guelf league, Oddo intensified his relations with the Guelfs and
with the Angevin rulers, Charles I and later Charles II and Charles
Martel, supplying them with arms (*pavenses*) in large quantities.[8] At
the same time he became a *familiaris*, as he was expressly termed,
of Cardinal Benedetto Gaetani and of Charles Martel (the son of
Charles II and regent for him during his years of captivity), granting
them large loans.[9] In an effort to expand these financial operations,
Oddo moved to Naples and then to Rome, where from 1292 to 1303
he made the transition from merchant to banker.[10] A second banking
company, closely associated with the *Societas Benedicta*, was
directed by the Cavalozzari, an important *popolano* family.[11] Its

partners also included members of the Falcone family, whose importance in the production of wool and furs has been emphasized by David Herlihy in his book *Pisa in the Early Renaissance*.[12]

The closeness of the relationship between these banking companies and Boniface VIII is also shown by the fact that Oddo Gaetani resided in the Lateran[13] and by the participation of several Tuscan banks in the major financial operations ordered by the pope for the archbishops of Pisa and Torres. Tuscan banks provided 2,500 florins and, later, 3,000 florins, just when the pope was making increasingly assertive claims to sovereignty over Sardinia, partly as a consequence of the war of the Sicilian Vespers and the investiture granted to James II of Aragon.[14] Special licenses were also granted for major funding for the archbishop of Patras.

Robert Davidsohn, the historian of Florence, records that, in the famous legal proceedings against Boniface VIII brought by the French king, Philip the Fair, there was stressed the accusation that the pope had forced public bodies and individuals to agree to loans at rates of interest as high as 60%. These loans applied also in France and various other European territories, as in the case of the powerful archbishop of Toulouse, who obtained 4,000 florins from the *Societas* in 1299 and a little later the sum of 11,000 florins from the Spini of Florence.[15] Between 1285 and 1299 papal favor and support for Oddo Gaetani also extended to his sons, Iacopo and Benedetto (who, as one can see, had the same name as Benedetto Gaetani). They were granted rich prebends and exemption from the obligations of the cure of souls while they were studying civil law at the university.[16]

In 1299 the noble Gaetani killed one of the *popolano* Cavalozzari in a vendetta, or private war, in Pisa and were put on trial for the murder. It seems, then, that the rivalry between the two banking firms was accompanied by a reciprocal hatred of the two families or *consorterie*. However, as a result of the intervention of two cardinals of the sacred college who had links with Boniface VIII, the commune absolved the Gaetani on the grounds of the "multa servicia" that they had done for the city at the Roman Curia.[17] The political and banking activities of the Gaetani were therefore so important that, even though family members were responsible for this homicide, they were exempted from the anti-magnate decrees, which were in force in most Italian communes.

Iacopo, son of Oddo Gaetani, was named councillor of the kingdom of Sicily by Charles II of Anjou, and his ship was granted special public protection. The king later assigned him annual revenues of 40 gold *oncie* and the use of the castle of Monteacuto in Val di Fiora for three generations. In 1302 he was entrusted with a special mission in Sicily immediately after the peace of Caltabellotta,[18] a mission for which he received a loan of 1,473 florins from the Spini company.

In the course of the negotiations regarding Sicily and Sardinia, the whole of the Guelf faction gradually came to side with James II of Aragon. In fact, Guglielmo Ricoveranza dei Visconti of Pisa was also a councillor of the king of Naples. In 1301 an Aragonese ambassador noted in his diplomatic dispatches that Iacopo Gaetani still had great influence over the Commune of Pisa and was in a position to ensure that the Pisans would not oppose the forthcoming Aragonese conquest of Sardinia.[19] In the early years of the fourteenth century, after the famous Florentine expedition of Charles of Valois, all these operations became clearly linked to that current of Tuscan Guelfism designated as the Black party, which included the opponents of Dante. The chronicler Dino Compagni, who believed Iacopo Gaetani to be an actual kinsman of Boniface VIII, bears witness to this.[20]

In 1300 the *Societas Benedicta* embarked upon the enormous enterprise of the so-called tenths "pro subsidio Terre Sancte." Boniface VIII had complained that the collectors of these tenths had been negligent in exacting them and he therefore entrusted the post of collector to one of the most important imperial electors, the arch-

bishop of Cologne, who was to forward the money raised to the
"mercatores de Florentia et Pisis."[21] Immediately afterwards the
pope specified that these were to be the Spini of Florence and
Iacopo Gaetani, Giovanni Falcone, and Guido Balsano *de Societate
Benedicta de Pisis.* The scale of these operations can be shown by
comparison with another figure: the pope was in debt to the Scali
banking company of Florence to the extent of 579,000 florins.[22]

The Gaetani also served as intermediaries between the Roman
Curia and the king of Aragon and received special acknowledge-
ment of this from James II. Boniface VIII's sudden death in 1303
was an unexpected setback to the Gaetani. It caused Iacopo to
make a special journey to the conclave in Perugia in order to support the Bonifacian faction headed by Cardinal Francesco Gaetani,
which hoped for the election of a successor who would continue
the political line of Boniface VIII.[23] But the opposite current of
Benedict XI and, later, Clement V prevailed; Cardinal Francesco
himself had to leave Rome. Iacopo fell back to the *rocca* of Pietracassa in Tuscany, from whence he conducted various armed expeditions against San Gimignano and against the Pisan *contado.*[24]
Since diplomacy had by now become unthinkable and impractic-
able, he passed in this way to open warfare.

In Pisa Iacopo was now considered an "exbannitus," and the
commune proceeded to enact harsher sentences and confiscations
against all the Gaetani. The property of Iacopo and Benedetto was
confiscated by the treasury or assigned to creditors. It was no acci-
dent that these creditors included Cardinal Napoleone Orsini, of
proven Ghibelline faith, who had been one of the opponents of the
Gaetani at the conclave of Perugia.[25] In 1306 Iacopo prepared for
further military operations, designed to coincide with the operations
of Florence against Arezzo, and in 1309 the *rocca* of Pietracassa,
with Iacopo still present there, again received aid from Florentine
and Lucchese forces.[26] The *rocca* did not return to Pisan control,
however, until Iacopo's death, which took place about 1322. In the

meantime the counts of Donoratico had established their control over the government of Pisa. It is well known that there were moments when the Ghibelline tradition of Pisa enjoyed a partial revival under the lordship of the Donoratico and especially owing to the activities of certain famous military leaders, such as Guido de Montefeltro and Uguccione della Faggiola.[27]

Between 1314 and 1316 and later in 1342 Pisa succeeded in securing control over Lucca, which it maintained for a couple of decades. But it was at just this point in the mid-fourteenth century that the trend favorable to agreement with Florence, which had been slowly developing in previous decades, firmly established itself within the ruling circles of Pisa. Thus the pro-Guelf initiatives, which at the end of the thirteenth century had emerged in opposition to traditional Ghibelline intransigence, constituted an anticipation of a different policy towards the Guelf league by Pisa, a policy that allowed for a greater degree of recovery for her trade and commerce.

Relations with Genoa were also undergoing modifications in the first decades of the new century. A peace treaty of 1341 declared that the two cities were no longer in a state of war but, rather, felt the need for a common defence against the Aragonese.[28] Thus pro-Guelf initiatives that arose in Pisa after the battle of Meloria gradually pushed the commune in the direction of cooperation with Lucca, Florence, and Genoa, which contributed to the survival of Pisan trade and commerce.

NOTES

The author would like to express his thanks to Professors Christine Meek, Maureen Mazzaoui, and Thomas W. Blomquist.

1. *Genova, Pisa e il mediterraneo tra Due e Trecento: Per il VII° centenario della battaglia della Meloria: published by the Società Ligure di Storia Patria* (Genoa, 1984).

2. O. Banti, "I trattati fra Genova e Pisa dopo la Meloria fino alla metà del secolo XIV," in, *Genova*, pp. 355–58.

3. *Genova*, pp. 362–63.

4. E. Cristiani, "La situazione storica dell'Elba alla fine del secolo XIII," in *Atti del Convegno di Storia dell'Elba, Rio Marina 29 ag.–1 sett. 1982* (Pisa, 1987), pp. 35–41.

5. G. Ciccone and S. Polizzi, "La casata dei Dodi-Gaetani nelle lotte politiche in Pisa alla fine del XIII secolo," *Bollettino storico pisano*, 53 (1984), 109–46 and "Le vicende di un nobile pisano alla corte di Bonifacio VIII," *Bollettino storico pisano*, 55 (1986), 65–83.

6. Ciccone and Polizzi, "La casata," pp. 122–25.

7. Ciccone and Polizzi, "La casata," p. 128.

8. Ciccone and Polizzi, "Le vicende," pp. 69–70.

9. Ciccone and Polizzi, "Le vicende," pp. 69–70.

10. Ciccone and Polizzi, "Le vicende," pp. 70–71.

11. Ciccone and Polizzi, "Le vicende," pp. 72–73.

12. Ciccone and Polizzi, "Le vicende," p. 75; D. Herlihy, *Pisa in the Early Renaissance* (New Haven, 1958), pp. 121–23, 199.

13. Ciccone and Polizzi, "Le vicende," pp. 70–71.

14. Ciccone and Polizzi, "Le vicende," pp. 72–73.

15. Ciccone and Polizzi, "Le vicende," p. 73; R. Davidsohn, *Storia di Firenze* (Italian trans. Florence, 1972), pp. 25–30.

16. Ciccone and Polizzi, "Le vicende," p. 76.

17. Ciccone and Polizzi, "La casata," p. 142.

18. Ciccone and Polizzi, "Le vicende," p. 78.

19. Ciccone and Polizzi, "Le vicende," p. 78.

20. Ciccone and Polizzi, "Le vicende," p. 74; Cf. p. 83: "sanctissimi patris domini Bonifacii egregius miles."

21. Ciccone and Polizzi, "Le vicende," p. 74.

22. Ciccone and Polizzi, "Le vicende," p. 75.

23. Ciccone and Polizzi, "Le vicende," p. 75.

24. Ciccone and Polizzi, "Le vicende"; G. Arias, "I banchieri toscani e la Santa Sede sotto Benedetto XI," *Archivio della R. Società Romana di Storia Patria*, 24 (1901), 499.

25. Ciccone and Polizzi, "Le vicende," p. 80.

26. Ciccone and Polizzi, "Le vicende," p. 82.

27. E. Cristiani, *Nobiltà e popolo nel comune di Pisa* (Naples, 1962), pp. 296 ff.

28. Banti, "I trattati," pp. 363–66.

Siena in the Fourteenth Century: State, Territory, and Culture

MARIO ASCHERI

Wherever this holy virtue justice rules, she persuades many souls to unity and these, gathered together for such a purpose, choose a common good for their lord. This lord, in order to govern the state, chooses never to keep his eyes turned from the splendor of the faces of the virtues surrounding him.[1]

From the Thirteenth to the Fourteenth Century:
The Guelf Turning Point, the Mercantile Triumph and Crisis

Before turning to the main topic at hand, it is necessary to review the background events of the period in Sienese history under review since they do not conform completely to the normal Italian political and institutional picture of the fourteenth century. The real foundations of fourteenth-century Siena are to be sought between 1270 and 1280. Starting with the battle of Colle in 1269, those years witnessed the decline of Sienese Ghibelline leadership, the return of political exiles, the formal weakening of the *Populus* and the Guilds (1271), abolition of the office of the Captain of the People (1274), and promulgation of a statute in which the organization of the Popolo is missing and the Guelf Party dominates. These events culminated in the installation of the rule of the merchants in the form of the government of the Thirty-six Guelfs, the so-called "Governors and Defenders of the City and Commune," who replaced the preceding College of the Twenty-four.[2]

163

In 1289 the *Popolo* reappeared, along with its Captains during the early period of the Nine (now styled "Governors and Defenders of the Commune and the People of Siena"). But the Popolo, it would seem, was by that time thoroughly controlled by the oligarchic Commune, which, while fostering a popular ideology, proved itself quite adept at keeping the more extreme Guelf exponents in check. The nobility and magnates appear to have been similarly kept under control. They were excluded from the supreme magistracies of government and identified officially by name in 1277. In short, the government of merchants and "mezzana gente" ruled the city until 1355.

In 1355, the first Sienese sojourn of Charles IV prompted a general revolt and a subsequent search for a new political equilibrium. The possibility of forming a lasting coalition was crushed, and groups once outcast took, or waited for, the opportunity to gain the upper hand. A turbulent period began and characterized the subsequent decades of the century, as various rebellions espoused by politically diverse groups broke out. The abandonment of the traditional alliance with Florence—caused by disagreements over control of Montepulciano, Arezzo, and Cortona—occurred during this period. An alliance with the Visconti, formalized in 1389, seemed natural enough at the time but was transformed into a brief surrender of Sienese autonomy in 1399. In the same period, various political upheavals began to bring to the fore the five *Monti*, that is, the more or less broad groups of citizens that from then on controlled the Sienese political situation through and despite intense periods of alternate cooperation and disagreement. The *Monti* were parties based on and called respectively the Nobles, the Nine, the Twelve, the Reformers, and the People.[3]

Thus from the late thirteenth and through the first half of the fourteenth century, a single leading group, formally composed of merchants and "mezzana gente" but also, in reality, supported by several magnates, ruled supreme. Later a more politically complex society evolved, a society in which the struggle between the Nobility and the People again arose, but by then it was a rivalry much more complicated and obscured by the various *Monti* and with more political than social ends.

The year 1355 was a turning point in the organizational forms of political life, but it nevertheless did not change fundamentally the state structure inherited from the preceding period. This structure had been basically stabilized and improved between the late 1200s and early 1300s, a time of relative prosperity and political and institutional stability. The collapse of the Nine in 1355 does, however, represent a fundamental split in Sienese history from a political point of view. Only at the beginning of the fifteenth century do we again find an era of stability such as that of a century earlier.

The period of the Nine is a crucial era in the history of the Sienese state, and it is that era, therefore, upon which we will concentrate in the following discussion.[4] The division at 1355 is also historiographic in that study of the subsequent period is haphazard and sectoral and editions of sources are conspicuously lacking.[5]

In 1355 the documentation of public institutions, such as the *Mercanzia* and the Wool Guild, were destroyed; even the emblems that decorated the homes of the *Noveschi* were struck down during the revolt, with an iconoclastic violence never repeated in Sienese history. These are well-known facts.[6] For example, the official copy of the collection of statutes in force in 1355 was apparently defaced on the illuminated folio, and the caption *Novem* was erased and substituted with that of the new office.[7] Such events do not seem to have been repeated during subsequent rebellions and the frequent modifications of the government's composition. At this point we should note that the presumed respect for the fresco of the famous *Guidoriccio* in the Palazzo Pubblico, a tribute to the most well-known *condottiere* of the Nine, seems unlikely to have existed, especially since the frescoes of other castles conquered at the time of the Nine have not been preserved.[8] It is easier to explain the preservation of the "Allegories of Good and Bad Government" painted in the Palazzo during the period of the Nine. The "commitenti" are absent in the representations, whose message is more cultural than political and not directly connected to a specific group within the government.

The Central Organization of the State

We have already referred to apparatuses of the central government essentially inherited from the thirteenth century. We may add that an almost constant tendency to control the intruding powers of the General Council of the Commune (composed of magnates and the "people") appears to emerge, even if its general competence was respected. The General Council had the final word on legislation and was the government's source of legitimacy. A centralizing trend, however, was expressed during the period of the Nine by the frequent conferrals of power on commissions appointed by the government for resolving specific problems, while the Council took on only generic matters surfacing there or dealing directly with governmental laws. This delegation of power was in favor of the Nine and, often, of the Orders or *ordines*; that is the heads of the most important central offices, such as the *Biccherna*, the main financial board, and the *Mercanzia*, the organization which claimed to represent the mercantile world. The councils of the Knights or of the Guelf Party also played a considerable role at the top of the government, but it is difficult to estimate the powers of these organizations and their particular interests because of the absence of documentation. The fact that their nomination was dependent on the Nine and the other Orders leads to the conclusions that the Guelf party and the Council of the Knights were not, in fact, autonomous and that the Sienese state had a "corporate" character much less clearly articulated than that of Florence.[9]

As was customary in the medieval tradition, the Nine and the

Orders of the city had very brief and rotating shifts, lasting two to six months and alternating with periods of ineligibility, here referred to as "vacations." In order to assure the continuity of the line of government and contacts between its supporters and the Nine, who were isolated in the Palazzo Pubblico, frequent convocations of formal advisory councils were necessary.[10] The most prominent members of the leading group apparently participated in these councils. Unfortunately, little is known about the membership of these councils and then only through second-hand references. Likewise, the membership of the Council of the People is rarely known except from a few lists.[11] According to the documentation examined by Bowsky, moreover, the organization of the guilds and Popolo seemed to depend completely on the regime and confirms once again the limited "corporate" character of the state at the time of the Nine.[12] But we know very little about the function of the Popolo's structure and even less about the methods of electing political personnel, though we can postulate a prevailing cliental co-option. In any event, the popular "compagnie" that should have theoretically constituted the leading structure of the regime do not seem to have played a decisive role at the critical moments faced by the government. The regime was perhaps saved more by the troops at its direct service sent from allies and from the *contado* than by *popolani* who would have been legally obligated to it.[13]

In the instance of particularly delicate occasions—for example, when dealing with rules regarding election of the Nine—the government felt the need to consult those who had already filled the highest office. In this ad hoc fashion we find that the Council of the *Riseduti* came about, a body that was to play an important role after the Nine and would take shape in the fifteenth century as The Council of the People, a true Senate and center of official political deliberation.[14] This was not the only new concept put into effect in the period following the Nine. The special powers that the Nine and the Orders occasionally exercised were now granted to special committees: the *Balie*, bodies elected for one term that was often extended. Their appointment was governed by exceptional laws, which permitted the government to employ members of the nobility—normally excluded from government even after the Nine—and other citizens unable to take office because of the rules regarding vacations and ineligibility.[15] Nevertheless, the employment of *Balie* did not seem to bring about substantial changes in the process of centralization of the powers of government that had begun during the time of the Nine. Major changes were simply rendered less necessary with the absence of formal parties such as the later *Monti* (excluding that of the magnates), on the one hand, and the control exercised over the General Council (which was elected by the Nine and Orders), on the other.

In short, the *Balie* seem to represent a new institution, associated with greater formalization and sophistication for decision making, rather than an actual turning point in depriving the councils of authority. The increased formalization and complication in their turn were connected with political difficulties, the growing complexity of the public apparatus, and the presence of the *Monti*. The keeping of the so-called "lion's books," the official register of the *Riseduti*, existing since the late fourteenth century, was probably due to the fact that membership in the *Monti* was hereditary. The growing regularization of offices, particularly concerning qualifications of age, could instead be accredited to the availability of registrations of the baptized in the city.[16] In this context it is not surprising to find the organization of a stable magistracy for the accounting of all the offices of the state (probably associated, in addition, with the rearrangement of public debt) and for assigning various powers especially regarding territorial government.[17]

· As far as bureaucratic structure and its personnel are concerned, in the absence of records it is difficult to make a precise statement about the decisions and appointments made by the Nine. But it is clear that beyond rotation of the lower offices—especially that of the notaries—the more sensitive jobs that required a familiarity with communal documentation were becoming better defined. Thus the Notary of the *riformagioni* increased in importance. The Notary was a foreigner but, as a rule, a Tuscan, with experience in the problems that he would have to face. One from Pistoia held the office for about ten years, another from San Gimignano for fifteen years.[18] Another office was that of Chancellor, then in charge of correspondence and embassies. Is it by chance that the only Chancellor we can trace effectively was the Sienese, ser Francesco di Ser Ghino,[19] who appears in each of the three registers of 1338, 1347, and 1351? This office continued to play a major role even after the Nine.[20]

The Captain of the People was also Sienese, though only after the fall of the Nine. Before that he was a foreigner like the *Podestà*; and like the *Podestà*, he filled a highly judicial but secondary office, no longer at the apex of the state as in the thirteenth century.[21] In 1355 the office of the Captain took on a definite physiognomy in Sienese history and became decidedly more political and highly distinguished by the new name of Gonfalonier of Justice. The events of 1355 had suggested that an authoritative Sienese citizen should lead the Popolo and state. The year 1355 also represented an important turning point for the *Mercanzia*. Previously its consuls had been ubiquitous among the Nine. The *Mercanzia* then became an office of the state, though still preserving its autonomy as an *universitas* and, therefore, its corporate foundation. But the consuls, at that point significantly called officers, were excluded from the Orders.[22]

A turning point for another important office also seems to have come about during the period of the Nine (in 1323 or earlier). It is the office of the General Captain of War, a foreigner who controlled both the *Podestà* and the Captain of the People and who had at his disposal an armed force larger than that provided for either the *Podestà* or the Captain of the People. His main role was that of the government's principal enforcer of public order. Of minor importance was his leadership and conduct of the communal army, a job that, moreover, would have required an officer with a longer term. He was the *salus, securitas et defensio* of the *domini Novem*, as presented in a 1338 text.[23] He was a noble who came to Siena often first as *Podestà* and then was kept on as the Captain of War after having had his fidelity and capabilities tested. As previously mentioned, Guido-riccio was one of them around the year 1330, and then again before his death and the fall of the Nine in the 1350s. Because of the type and duration of the office, subjected neither to vacations nor to checks, the Captain of War personified the fearsome face of the mili-tary and police power of an otherwise anonymous government.

We must, indeed, wonder how much importance to give to a pas-sage written by the great lawyer Bartolo da Sassoferrato immediately after the fall of the Nine, in which he admits that they had governed *bene et prudenter* for about seventy years, but that they formed a government of but a few, of the *ordo divitum* for which the *popoli multitudo indignabatur*. Therefore, it had been necessary for them *semper stare cum magna fortia militari*.[24] Bartolo was probably re-porting information filtered through to him in Perugia (where he died in 1357) or perhaps gathered mainly at the imperial court and spread to justify the Nine's *depositio* as ordered by the Emperor, his pro-tector, and it was therefore difficult, in Bartolo's judgement, to con-cede a legitimate foundation for their success. We shall see the ef-fectiveness of the Nine more clearly later, when we discuss the *con-tado*. The Captain of War's character and office during the rule of the Nine stand out even more if we note that in the period following such pre-eminent and lasting figures cannot be identified. Moreover, the office itself was reduced to purely military functions and limited by the presence of several salaried *condottieri*.[25]

The Government of the Sienese Territory

The history of the territory of the Sienese state beginning with the *contado* requires a relatively lengthy explanation, because less scholarly work exists for this subject than for other topics. The first

impression that we receive from the documentation and literature
is that there was a *contado* conceived of in Siena as a homogeneous and unitary reality, a great economic area of a regional type,
at the city's service, open to the penetration of its *cives*, and whose
conservatio est augmentatio civitatis.[26] It adopted the same weights
and measures during the thirteenth century[27] and in 1291 a tax, or
general gabella, was imposed and called "that of the contado."[28] In
the following decades it was divided into districts for conscription
(with an enlistment of up to 7,000 *pedites*) through the vicariates
guided by Sienese citizens first called Vicars and later called Captains.[29] Another jurisdiction was created by dividing the countryside
into nine districts for the control of public order and criminality by
means of podestarial cavalrymen assisted by special armies.[30]

The two district divisions did not coincide. It is reasonable,
however, to assume that a kind of cross check by various concur-
rent territorial officials existed, with an overlapping that imitated
the one between the duties of the *Podestà*, the Captain of the
People, and, later, the Captain of War. The two series of districts,
however, had nothing to do with the same communities when considered altogether.[31] But yet another territorial division was fundamental to the organization of the *contado*. Borders were given to
single communities. These were fundamental to defining the
spheres in which the inhabitants of communities legally lived and
the territorial limits of the power of the Vicars. The Vicars, always
Sienese *cives* and usually notaries, were envoys to the local governments of small communities or groups aggregated precisely for this
purpose.[32]

These communities were subject to general legal restraints; such
as those which reserved high criminal justice for the Sienese
courts, protected the property of the *cives* with their *mezzaiuoli* and
tenants, or imposed forms of collective responsibility and disci-
plined the break-up of communities. Some rural populations no
longer capable of facing their tax obligations to the governing city

were subsequently grouped together with other communities in order to limit evasion of fiscal responsibilities.[33]

The *contado*, therefore, appears as the area directly subject to the city. Its own status was different from that of the city and the villages of the so-called Masse and Cortine immediately adjacent to it.[34] In short, it is in the territorial state that Sienese power seemed exclusive and unconditional. But this was true only for the *contado* in the strict sense, because the Sienese state also included *civitates* or large communes such as Grosseto, Massa, Montepulciano and Montalcino. They had entered into the political and military orbit of Siena but were not directly administered by her. They should not, therefore, be included in the *contado*.[35]

These communes were, instead, important centers outside the *contado* with military and financial services imposed by the governing city. Siena controlled these towns by specially constructed fortified towers and by quartered troops and officers. Such towns, soon to be called *accomandate* (derived from feudal language) had a formal and contractual relationship with Siena that retained for them a more-or-less ample administrative autonomy, their own *contadi*, and their own elites. Every one of these posed different problems for Siena and required constant political attention, particularly Montepulciano and Montalcino.[36] Montepulciano was eventually to be lost to Florence, while a solution to the problem of Montalcino was attempted in 1361 by new articles of association and the concession of Sienese citizenship.[37]

These cities were not intended to be a part of the *contado* in the narrowest sense. With reference to them we should speak rather of Sienese *iurisdictio* and *districtus*. Their inhabitants were not *comitatini* but rather *distrectuales*.[38] In the language of Sienese public law as found in official communal documents, *comitatus* and *iurisdictio* were often interchangable, but it seems clear that *iurisdictio* and *districtus* in some contexts covered a wider field than the actual *comitatus*.[39] An overlapping rather than an opposition existed between the two areas, almost as if they were concentric circles of different measures. In the *comitatus* the Sienese *iurisdictio* and *districtus* also applied, but these jurisdictions outside the strictly defined *comitatus* acquired a different content since they resulted from specific agreements stipulated between the parties involved.[40] For reasons that we shall attempt to clarify, the above distinction between the two, however, was not always evident, or at least the communal officers did not always act as though they were. A concrete example of the situation is the matter of personal property belonging to a powerful family of Grosseto, the Abati del Malia, which the revenue officers claimed to be able to tax, having in mind Grosseto's subordination in the Sienese *iurisdictio*.[41]

The distinction between *contado* and *districtus* is extremely important. So much so that some Sienese with castles in their possession were not considered among the legal nobility of the *contado*. However, non-Sienese owners with seigneurial rights outside the *comitatus*, but within the area of Sienese *iurisdictio*, could be included as *contado* nobility.[42] But the problems of the non "comitatine" areas included in the political and military sphere of Siena went beyond the federate cities; they were more numerous than we would imagine at a glance and do not conform to a precise model. Having a different status from the moment of absorption, these areas were influenced by diverse circumstances and also by various written settlements following the political customs and requirements observed at any given time by the Sienese government. The result was a different treatment by the commune. The non-"comitatine" areas evolved in a different way from that of the *contado*'s strictly defined community-type. There was a relatively liberal recognition of their administrative autonomy and of seigneurial rights already exercised over them.

The case of Abbadia S. Salvatore is a typical example of subordination to the Sienese *iurisdictio*. Siena kept the *guardia* and *signoria* of the locality for itself, but did not weigh heavily upon, or question, abbatial rights as far as the local commune was concerned, claiming only explicitly enumerated services.[43] More ambiguous was the situation of the castles located a few kilometers south of Siena, enclaves in the *contado* claimed by the bishop of Siena. These castles, therefore, had a kind of joint ownership between two competing lords with episcopal supremacy on the patrimonial side of the management. Despite repeated clashes and compromises, there were no open declarations of principles of sovereignty that might attract dangerous reactions and clerical sanctions.[44]

But how many other similar situations were there? There have not been any inventories compiled that can satisfy our curiosity as to the heterogeneity of such relationships. Nor, unfortunately, can we be certain that they can all be identified through the *Caleffi*, that is, the Sienese *liber iurium*, all presently unpublished except the oldest one. This is because not all deeds considered expired were included in them, and partly because they normally comprised bilateral acts. At the same time the unique relationships such as we have referred to above could have been created by statutory laws, decisions of the Councils, and the like.[45]

Such were the conditions existing in new lands or lands under colonization during the latter part of the century, for example, Monteriggioni, earlier Paganico, Montemassi, and Castelnuovo Berardenga.[46] But here we also encounter predictable exceptions; specific and pressing political, economic, and military reasons seem to have justified these differences. There are also, in the old *Caleffo*, acts by which, within a few years of each other, around 1330, the subjection to Siena of Sticciano, Giuncarico, Travale, Casole, and Gerfalco in the Maremma, and of the mining areas towards Massa Marittima was decreed. The relationships with these communities and their lords were all very different from one another.[47]

This deserves to be emphasized, and not just for the period that directly concerns us, since several unusual situations dragged on for a long period of time. A careful and comprehensive survey of the peculiarities under the unitary politico-military Sienese leadership is essential. The diverse institutional organization of the communities brought immediate consequences to the lives of their inhabitants in a variety of ways. The character of the relationship with Siena could give rise to various alternatives in the structure of the local commune, in the dealings with its lords if there were any, and in the different possibilities of social, economic, and demographic development. The relationship was likely to influence the expansion of Sienese penetration and the activities of the *contado*'s communities themselves. These differentiations are reflected in the numerous petitions turned over to Siena by individual communities and conserved both in the registers of the General Council and in the series of the so-called *concistoriali* documents. These special pleas are not necessarily representative of a homogeneous reality, and it is perhaps only our own perceptions that lead us to consider them similar to one another. During this period, the expansion of the political and military borders, the enlargement of the economic sphere, and the consolidation of the means of communication were critical. To be specific, it was of importance to the Sienese government to take advantage of crises involving Massa, the Aldobrandeschi, Orvieto, and Arezzo in order to expand an area subject to its dominance. Probably because of the politically dominant mercantile interests, expansion in and of itself was the primary objective of the Commune rather than the consolidation of power already established.

What is more important from our perspective is that these observations also apply to a certain extent to the *contado* in its strict sense, a *contado* that was unitary and homogenous only in regard to certain aims of the government and not in many other aspects. Meanwhile it is obvious that local communities had particular and individual political, social, and economic backgrounds. This is especially evidenced by the extreme differentiation in taxation to which each was subjected. The figures that we find are a result of balances produced by unknown factors such as the reimbursement of military costs, expenses for bridges and roads, fortifications or deductions for *comitanti* turned citizens, etc. In any case, the 252 entries of the second semester of 1344 record ninety-eight communities, that is, no more than one-third, with a tax up to only 30 lire, and almost as many, ninety-three, up to 100 lire (which means that more than two-thirds of the communities enter into this category). Then we find thirty-four included between 101 and 200 lire, sixteen between 201 and 400, and ten over 400 lire, with Asciano at 950 and Radicondoli at 916 lire reaching the highest amounts among these.[48] What did the towns in the former categories have in common with those of the latter categories, save an abstract judicial form?

Another important factor to take into consideration is the method of absorption into the state. In this case, conditions of war or peace were decisive. For example, Arcidosso and Castelpiano are jointly registered in the old *Caleffo* within a few days of each other according to the same formula. There is a clause, however, which must have had several practical consequences. Some immunities were granted in Arcidosso alone, yet both communities were considered a part of the *contado*.[49]

This differentiation is further accentuated if we take into account the fact that seigneurial families were present only in some areas, and obviously not all of them were equally capable of influencing local events. This phenomenon was extensive, but not always clearly documented at the public level as we shall soon see. The siegneurial rights noted in the Table of Possessions around the second decade of the century are therefore of considerable interest.[50]

Even as early as 1307, however, some localities were not able to fulfil their duties, as acknowledged officially, because they were oppressed by *potenti*.[51] The Commune had to intervene in order to avoid losing tax revenues, not to mention its credibility. But the political compromises reached with the former leading Sienese magnates, the owners of castles and estates, necessitated caution. It was certainly easier to intervene where foreigners were concerned, as in 1309, when Trequanda was kept from falling into the hands of the Franzesi's Florentine creditors.[52] Or when, in 1314, after the defeat of the Ghibelline leader, Filippo Bonsignori, his fortifications of southern localities were destroyed by Siena and were turned over to the Commune.[53] Filippo was ultimately freed from fines and penalties and reinstated as "citizen and true Guelf," in exchange for the control of Montegiovi—important for the future expansion around the Mount Amiata—and the waiver of privileges and immunities granted him by the "alto Arrigo" (Henry VII).

These were exceptional cases, however. We have proof that citizens obedient to communal politics with legitimately acquired rights over their castles were regularly respected in those rights within and outside the *contado*.[54] These citizens were the *domini naturali*, titles with implicitly positive connotations. A census might be taken of their possessions for fiscal purposes, perhaps with the political and military aim of identifying areas from which potential dangers could originate. In 1319 it was decreed that *fortilitia, cassera, muramenta, domus et hedifitia terre et possessiones* be registered, whatever the claim held by citizens and *comitatini* within and outside the *contado* and Sienese jurisdiction.[55] We also know that an extra register with *fortilitia* was compiled, but unfortunately it has not been preserved.[56]

The Commune could have bought these rights or at least imposed a prohibition to alienate them in such a way as to avoid threatening concentrations of power or their indefinite existence. Instead, none of this was done, and those rights continued to be alienable (even in favor of the Commune of Siena) by simple acts of common private law guaranteed by communal sanction. We have some knowledge of a few transfers,[57] but only additional research through the diplomatic and notarial sources can explain such actions, because of the irregular and casual preservation of family ar-

chives. The state does not seem to have kept a copy of these transactions. Information about the transfers of rights would clarify
many things; their value, the strategies of families, investment
interests, etc. It does seem certain, in any case, that they were very
important when one compares surviving information with what is
written in the Table of Possessions in which important Sienese
families, the owners of numerous castles within and outside the
contado appear.[58]

In order to clarify the role of these private jurisdictions, we
should also point out that they were always owned by citizens subject to communal control, and in this manner the Commune
avoided the costs of upkeep and custody of castles in non-strategic
locations. In such a way, however, these families maintained an
economic and military clientele in bases which could potentially be
used against the Commune,[59] as actually happened, particularly during the second half of the fourteenth century. Above all, examples
of governmental autonomy given to successful *popolani*, whose
strong garrisons in and outside the *contado*, duly chosen in such a
way as to reduce overall risk, were viewed as a status symbol and
a wise investment against an uncertain economic and political
future.

The Commune made a political choice, perhaps inevitable for
the most part, that seemed to reconcile public and private interests.
The dangers hidden in those recognitions were surely understood.
In 1321, for instance, through a law solemnly reproduced about
twenty years later, the Commune, aware, no doubt that one could
not serve two masters at one time, levied a fine of 1,000 florins on
whomever, person or corporation, was guilty of reducing societies
and individuals in the city, *contado*, or jurisdiction to conditions of
servitude or vassalage. All agreements not entered into by *liberi
homines* were considered null and void.[60] This was a novel act at
a time when servile bonds were still recognized in particular instances.[61] It is probable that the law was to be valid only in the

future. Furthermore, it seems that servile status could not be easily verified in such a large *contado*, since it was not a simple task for the state to avoid the usurpation of public property.[62] The transfer, for example, of real estate in the city and in the *contado* to foreigners and citizens not listed on the tax rolls was forbidden.[63] But how could the Commune check the great power of the lords or castle owners, or control the myriad ways in which the communities' unsatisfied creditors could erode the law or judicial sanctions? The former were guaranteed recourse to impersonal judicial procedures, but how useful these sentences were to individual communities is problematic. Significantly, the government intervened between creditors and communities in cases that threatened public order or a community's ability to honor its obligations to the Commune.[64] The city's relationship with the two parties was political, and mediation served political purposes, through the grant of extensions, discounts, etc. in favor of the communities.[65]

As with the often rebellious magnate families who were given bonuses in the form of discounts and amnesties,[66] so also for the communities the state tried to create an image of a supreme *paterfamilias* who in case of necessity knew how to punish and reward. This was essentially the function of *iustitia* and *aequalitas*, which reoccur with obsessive monotony in the public documents of the time.[67] This did not mean that everyone was to be treated in the same way. On the contrary, it was meant to transcend an apparent identity to note similarities but also to recognize differences.[68]

Ius strictum should have been administered by the courts, but *iustitia* and *aequalitas* required judgements that we today would call discretionary or political, the kind of decisions that only the groups forming an oligarchical government can make. Therefore, ordinary judicial authority was often blocked by politicians' decisions,[69] not on the basis of a failure to discriminate among the functions of state, as a modern theorist would say, but on the basis of sovereign power vested in the political offices of the city.

But let us return to our discussion of territorial concepts. There were lords' rights that the city tried to keep at a minimum. These included rights that inhibited the free circulation of products and those that inhibited the collection of gabelles, tolls, and other taxes in the city, *contado*, and jurisdiction. In 1331 it was decreed that legitimate ownership of those rights had to be legally demonstrated,[70] not before a judge (which would have caused fewer problems) but before the formally supreme political body, the General Council. Some such presentations were made soon after[71]; but how this law was applied remains obscure. The communities that were subjected to rights pertaining to the lords are listed a few years later in the military and police districts, but not always in the subsequent tax assessment on the *contado*.[72] The rights of the Sienese state overlapped one another and competed with the natural seigneurial and local community structures,[73] creating conditions similar to those which we have considered for the jurisdictions outside the *contado*.

These distinctions became progressively more obscure as a consequence of closer and more careful definition of these relationships. The final blow was given by the law that decreed that a community's vicariate itself could be held by the "natural lord" in the name of Siena.[74] At this point the community of the *contado* was structurally closer, almost assimilated, to that of the Sienese *iurisdictio* with its own local lords. The method of imposing fiscal and military services changed or could change, but the relationships remained the same. I hypothesize that this reality has inhibited the clarification of technical distinctions among *comitatus—iurisdictio—districtus*.

Different local conditions, however, remind us that we must approach with caution the evidence regarding the so-called *contado*. The Sienese countryside can be characterized at any time by the joint presence of communities in ruin and others relatively flourishing, though with the levels of differences varying according to the general economic trends. An undifferentiated consideration of individual conditions can lead to serious misunderstandings. It is necessary to realize that each locality had a diverse structural strength and, therefore, a dissimilar capacity to respond to the inter-action between lords, creditors, and the dominant city.[75] This gave each community a special character, just as did climate and local agriculture. There were situations that, unfortunately, contemporary politicians did not set down in writing. We must, therefore, recreate the special character of each community on the basis of hetero-geneous and often ambiguous sources. Almost every avenue of re-search remains open, in spite of the important works currently available to us.[76]

We know very little about subsequent developments after 1355, although documents attest that a crisis occurred that, on the one hand, strengthened the noble presence in the territory and, on the other, led to an intense but selective fortification on the part of the Commune. The communal defensive system ultimately proved itself stronger, but the consequent shifting of population from one area to another led to the abandonment of certain communities.[77] In short, the rearrangements that occurred during the crisis seem also to have provoked the renunciation of the two-fold military and police division of districts as they existed at the time of the Nine. The Captains of the Vicariates then assumed more clearly the attributes of the central government's provincial agents.[78] Mean-while, in order to spare capital and men, the smaller rural commu-nities were grouped in podestariates and vicariates for ordinary ad-ministration in imitation of the districts of the towns such as Montalcino and Massa, which were part of the state.[79] The practice of granting Sienese citizenship to entire communities, even the larger ones, continued; after Montalcino (already mentioned), Chiusdino followed in 1361, Asciano in 1369, and San Quirico in 1385.[80] We still lack, unfortunately, a detailed study of what really took place in this period.

These new conditions did not, however, alter the regional

nature of the state, since they were controlled only by the citizens of the capital: forms of institutional representation from the territory had not as yet been introduced. Just as the reduction to the status of being part of the *contado* was understood as punishment for the affected community, the grant of citizenship was seen as a *beneficium-privilegium*,[81] even if it did not have the same meaning for all of the grantees.

The *res publica* remained based upon the *civitas*, the proud capital, Siena. Political representatives from the territory were excluded, and even though a culture and hierarchy based on class and policies of and for classes existed, representatives in the state offices were not divided according to class.[82] The city, strongly distinguished by social and cultural divisions, had discovered a means to avoid disintegration: citizenship on the legal level and on the cultural level. This strategy transcended class differences and created a consolidated urban and civic culture whose values derived from the church, local saints, and traditions. Here we find a common cultural patrimony necessarily bringing together very diverse elements that emphasized strongly the majesty of the public corporation and its representatives.[83]

Culture and Tripartite Society

Thus we come to the matter of the "focus" of the Nine and their state in Sienese history. Their era had already become a myth in the fourteenth century,[84] and the period still exercises a strong hold upon the scholarly mind.[85] The state, built on the solid foundations of the thirteenth century, possessed exceptional vitality and strength, making sound investments that served Siena well through the following centuries, including those after the loss of liberty and the modernization attempt of Peter Leopold.[86]

The late thirteenth and early fourteenth centuries formed a period in which there was a pronounced growth in civic and public conscience, verifiable in Siena in many ways. Examples can be found in the concern for urban order and in the great artistic commissions of public origin. One should note the stress placed on complete state sovereignty, on civic grandeur, and on the possession of supreme authority regarding resolutions of conflicts.[87]

The she-wolf with twins circumspectly appeared in those days, perhaps for the first time around 1315 in the great *Maestà* in the Palazzo Pubblico.[88] Later it was directly linked, in the late 1330s, to the Commune in Lorenzetti's cycle found today in the Palazzo Pubblico. Here it seems that the objective is not so much to indicate Siena's descent from Rome, but that Siena was another Rome, in other words, on the same level. Rome was the symbolic center of complete, legitimate power, and Siena wanted to stand proudly alongside her. The emperors of that time, crowned or not, legitimate or not, were nothing but objects of apprehension and sources of trouble for Sienese civil life, while the supreme function of leadership claimed by the papacy in the temporal sphere was not able to take effect in a practical way. These authorities, empire and papacy, discredited themselves in turn. Now the only possibility left was to rebuild the new Rome in a more limited sphere, the *res publica* par excellence.

At this time the Roman imperial model exercised a strong cultural attraction in spite of the necessary, violent resistance to the actual empire. Some details are important. It seems to me that in this period Siena began to think of the *concistoro* as the site of governmental power.[89] Conspirators themselves in 1318 had even thought of setting up an office of "proconsul" once the Nine had been eliminated.[90] But calls to the *res publica*, to the *bene commune*, to the government seen as *ufficium*, were constant until the end of the 1330s, when the great new elaboration of the city statutes intended to represent the Nine's apotheosis in the legislative sector was introduced.[91] The statutes began with an extraordinary *Deo auctore*, that is, literally employing a text of the emperor as legislator by antonomasia.[92]

At the same time Lorenzetti described Siena as the *civitas virginis*, reviving and reasserting the thirteenth-century tradition embodied in the Palazzo's *Maestà*, but giving it a greater significance in the new, fully laic, context. The absence of the empire and the papacy, the traditional sources of legitimation of power, brought the Virgin into direct touch with Siena. Siena was recognized as a legitimate part of the divine order, above titles and earthly mediations. It was not an earthly power that reminded the Sienese government, *Diligite iustitiam qui iudicatis terram* in its two frescoes executed more than twenty years apart in the Palazzo. Was not Lorenzetti's *Gran Vecchio*, as a representative of the Commune with crown and globe, intended as an image of absolute supremacy and independence?[93]

There was obviously a strong learned component behind these representations that utilized ancient and not so ancient elements. The sources and transmitters of this new, basically eclectic culture certainly are a problem for the historian, even though we have a clear picture of the setting in which they are placed. It was hardly fortuitous that a statue of Aristotle, a work of Niccolò Pisano, adorned the facade of the *Duomo*.[94] The liberal arts framed the fresco of the Good Government, where, among other things, a university professor was depicted in the act of teaching and the atmosphere was receptive and sensitive to cultural messages originating from preachers or theologians, lawyers or notaries.[95] When Lorenzetti's cycle on justice is referred to as "propaganda," a very narrow judgement is made; forgetting, moreover, that it has yet to be demonstrated that the message was directed at the general public. It seems more probable that the purpose was to give daily warning to the rulers of the state, many of whom were new office holders.[96]

It was in this new Rome, therefore, that Lorenzetti's harmonic pictorial representation depicted the various social groups as mutually functional and yet graphically different one from another, in features and appearance. These components referred to a great cultural heritage, now to be perceived at a political level. The cultural synthesis was happily joined with political opportunity and the maturity of a leading group that orchestrated a cultural program for political purposes.

Sienese society was already tripartite economically, if not socially and politically, in the thirteenth century. Then a further step was taken. If the magnates were violent and domineering and increased the risk of tyranny, the masses were no less dangerous considering their ignorance, unruliness, and envy of wealth.[97] The "pacific state" of the "People" and Commune could be assured only by a middle class as a just mean between the two extremes. It was a middle class that had already demonstrated its providential vocation for sovereignty through the *Mercanzia*, which fostered the public's well being and allowed every class to live happily in the "Good Government."[98] The interests of all coincided with the interests of the merchants who represented the productive forces of the whole city.[99]

The regime of the Nine produced a great cultural edifice that succeeded in clarifying a number of political anomalies: for example, the exceptional position of the *Mercanzia* at the time, and the ambiguity of the notion of *mercator* itself. These matters, however, must be described elsewhere. For now another observation is appropriate. The regime's credibility grew when it was ultimately able to assert its authority over the magnates,[100] whose constant unruliness indirectly resulted in strengthening it, and over the *minuti* as well.

Certainly the implementation of such an objective scheme required a solid hegemony of the mercantile groups and a simplified political, institutional, social, and economic ambience. Once accepted, this cultural plan had to be carried out daily in real and practical political life. We know that the problems of management after the Black Death worsened to the point of bringing about the fall of the Nine in 1355,[101] and then led to the forced abandonment of the political program developed by and for the merchant element.[102]

However, their program had held sway for many decades and, applied with political astuteness, had overcome numerous difficulties. How hard it was to replace this regimen can be shown by the events of the period following 1355, with its crises and political oscillations. The state nevertheless survived as a result of the strong institutional basis developing out of the extraordinary union of business, politics, and culture realized in the early Trecento by the government of the Nine.

NOTES

A first and shorter version of this work was published in the Proceedings of the conference *La Toscana nel Trecento*, held October 1986 in San Miniato, sponsored by the *Centro di studi sulla civiltà del tardo medioevo: La Toscana nel secolo XIV: Caratteri di una civiltà regionale*, ed. S. Gensini (Pisa, 1988), pp. 165–81.

1. "Questa santa virtù (la Giustizia) là dove regge induce ad unità li animi molti, et questi acciò ricolti un Ben Comun per lor Signor si fanno, lo qual per governar suo Stato elegge di non tener giamma gli ochi rivolti da lo splendor de volti de le virtù che torno allui si stanno. . ." (Siena, Palazzo Pubblico, 1338/39).

2. W. M. Bowsky, *A Medieval Italian Commune: Siena under the Nine, 1287–1355* (Berkeley, 1981), esp. p. 172 and, for what follows, pp. 34 ff., 299–314. Also V. Wainwright, "The Testing of a Popular Sienese Regime: The 'Riformatori' and the Insurrections of 1371," in *I Tatti Studies: Essays in the Renaissance*, 2 (Florence, 1987), pp. 107–70. The twenty–four governors are painted in Lorenzetti's fresco. The symbol of the People, the rampant lion, is everywhere (but not in the so-called "Guidoriccio") in the Palazzo Pubblico.

3. The second half of the fourteenth century is not well understood; see the bibliography in my *Siena nel Rinascimento: istituzioni e sistema politico* (Siena, 1985). On the *Monti*, see my introduction to *Siena e il suo territorio nel Rinascimento*, ed. M. Ascheri and D. Ciampoli, vol. 1 (Siena, 1986), pp. 1–53, and the

documents, pp. 343–62.

4. For the period of the Nine, see Bowsky, *A Medieval Commune*. See pp. xiii–xiv for Bowsky's previous works. Some of his interpretations, however, have been questioned; see my "Siena sotto i Nove in un libro di W. M. Bowsky," *Nuovi studi cateriniani*, 3 (1988), 126–33.

5. The oldest *Liber iurium*, for example, was published as *Il Caleffo Vecchio del Comune di Siena*, ed. G. Cecchini, 4 vols. (Siena, 1932–84), the last vol. was edited by M. Ascheri, A. Forzini, and C. Santini. The indicies were edited by M. Ascheri, as vol. 5, which includes an introduction by P. Cammarosano, "Tradizione documentaria e storia cittadina: una introduzione al 'Caleffo Vecchio' del Comune di Siena," that also appeared separately under the same title (Siena, 1988).

6. See the Epilogue in Bowsky, *A Medieval Commune*. For a detailed discussion of Lorenzetti's frescoes, see C. Frugoni, *Una lontana città: sentimenti e immagini nel medioevo* (Turin, 1983), pp. 136–210; L. Carbone, *Note sull'ideologia e la prassi politica di un'oligarchi borghese del '300*, 2 vols. (diss., University of Florence, 1976–77); Q. Skinner, "Ambrogio Lorenzetti: The Artist as Political Philosopher," *Proceedings of the British Academy*, 72 (1986), pp. 1–56 (of the off-print); and R. Starn, "The Republican Regime of the 'Room of Peace' in Siena, 1338–1340," *Representations*, 18 (1987), 1–32. In C. Frugoni's *Pietro e Ambrogio Lorenzetti* (Florence, 1988), p. 68, I detect the acceptance of my opinions expressed at the San Miniato conference (see note at beginning of endnotes) identifying the "Great Old Man" with the "Good Government."

7. See, for example, the illumination in D. Ciampoli, *Il Capitano del popolo a Siena nel primo Trecento* (Siena, 1984), p. 112–13 and on fols. 59–60 of the manuscript.

8. On the *querelle*, see M. Mallory and G. Moran, "New Evidence Concerning 'Guidoriccio'," *The Burlington Magazine*, 128 (1986), 250–59, who argue against the traditional attribution to Simone Martini; and A. Martindale, "The Problem of 'Guidoriccio'," *The Burlington Magazine*, 128 (1986), 259–73, who supports attribution to Simone. See also my *Siena nel Rinascimento*, p. 19, n. 11; C. B. Strehlike, "Niccolò di Giovanni di Francesco Ventura e il 'Guidoriccio'," *Prospettiva*, 50 (1987), 45–48; L. Bellosi, "Ancora sul 'Guidoriccio'," *Prospettiva*,

50 (1987), 48–55; J. Polzer, "Simone Martini's Guidoriccio Fresco: The Polemic Concerning Its Origin Reviewed," *Racar*, 14 (1987), 16–69; and H. B. J. Maginnis, "The 'Guidoriccio' Controversy: Notes and Observations," *Racar*, 15 (1988), 137–44. Also see the proceedings of the conference on Simone held in Siena in 1985, ed. L. Bellosi (Florence, 1988), and my observations in M. Ascheri, *Dedicato a Siena* (Siena, 1987), pp. 61–78.

9. On the General Council, see Bowsky, *A Medieval Commune*, pp. 85–103 and passim for delegations to the Nine and *Ordines*. See also his *The Finance of the Commune of Siena, 1287–1355* (Oxford, 1970), as well as his "The *Buon Governo* of Siena (1287–1355): A Medieval Italian Oligarchy," *Speculum*, 37 (1962), 368–81, and "The Impact of the Black Death upon Sienese Government and Society," *Speculum*, 39 (1964), 1–34. For appointments from the Council, see Bowsky, *A Medieval Commune*, p. 96. For commissions and the autonomous legislative powers of the Nine, see M. Ascheri and E. Ottaviani, "Le provvisioni della raccolta 'Statuti 23' (1323–39) dell'Archivio di Stato di Siena," *Bullettino senese di storia patria* (henceforth *BSSP*), 88 (1981), 206–33. For the collateral councils of the government see, for example, the fifty-six men summoned for foreign affairs in 1351 (Bowksy, *A Medieval Commune*, pp. 169 ff.). On the 'Ordines,' see Bowsky, *A Medieval Commune*," p. 23; and on 'Executores gabelle,' see Bowsky, *A Medieval Commune*," p. 78. For the Consuls of knights, see Bowsky, *A Medieval Commune* and *The Finance*.

10. Ascheri and Ottavini, "Le provvisioni," passim.

11. Bowsky, *A Medieval Commune*, p. 37.

12. Bowsky, *A Medieval Commune*, pp. 37–42, 133, 309.

13. Bowsky, *A Medieval Commune*, pp. 45, 132.

14. Bowsky, *A Medieval Commune*, pp. 130 ff.: after an aborted revolt in 1318, a *magnum consilium de eorum gente, de ordine dominorum Novem*, deliberated (the vote was 109 to 5) to bring into the General Council the problem of government *mutatio*, since many people *de diversis conditionibus* were not satisfied with the rule of the "middle people." See also Carbone, *Note sull'ideologia*, 2:22. For succeeding Councils of the People, see my *Siena nel Rinascimento*.

15. For bibliography, see my *Siena nel Rinascimento*, pp. 29 ff.

16. The 'books of lions' are in *Archivio di Stato di Siena* (henceforth *ASSi*) *Concistoro*, 2, fols. 333 ff. (from 1371); for books of baptisms, see *ASSi, Bicchema*, 1132 ff. (1380).

17. G. Catoni, "I 'Regolatori' e la giurisdizione contabile nella Repubblica di Siena," *Critica storica*, 12 (1975), 46–70.

18. Bowsky, *A Medieval Commune*, p. 95.

19. *AASi, Concistoro 1* (Jan.–Feb. 1338), fol. 2^v; 2 (Nov.–Dec. 1347), fols. 2^r–3^r and (Sept.–Oct. 1351), fol. 3^r. During the thirteenth century the Chancellor appears with different functions; see Cammarosano, "Tradizione documentaria." In the 1309–10 statutes, *Il costituto del Comune di Siena volgarizzato nel* MCCCIX–MCCCX (Siena, 1903), ed. A. Lisini, vols. 1–2, the Chancellor appears only once (distinzione IV, cap. 91) when it is clear that the Commune's seal is to be preserved close by the Nine "nonostante el capitolo el quale favella d'elegere el cancelliere."

20. See my *Siena nel Rinascimento*, p. 43, n. 63.

21. Bowsky, *A Medieval Commune*, pp. 33–34.

22. See "Giustizia ordinaria, giustizia di mercanti e la Mercanzia di Siena nel Tre-Quattrocento" in M. Ascheri, *Tribunali giuristi e istituzioni dal medioevo all'età moderna* (Bologna, 1989), pp. 23–54.

23. Carbone, *Note sull'ideologia*, 1:16. On this office, see Bowsky, *A Medieval Commune*, pp. 45–54.

24. In his widely circulated *Tractatus de regimine civitatis*; see the edition in D. Quaglioni, *Politica e diritto nel Trecento italiano: Il 'De tyranno' di Bartolo da Sassoferrato (1314–1357)* (Florence, 1983), p. 163.

25. We need detailed research on this point. I am presently expressing only personal impressions not as yet based on systematic research.

26. In a source from 1306; see Bowsky, *The Finance*, p. 357; also his *A Medieval Commune* and his "Medieval Citizenship: The Individual and the State in the Commune of Siena, 1287-1355," *Studies in Medieval and Renaissance History*, 4 (1967), 193-243; and his "City and Contado: Military Relationships and Communal Bonds in Fourteenth-Century Siena," in *Renaissance Studies in Honor of Hans Baron*, ed. A. Molho and J. A. Tedeschi (Florence, 1971), pp. 75-98.

27. For this and other problems of the thirteenth century, see O. Redon, *Uomini e comunità del contado senese nel Duecento* (Siena, 1982), p. 202.

28. But existing taxes on bread, wine, meat and markets were maintained: Bowsky, *The Finance*, pp. 114 ff.; and his *A Medieval Commune*, p. 141.

29. Bowsky, *A Medieval Commune*, pp. 130, 146. For the boundaries of the nine districts in 1337-39, see Ascheri and Ciampoli, *Siena e il suo territorio*, vol. 1, with map annexed. On these districts and those of the police, see Bowsky, "City and Contado."

30. On these, see *ASSi, Statuti di Siena 26*, fols. 18^r-21^r; fols. 21^v-22^v for the districts of "milites." The rubrics of this important statute are published in Ciampoli, *Il Capitano del popolo*, pp. 59-121. See also my introduction to the same, pp. 7-21.

31. A map that I constructed and that appeared in *BSSP*, 95 (1988), makes this clear.

32. In 1342 the communities were formed into forty-four groups of five to six each; see *ASSi, Consiglio generale 131*, fols. 92^r-94^r. Later the importance of communities was confirmed by differentiated "choice" (*cerna*) for their officers; see, e.g., the major "choice" of notaries in 1372 in *ASSi, Concistoro 65* (with about seventy communities).

33. For the late thirteenth century, see Redon, *Uomini e comunità*, p. 196; and Bowsky, *A Medieval Commune*, p. 107. On the 1309-10 statutes, see Lisini, *Il costituto*, 1:282; 2:166, 169, 314. For the 1337-39 statutes, see *ASSi, Statuti di Siena 26*, fols. 136^v-37^r. For sources on the communities, see P. R. Pazzaglini, *The Criminal Ban of the Sienese Commune 1225-1310* (Milan, 1979).

34. For some basic observations, see Bowsky, *A Medieval Commune*.

35. In the 1309–10 statutes the *Podestà* elected for those towns' General Councils; see Lisini, *Il costituto*, 1:343. By 1404 (at least) these towns and Lucignano di Valdichiana had chancellors; see *ASSi, Statuti di Siena 38*, fol. 16ᶠ. The essential historical data on these towns and communities, even the smallest in the Sienese State, can be found in the reference work by P. Cammarosano, "Repertorio," *I castelli del Senese*, vol. 2 (Siena and Milan 1976), 275–402 and the second edition (Milan, 1985), with an appendix, pp. 411–17.

36. I. Calabresi, *Montepulciano nel Trecento: contributi per la storia guiridica e istituzionale* (Siena, 1987).

37. We await a modern work on this important town, but for now see A. Cortonesi, "Demografia e popolamento nel contado di Siena: il territorio montalcinese nei secoli XIII–XV," in *Strutture familiari epidemie migrazioni nell'Italia medievale*, ed. R. Comba, G. Piccini, and G. Pinto (Naples, 1984), pp. 153–81.

38. For a clear example, see my *Chianciano 1287: uno statuto per la storia della comunità e del suo territorio* (Rome, 1987).

39. For such documents, see Cecchini, *Il Caleffo Vecchio*, passim; and Ascheri and Ciampoli, *Siena e il suo territorio*, 1:83–249, passim.

40. The *liber censuum* of 1400 distinguishes rightly between "sottopositi et racomandati" and is written "ad honore et stato et incremento felice del magnifico Comuno et Populo senese de la città di Siena, suo contado, forca [this translates, 'jurisdictio'] et distrecto"; see Ascheri and Ciampoli, *Siena e il suo territorio*, 1: 91–92. For more recent work on the problem, see M. Ascheri and D. Ciampoli, "Il distretto e il contado nella Republica di Siena: l'esempio della val d'Orcia nel Quattrocento," in *La val d'Orcia nel medioevo e nei primi secoli dell'età moderna*, ed. A. Cortonesi (Rome, 1991), pp. 83–112.

41. On this question, see W. Bowsky, "A New Consilium of Cino of Pistoia (1324): Citizenship, Residence and Taxation," *Speculum*, 42 (1967), 431–41.

42. As noted by G. Cherubini, *Signori contadini borghesi* (Florence, 1974), pp.

292 ff.; for example, the Elci, but also the Ubaldini and Pazzi.

43. See M. Ascheri and D. Ciampoli, "Il Comune di Abbadia S. Salvatore nella Repubblica di Siena (secc. XIV–XV)," in *L'Amiata nel Medioeveo, Abbadia S. Salvatore* (Empoli, 1986); and a recent collection of documents: *Abbadia San Salvatore: Commune e Monastero in testi dei secoli* XIV–XVIII, ed. M. Ascheri and W. Kurze (Siena, 1986), pp. 11, 19. The case of Chianciano is studied in my *Chianciano 1287*.

44. On these 'feudal' communities, see V. Passeri, *I castelli del Comune di Murlo* (Radda in Chianti, 1985); and N. Mengozzi, *Il feudo del Vescovado di Siena* (Sienna, 1911; repr. Florence, 1980). In Vico and Montechiaro, Sienese canons were lords; see Bowsky, *A Medieval Commune*, pp. 178, 268.

45. See Cammarosano, "Tradizione documentaria."

46. Cammarosano, "Repertorio," s.v.; see also his *Monteriggioni: storia architetura paesaggio* (Milan, 1988), and P. Angelucci, "Genesi di un borgo franco nel Senese: Paganico," in I Deug Su and E. Menestò, eds., *Università e tutela dei beni culturali: il contributo degli studi medievali e umanistici* (Florence, 1981), pp. 95–140.

47. See documents in Cecchini, *Il Caleffo Vecchio*, 4:1671–78, 1686–1700, 1727, and 1747 ff.; and Bowsky, "Medieval citizenship," pp. 218–21, and *A Medieval Commune*, p. 219. For the duty to enlarge the *contado*, see, for example, *ASSi, Statuti di Siena 5*, fol. 290ᵛ, and *21*, fol. 27.

48. *ASSi, Gabella 21*.

49. See documents in Cecchini, *Il Caleffo Vecchio*, 4:1799–1804.

50. Listed in Cammarosano, "Repertorio."

51. Bowsky, *The Finance*, p. 244, n. 51.

52. Bowsky, *A Medieval Commune*, p. 253.

53. Bowsky, *A Medieval Commune*, pp. 71, 172–73.

54. For example, the case of Stertignano; see Cherubini, *Signori contadini*, pp. 177–99; or that of Poggio alle Mura, close to Montalcino; see I. Polverini Fosi, "Proprietà cittadina e privilegi signorili nel contado senese," *BSSP*, 87 (1980), 158–66. For the legal prescriptions, see Lisini, *Il costituto*, 2:170.

55. Bowsky, *The Finance*, p. 77, n. 30.

56. Cherubini, *Signori contadini*, p. 289.

57. These are only indirectly known, at least from looking at data from the 'Tavola delle possessioni' and also the material in Cammarosano, "Repertorio."

58. Suggested first in Cherubini, *Signori contadini*, pp. 389–95.

59. See especially P. Cammarosano, "Le campagne senesi dalla fine del secolo XII agli inizi del Trecento: dinamica interna e forme del dominio cittadino," *Contadini e proprietari nella Toscana moderna*, Proceedings of the conference in honor of Giorgio Giorgetti, vol. 1 (Florence, 1979), pp. 153–222.

60. Bowsky, *A Medieval Commune*, p. 256. For 1337–39, see *ASSi, Statuti di Siena 26*, fol. 137.

61. Lisini, *Il costituto*, 2:178–79.

62. Bowsky, *A Medieval Commune*, p. 102; and his *The Finance*, p. 264.

63. A rule such as this (therefore from before 1324) appears in Bowsky, "A New Consilium," p. 436.

64. Bowsky, *A Medieval Commune*, pp. 104, 112, 130.

65. Bowsky, *The Finance*, pp. 247–50; and his "The Impact of the Black Death," p. 23, n. 133.

66. For the earlier period, see Pazzaglini, *The Criminal Ban*; Redon, *Uomini e comunità*; see also Bowsky, *The Finance*; and his *A Medieval Commune*.

67. Informative documents may be found in Carbone, *Note sull'ideologia*, and in

footnotes of Bowsky's works; see especially the chapter on "The Civic Ideal" in his *A Medieval Commune*, pp. 260–98.

68. Unfortunately, Sienese cultural and religious life remains unstudied.

69. See, for example, Bowsky, *A Medieval Commune*, pp. 104, 105, 130. For a specific case, see *ASSi, Consiglio generale 131*, fols. 50^v–51^v (1342); *Concistoro, 65*; fol. 10^v.

70. Bowsky, *The Finance*, pp. 128–29.

71. For example, rights on a market at Fercole and on the Pari district were granted to a Malavolti and on S. Gimignanello to a Gallerani; see Bowsky, *The Finance*, pp. 124–25; and his *A Medieval Commune*, pp. 254–55.

72. For the military districts, see Ascheri and Ciampoli, *Siena e il suo territorio*, 1:57–67; for police districts and a tax on the *contado* in 1344, see the forthcoming vol. 2. As stated above, the exception is S. Gimignanello.

73. We have already suggested cases such as Abbadia, Chianciano, and Vescovado, but more research is necessary.

74. For the second the half of the thirteenth century, see Redon, *Uomini e comunità*, p. 183. In the 1309–10 statutes it seems clear; see Lisini, *Il costituto*, 2:169. A sure proof can be found in *ASSi, Gabella 2*, fol. 110^r, where *domini naturales* are paid as *rectores*. Unfortunately, inclusion in a military district does not mean the exclusion of *dominus naturalis*; see Bowsky, *A Medieval Commune*, p. 150.

75. For how different conditions could be, see Bowsky, *The Finance*, pp. 94, 232–33, 235.

76. Such as those by Cammarosano, Cherubini, and Redon.

77. There are many entries in Cammarosano, "Repertorio," and in the recent demographic works by M. Ginatempo, "Motivazioni ideali e coscienza della 'crisi' nella politica territoriale di Siena nel XV secolo," *Ricerche storiche*, 14 (1984), 291–336, and "Per la storia demografica del territorio senese nel Quattrocento:

problemi di fonti e di metodo," *Archivio storico italiano*, 142 (1984), 511–87.

78. Some of their letters are published in S. Sbarra, "Documenti inediti dell'Amiatino tre-quattrocenterco," *Studi di filologia italiana*, 33 (1975), 15–188.

79. For the final moment of this process, see Ascheri, *Siena nel Rinascimento*, pp. 87–88 and 90.

80. At the beginning of the fourteenth century, these towns were exempt from the tax on the *contado*; for example, Monteriggioni, Frosini, and Mensano; see *ASSi*, *Lira 11* from 1342. About 1390 there were also Chiusdino, Castello della Selva, and S. Quirico d'Orcia; see *Lira 289*. For citizenship in Chiusdino, see Ascheri and Ciampoli, *Siena e il suo territorio*, 1:105, and see p. 112 for Casole's promise in a 1352 agreement to be taxed together with the city; for Asciano, see the local publication by G. Tanganelli, *Asciano e le sue terre* (Siena, 1970), pp. 84–85.

81. For an example, see the response to the rebellion according to the chronicles of Massa Marittima after the fall of the Nine, in O. Malavolti, *Dell'historia di Siena*, vol. 2 (Venice, 1599; repr. Bologna, 1982), pp. 113–14.

82. Bowsky's hypothesis on this point (*A Medieval Commune*, p. 88) seems hazardous.

83. Some noteworthy documents are in Carbone, *Note sull'ideologia*, passim.

84. See, for example, the footnotes in my *Siena nel Rinascimento*, pp. 13 and 19.

85. The observation on Bowsky's research by J. Hook seems hasty; see my "Siena sotto i Nove."

86. In 1786 Peter Leopold tried to modernize the Sienese Commune, but we lack research on these efforts.

87. See, for example, documents in Carbone, *Note sull'ideologia*; but one should also view Lorenzetti's "Buon Governo."

88. See in the border, below, on the left.

89. One of the first references could be in the 1309–10 statutes; see Lisini, *Il costituto*, 2:495; then see Cecchini, *Il Caleffo Vecchio*, 4:1805 (year 1332) and the first preserved register of the records of the Nine itself, *ASSi, Concistoro 1*, fol. 1ʳ (Jan.–Feb. 1339).

90. W. Bowsky, "The Anatomy of Rebellion in Fourteenth-Century Siena: From Commune to Signory," in *Violence and Civil Disorders in Italian Cities 1200–1500*, ed. L. Martines (Los Angeles, 1972), pp. 229–72, esp. p. 257.

91. See again Carbone, *Note sull'ideologia*; and Bowsky, *A Medieval Commune*, esp. the chapter on "The Civic Ideal." Of course one should bear in mind the inscription discussed above.

92. *ASSi, Statuti di Siena, 26*, fols. 1ʳ–2ʳ.

93. This important point does not seem always clear in the current interpretations of the fresco.

94. Bowsky, *A Medieval Commune*, p. 288, n. 94.

95. The laws against lawyers and notaries had a political basis, not a cultural one.

96. *Diligite justitiam*, for instance, could be addressed only to the government; at any rate, we do not have a study on the use of space in the Palazzo Pubblico during the Middle Ages.

97. This is in the Aristotelian and Thomistic background of contemporary thirteenth-century culture. For the three fiscal *lire* in the 1262 and 1309–10 statutes, see Bowsky, *A Medieval Commune*, p. 21, n. 56 and pp. 52, 92, 169; also his *The Finance*, pp. 82–87.

98. In the 1309–10 statutes we read that "de le principali belleze è di ciascuna gentile città che abiano prato o vero luogo a deletto et guadio de li cittadini et de' forestieri . . . per le mercanzie di gualungue conditioni et fiere spetialmente ine tenere et fare per onore et utilità de la sua città et cittadini, et guadagni et altre cose abondevolmente sieno dotate e crescano . . . uno prato . . . molto bello et dilettevole, per le fiere et mercati ine tenere et fare, a belleza et pro del Comune et de li cittadini de la città di Siena" (Lisini, *Il costituto*, 2:135). Without the

bankers the city would become a *vilissimo castello*; see Carbone, *Note sull'ideologia*, 1:145.

99. See my *Siena nel Rinascimento*, p. 129.

100. After the 1318 crisis, three well-known "magnates" spoke in the General Council against the proposal to widen political participation; see Carbone, *Note sull'ideologia*, 2:22.

101. See especially Bowsky, *A Medieval Commune*.

102. An earlier project was, for instance, the *Tavola della possessione* program, *salus et vita Communis Senarum*, as said in 1319; see Carbone, *Note sull'ideologia*, 2:130.

From Development to Crisis: Changing Urban Structures in Siena between the Thirteenth and Fifteenth Centuries

DUCCIO BALESTRACCI

Siena, by the first half of the twelfth century, like so many other European cities, was experiencing the effects of the general economic expansion that was in the process of changing the economic shape of the West. Well-to-do peasants from the surrounding countryside were flocking to the city, contributing to the growth of the boroughs lying outside the walls of the early medieval *castrum*. As population spilled out from Siena's earliest settlement on the hill of San Quirico, the city gained control of the strategic Via Francigena that ran beneath the original walls. On another front, towards the north, the city spread out into a wedge-shaped area that was quickly walled in, for it was from this direction that the greatest threat to Sienese liberty traditionally had—and would—come. Only a few kilometers north of this new borough of Camollia lay the border with Florence. For centuries it was the point of demarcation and contention with a powerful and dangerous neighbor from whom, because of her proximity, Siena could hardly anticipate anything but threatening relations.

When Siena undertook to build her new walls at the beginning of the 1200s, the city had practically doubled her population over that of the preceding century. As well as the above-mentioned

areas, the city had also acquired a portion of territory to the east
and an annex to the south that included yet another section of the
vital Via Francigena. When Ernesto Sestan observed some thirty
years ago that Siena was the daughter of this critical link in the
traffic flowing from the North to Rome, he was correct in that control of the road conditioned not only the initial growth of the city
but also its subsequent urban shape.[1]

Unfortunately, we know very little of the city in this early
period. Only the survival of some stone towers built by aristocratic
families, a few churches, and the cathedral—which was in a peren-
nial state of construction from the end of the eleventh century,
when work was begun to replace the small existing church, until
1179, when the new building was consecrated, and continually
under reconstruction and enlargement until the beginning of the
thirteenth century—remain to characterize the urban environment.[2]
On this meager evidence, might we, then, define late twelfth- and
thirteenth-century Siena as a city characterized by the architecture
of the magnates?[3] Like all generalizations, such a definition runs
the risk of oversimplification. A city, in any time and in its varied
forms, is an organism that responds to the needs of all social
classes living within its confines. Nonetheless, I see in Siena of the
Millecento and Duecento a style and function that reflects aristocratic dominance.

The conquest of the Via Francigena, and in particular that of
the northern part, was accompanied by the imposition of magnatial
control of transit along this stretch of the road. Control was reflected in the relocation of the consortial domiciles (*castellari*) of
the great aristocratic clans that, through participation in the consular commune, also dominated urban government.[4] It was hardly
fortuitous that many magnatial residences rose one next to another
along the section of the Francigena situated between the present
Porta Camollia and Croce del Travoglia. Here were located the
complexes of the Bandinelli, Paparoni, and Malavolti, while next

to these rose the residences of the Montanini, the Salimbene, the Rossi, Salvani, Tolomei, and the Ugurgeri. This was done in order to dominate the Francigena just as similar magnatial groups elsewhere controlled critical points within a city. The relationship between the aristocracy and the bridges of Pisa comes to mind in this context. Furthermore, it was the same magnatial residences, given the absence of public buildings such as a municipal hall, that furnished space for governmental entities such as communal offices and prisons; in short, the public preserve was housed within the private buildings of the political and social class that ruled the city. Thirteenth-century Siena thus consisted mainly of the *castellari* and other towers of the ruling elite: fortresses as well as residences, built of stone and decorated with the expensive *pietra serena* from the Montagnola Senese.

Alongside these dominating aristocratic buildings, however, were the houses of the less affluent classes. These were built of brick but also contained a large quantity of wood used for inner walls, window shutters, and balconies. More humble yet were the dwellings carved from the rock and tufa of the ample cliffs of Siena. These had probably been inhabited since the early Middle Ages and were still being used as homes and shops, as archeological studies at the University of Siena have recently brought to light. Some of these can still be seen today along the street leading to Camollia and next to the centrally located Baptistery. Although they are currently surrounded by other buildings, their presence is still quite evident.[5]

But it is nevertheless the towers—not only in Siena but also elsewhere, as the studies of Lupi for Pisa, Fiumi for Prato, and Volterra and Fanelli for Florence indicate—that give witness to the changing face of medieval Siena.[6] Gradually, with the rise of the mercantile bourgeoisie who took their place alongside the older aristocracy, towers lost their original class connotations and became primarily residential. Ownership of towers passed into the hands of the middle-class (*borghesia*), and while this was taking place, important changes in other sectors were occurring in Siena.

At the end of the thirteenth century Siena drastically altered her political alignment. The defeat of the Ghibellines after 1269 at *Colle Val d'Elsa* created an internal political crisis that resulted in the downfall of the aristocratic, magnatial, Ghibelline oligarchy and its replacement in political leadership by a new oligarchy, of a totally Guelph persuasion, drawn from the merchant-banking class. Within less than two decades of transitional rule, the Nine (which took its name from the number of the executive board) was firmly in control of the city, thus initiating a dominance that would last from 1287 until 1355 and would mark the longest period of institutional stability in the history of the Sienese Commune. And the government of the Nine utilized every means at its disposal to maintain this internal stability.

Perhaps the clearest indication of the government's passion for stability comes from the brush of Ambrogio Lorenzetti, who, at the end of the 1330s, depicted above his fresco, "The Effects of Good Government," in the Palazzo Pubblico the figure of "Securitas," who holds in her left hand a scroll upon which is inscribed:

> Let each free man walk freely
> And let each working man sow,
> While such a commune
> This lady will hold in her rule,
> Since she has taken all
> power from the criminal.

But the right hand of "Security" shows with graphic eloquence just what was implied here. In her right fist "Security" grasps a gibbet from which dangles a corpse.

This brief essay is not the place to go into a detailed analysis of the role of the Nine in the history of Siena. Above all, to do so would be simply a paraphrase of what we know of the period from

the comprehensive studies of William Bowsky and of my colleague, Mario Ascheri.[7] I will here limit myself to the observation
that a strong oligarchy, governing during a period of unrivaled
economic prosperity and having lost the political contest for
supremacy over Tuscany, turned the city inward, concentrating on
promoting the economy and perfecting its internal organization.
The Nine had a clear conception of the type of city that they desired, and, at the same time, they proved themselves more than
capable of implementing their vision of a coherent urban landscape.
When Lorenzetti painted his fresco of the allegory of the *Buongoverno*, commissioned by the Nine, he made visually clear the political agenda of the oligarchy within which was subsumed a concomitant conception of how they wished their city to appear.
Lorenzetti reveals an orderly urban environment characterized by
the stone towers of the aristocracy and, above all, by the colorful
brick houses of the wealthy bourgeoisie: a city rich in ornamenta-
tion and in perfect harmony with the ideology of her governors.[8]

Between 1290 and 1298 the Commune began an impressive program of reorganizing and straightening the city's streets. The various
access routes to the Cathedral were redesigned. Urban streets were
connected to the part of the Via Francigena that passed through the
city proper. From the end of the Duecento, access from the various
citizen quarters to wells was improved. During the entire first half
of the fourteenth century, there was an effort to link the city center
with Fontebranda, where there was not only a spring but also ponds
around which wool and hides were prepared. Also, the beginning of
the Trecento saw the planning and completion of the entryways to
the Piazza del Campo. Finally, from 1328 onward Arco, Abbazia
Nuova, San Vigilia, and San Domenico were enlarged.

The government of the Nine, extending a program begun in the
1240s, continued paving the streets in brick. This work went forward intensely until the end of the century. Although it slowed at
the beginning of the next, it was again started up during the 1330s

and, as a concomitant to this, during the entire period of the Nine
there proceeded without interruption efforts to clear the streets of
vagrants, groups of prostitutes, and other perceived undesirables.

Another program, initiated before the regime of the Nine but
pursued under its tutelage, involved the discouragement of building
in wood. Wooden houses were especially vulnerable to fire while,
at the same time, they detracted from the beauty of a city that the
government desired to make the most glorious in Tuscany. Thus,
the first decades of the fourteenth century witnessed a massive substitution of brick for wood in construction. Brick was also used in
the building of towers and the more important public edifices.
Moreover, the Nine carried on a campaign against those structures,
such as storerooms attached to houses, balconies, and window
shutters that jutted too far into the urban streets. Judging, however,
from the frequency with which these injunctions were repeated for
decades and the fact that the battle continued after the fall of the
Nine, it would seem that the war against such additions was a
losing proposition.[9]

Another major concern of the Nine was provisioning the city
with water. Indeed, this concern reached nearly obsessive levels in
this period. If, up until the government of the Nine, hydraulic projects had been sporadic or utopian—one may cite the earlier impossible scheme to carry water from the distant river Merse—there
was now put forth a more rational and practical plan to provide the
city with water. In the 1330s work was begun on the *bottino*, the
underground aqueduct that, running north, was designed to supply
the central city rather than just the wells of the periphery, as had
been the case before.[10]

The extension of the *bottino* was a considerable undertaking: it
necessitated twenty-five kilometers of underground tunnels of brick
vaults high enough to allow workmen to walk in them while clean-
ing. Built at a considerable cost in public monies and human
energy, the *bottino* radically altered the distribution of water in

Siena. As a consequence, the construction of new wells received a tremendous stimulus. In the years between 1252 and 1253, requests for the government to build wells increased dramatically. Solicitations came from Ovile, Stalloreggi, Casata, San Martino, Abbazia Nuova; while not all requests were honored, a great number of them were. This period marks the last phase in Siena of significant improvements in the means of water distribution. From the period of the Nine on, subsequent governments limited themselves to the maintenance of the aqueduct and existing wells. Practically speaking, no further work of any significance was undertaken.

The urban program of the Nine, however, achieved its most impressive expression in the elaboration of the grand architectural projects undertaken during its regime. At the beginning of the thirteenth centu: work on the site of the Palazzo Pubblico was already underway. Here would be housed the offices of the public magistracies, thus freeing them from the somewhat awkward necessity of sharing space with private citizens that, as we have seen, had been the situation during the Ghibelline period. The first nucleus of the palace was completed in the Piazza del Campo by 1295, and in the first years of the Trecento, expansion of the building continued. Between 1300 and 1310 construction went on at a steady pace. In 1326 a lateral extension that would house the communal prison was begun. In 1325 construction of the tower was begun. The tower, in and of itself, was the symbol of the government's prestige, but it also provided a visible point of reference to the Piazza del Campo, which was the center of political power, the place where major commercial deals were consummated, the site of the money-changers, and the locus for the administration of commercial justice.[11] Heart of the city and showplace for displaying the regime's political power, the Piazza del Campo exemplified better than any other locale the urban ideal of the Nine. And it took good care of the *Campo*: the government constructed a fountain there and decreed that all new palaces built around it should harmonize architecturally with the Palazzo

Pubblico. The Piazza itself was paved with brick and stone, and the activities that could take place there, as well as those that could not, were minutely regulated.

Finally, the government of the Nine interested itself in the city's walls. It enlarged the thirteenth-century encirclement that, it was feared, would not hold the newcomers who continued to flock to the city. Thus, next to the area already protected, other walls were projected for uninhabited areas that could hold the new citizens. This undertaking, as we shall see, ultimately failed; it constituted, perhaps, the only significant error in urban planning during the reign of the Nine. It may be said, however, that the city of the Nine was definitive: definitive in the sense that after the mid-fourteenth century, alterations to the urban fabric were minimal. When Francesco Vanni laid out his asymmetric map of Siena, he revealed a city as it had been formed in the Trecento under the Nine, and this was the city that endured until the first two decades of this century.

If it is true that the epoch of the Nine marked the years of Siena's greatest urban development, it is also true that, at the same time, the specter of an impending crisis was looming on the horizon. The extended demographic growth that characterized the central Middle Ages came to an end around 1300. A Malthusian phenomenon? Probably so. Be that as it may, the trend of rising population had spent itself by the end of the Duecento, and its end brought a halt to the urban expansion of most cities of the West. Siena, from this point of view, hardly constitutes an exception. Rather, Siena might be said to be a paradigm of the general western European situation in the mid-fourteenth century.

It is hardly by chance, given the circumstances, that the circle of walls planned during the 1330s remained largely empty or that projects for future urbanization were abandoned in these years. The dale below the hospital of Santa Maria della Scala, for example, remained uninhabited, as did the valley of Follonica between the convents of San Francesco and Santo Spirito. Furthermore, the enclosure of this part of the city—also planned during the 1330s—was not accomplished until the next century. Similarly abandoned was the projected expansion to the south, which was intended by the Nine to contain in one region of the city the wave of expected new arrivals who, at the beginning of the century, were still requesting housing.

Precisely, too, in the early Trecento, the government of the Nine initiated the urbanization of the new quarter of Santa Maria, the valley that extended from the Convento dei Servi to Sant'Agostino. The plan envisioned a precise distribution of lots, each oriented after the classic fashion with the short side facing the street, which linked the inhabitants with the city gate to the south and to the north with the market square below the Palazzo Pubblico. The road also gave access to the church, the well, and other appurtenances in the region. The operation went forth despite some grumblings from the inhabitants themselves, who were irritated at the poorly planned disposition of the settlement in a kind of shell connected only by precipitous streets to the city center. By the turn of the 1320s the new *borgo* of Santa Maria, nevertheless, contained close to ninety houses.

The project, however, came to a halt and was even cut back when the population of Siena was decimated by the plague of 1348. How many Sienese became victims of the plague? An estimate is difficult, and contemporary testimony dubious. Perhaps not the 30,000 souls that Agnolo di Tura del Grasso would have us believe, but certainly a number sufficient to confirm the widely held impression that Siena was disastrously ravaged by the contagion. The plague left empty houses in the center of the city and wiped out the new borough of Santa Maria. Now that accommodations were available in more convenient locations, it obviously made little sense to dwell in that incommodious quarter.

Indeed, the plague had hardly ceased in December 1348 when some immigrants refused to comply with a law making it obligatory to build a house in the new quarter as a condition of obtaining citizenship. Within a few decades, Santa Maria had practically no inhabitants whatsoever. In 1385 the Commune officially decreed an end to the project. The futility of pushing settlement in this area was recognized, and it was decided that the area should be allowed to return to orchard. Sixteenth-century maps, in fact, show a total absence of habitation, revealing instead a condition identical to that which may be observed today in the same valley that has completely lost its urban character. In large part, its internal street pattern has disappeared. Relics of the old water system can only be traced with difficulty. Finally, accentuating the abandonment of any urban function whatever is the disappearance of the gate that connected Santa Maria with its neighboring territory.

The plague not only blocked urban development in Siena but also ended that part of the Nine's plan that inclined toward civic architectural ostentation and monumentality. The dream of a great cathedral—the largest in the whole of Christendom—had traditionally obsessed Sienese governments. Hardly forty years had elapsed since the consecration of the Cathedral in 1179 when work to enlarge it began. This expansion continued through much of the thirteenth century when, in 1285, it was decided to build a new facade. But while this work was progressing, the Nine determined in 1316 on an even further elaboration, employing the currently enlarged cathedral as a transept for a new church of a size equal to the whole of today's Piazza del Duomo. As it turned out, however, this construction was halted in 1322 by a governmental commission appointed to inspect the stability of the structure. Although the commissioners found serious geological faults in the slope behind the construction, this fact did not permanently halt the undertaking. Between 1331 and 1339, continuous purchases were made of houses destined to be torn down to make room for the new edifice. Not even the doubts expressed within the *Consiglio Generale* could bring the project to an end.

The program to construct the largest cathedral in the Christian world then was halted not by the government but rather by the plague. Indeed, work was once more commenced in 1355, but nothing significant came of it. Perhaps the temper of the post-plague times no longer favored these grandiose, triumphal, projects. Perhaps the political will to continue the effort was lacking, given the fact that the regime of the Nine, proponents of the scheme, had collapsed. But for whatever reason, in 1357 the more dangerous parts of the structure were demolished, and of the new Duomo there remains today only the skeleton of a nave and the incomplete facade.[12]

The second half of the fourteenth century was characterized by an extreme dearth of urban construction. There was no significant modification in the layout of the streets; work on public buildings advanced modestly; and virtually no great structures were erected. In sum, the political upheavals following the stability of the Nine, the often grave economic crises that the city suffered, the reduced population, and the inherent weakness of the fractionalized governments that successively rose and fell all seem to be reflected in the cityscape of Siena.

The government of the Nine had generated a strong urban program—analogous in this to cities in other parts of Italy, particularly during the Renaissance. The weak governments that followed the Nine failed conspicuously to generate any original projects. When they tried to conceive new designs on a grand scale, they merely fell back upon the worst schemes of the Nine, those that bordered upon the grotesque. In 1365, for example, the Commune planned to link the church of San Domenico to the quarter of Vallepiatta by means of a bridge of unheard of dimensions. It would have had to have crossed the whole of the wide and deep valley of Fontebranda. It is hardly surprising that the undertaking was never completed, nor, in all probability, could it have been completed, given the technology of the day.

In addition, when Sienese governments of the second half of the fourteenth century were not motivated by irrational ambition, they limited themselves to carrying out projects that, in reality, were only continuations of the ideas initiated by the Nine. An example of the lack of originality in the sphere of urban planning in the post-Nine era is the concept of decorum (*decoro*) inflicted upon the city. This notion of order and space was wholly unoriginal and almost completely inherited from the preceding period. Further, the post-Nine sense of decorum was essentially hostile to small industries, which were accused of producing waste and noxious odors despite the fact that powerful political groups existed to represent the artisan class. In sum, the last half of the Trecento saw no change in the physical image of the city as it had developed up to that point. Nor did this static situation change during the fifteenth century, a century during which Siena had to confront economic stagnation and the loss of status relative to the other states (regional and sub-regional) on the Italian political checkerboard.[13]

Siena, of course, enjoyed periods of internal stability in the Quattrocento, but stability in and of itself does not necessarily guarantee economic strength.[14] All sectors of Sienese life reflected this economic lethargy, including urban planning. Again, no changes or noteworthy additions to the architectural fabric of the city are to be found. True enough, the section of walls in the Valley of Follonica was completed, but, as noted, this was the fulfillment of a project begun in the early fourteenth century. The urban restructuring that characterized numerous other contemporary Italian cities had no significant impact upon Siena.

The only signs of the Renaissance style are to be found in a handful of architectural experiments undertaken by the aristocracy on their private buildings. For instance, the Piccolomini consortium transformed its houses in Via Banchi di Sotto into a unified Renaissance palace flanked by a loggia. The Piccolomini also rebuilt another of their palaces located in Via di Città in the new style. In these instances, the use of stone, in sharp contrast with the widely-used brick of the Sienese Gothic, underscores the nearly total absence of a Sienese Renaissance architecture. Indeed, the buildings of the Piccolomini, especially the facades and court of the palace in Via Banchi di Sotto, were pale imitations of the Florentine style. In their totality these innovations convey a sense of extraneity in contrast to the surrounding Sienese Gothic.

Finally, the *Ufficiali sopra l'Ornato*, those officials who in the fifteenth century were responsible for the urban landscape, have left written testimony to this lack of initiative insofar as the public authority was concerned. Their charge was basically to identify structures dangerously near collapse and to single out buildings that clashed with the prevailing sense of decorum, ordering their renovation on the occasion of the visit of a sovereign or a pope. Other than this, nothing.

The crises of the Middle Ages would seem to have left Siena in the backwaters of history. Of her ancient splendor, only a vainglorious memory remained. In place of the authoritarian but stable regime of the first half of the fourteenth century, succeeding governments tended to accent the authoritarian at the expense of stability—especially when the *Balìe* began to supersede the citizen councils. The years of growth were over. The great urban projects of a by-gone era were long past. Of the Nine, only the name survived in the public memory, and it was in this era that the myth of the *Buongoverno* began to take shape.

NOTES

1. E. Sestan, "Siena avanti Montaperti," in *Italia medievale* (Naples, 1968), pp. 151–92; P. Nardi, "I borghi di San Donato e di San Pietro a Ovile: 'populi,' contrade e compagnie d'armi nella società senese dei secoli XI–XIII," *Bullettino senese di storia patria*, 73–75 (1966–68), 7–59.

2. V. Lisini, *Il duomo di Siena* (Siena, 1911); E. Carli, *Il duomo di Siena* (Siena,

1979); and U. Morandi, *La cattedrale di Siena: ottavo centenario della consacrazione, 1179–1979* (Siena, 1979).

3. For reflections on the character of Siena at this time, see L. Bortolotti, *Siena* (Rome and Bari, 1983).

4. The term *castellari* in Sienese usage refers to a fortified enclave while elsewhere when employed with reference to medieval settlement it has the meaning of a ruined fortification. See V. Lisini, "Il castellare dei Salimbene," *Rassegna d'arte senese*, 18 (1925), 1–23; U. Morandi, "Il castellare dei Malavolti a Siena," in *Quattro monumenti italiani*, intro. by M. Solmi (Rome, 1969), pp. 79–99; D. Balestracci, "Il nido dei nobili: il popolo di San Cristoforo e la famiglia degli Ugurgeri in età comunale," in *Contrada Priora della Civetta: le sedi storiche* (Siena, 1984), pp. 97–102; and L. Franchina, "I misteri del Castellare," in *Contrada Priora*, pp. 103–08.

5. V. Lisini, "Note storiche sulla topografia di Siena nel secolo XIII," in *Dante e Siena* (Siena, 1921), pp. 245–347; and G. Chierici, "La casa senese al tempo di Dante," in *Dante e Siena*, pp. 349–86. For the excavated houses in the tufa rock, see C. Nepi, P. L. Palazzuoli, R. Parenti, and F. Valacchi, "Per lo studio della 'facies' rupestre della città di Siena," *Archeologia medievale*, 3 (1976), 413–28.

6. C. Lupi, "La casa pisana e i suoi annessi," *Archivio storico italiano*, ser. 5, 27 (1901), 264–314; 28 (1901), 65–96; 29 (1902), 193–227; 31 (1903), 365–96; and 32 (1903), 73–101. See also G. Fanelli, *Firenze* (Rome and Bari, 1980); and E. Fiume, *Demografia, movimento urbanistico e classi sociali in Prato dall'età comunale ai tempi moderni* (Florence, 1968). Various studies by the latter author have been published as *Volterra e San Gimignano nel medioevo*, ed. G. Pinto (Siena, 1983).

7. See, by W. M. Bowsky: "The *Buon Governo* of Siena (1287–1355): A Mediaeval Italian Oligarchy," *Speculum*, 37 (1962), 368–81; "The Impact of the Black Death upon Sienese Government and Society," *Speculum*, 39 (1964), 1–34; "Medieval Citizenship: The Individual and the State in the Commune of Siena, 1287–1355," *Studies in Medieval and Renaissance History*, 4 (1967), pp. 193–243; *The Finance of the Commune of Siena, 1287–1355* (Oxford, 1970) (Italian translation Florence, 1976); *A Medieval Italian Commune: Siena under the Nine, 1287–1355* (Berkeley, 1981) (Italian translation Bologna, 1986). See Ascheri's contribu-

tion to this present volume.

8. On the interpretation of the fresco, see C. Frugoni, "Immagini troppo belle: la realtà perfetta," in *Una lontana città: sentimenti e immagini nel medioevo* (Turin, 1983), pp. 136–210.

9. D. Balestracci and G. Piccinni, *Siena nel Trecento: assetto urbano e strutture edilizie* (Florence, 1977).

10. F. Bargagli Petrucci, *Le fonti di Siena e i loro aquedotti*, vol. 2 (Siena and Florence, 1903); and D. Balestracci, *I bottini: acquedotti medievali senesi* (Siena, 1984).

11. For the vicissitudes in building the Palazzo Comunale, see *Palazzo Pubblico di Siena: vicende costruttive e decorative* (Siena, 1983).

12. Carli, *Il duomo di Siena.*

13. G. Piccinni, "Modelli di organizzazione dello spazio urbano dei ceti dominanti del Tre e Quattrocento," in *I ceti dirigenti della Toscana tardo comunale: atti del III° Convegno, Firenze, 5–7, dicembre 1980* (Florence, 1984), pp. 221–36.

14. See the analysis of M. Ascheri, *Siena nel Rinascimento: istituzioni e sistema politico* (Siena, 1985).

Economy and Society in Southern Tuscany in the Late Middle Ages: Amiata and the Maremma

GABRIELLA PICCINNI

In recent years, studies of the Italian countryside in the late Middle Ages have followed two lines of investigation. First, an attempt has been made to provide a general overview, without which the integration of Italian data into a larger European synthesis is hampered. At the same time, the focus on smaller territorial units has underscored the diversity that regional and national surveys have suggested. Thus the traditional divisions between the history of the plains, the mountains, and the hills, based on distinct environmental and productive elements, have been further clarified by historical cross-sections of regions and sub-regions.

Studies based on the sub-region have proved particularly valuable for Tuscany, a territory differentiated from other parts of Italy not only by culture but also by geography and, in our period, by economic and social structures as well. The unification of the region such as we see it today occurred only between the end of the fourteenth and the beginning of the fifteenth centuries with the Florentine conquests of Pistoia, San Gimignano, Arezzo, Pisa, and Cortona in the north, while the defeat of Siena—the last major city toward the south—opened the way to the subjugation, in the course of the fourteenth century, of the section of the Maremma now known as Grossetana and of the mountain of Amiata. In the following discussion, the focus is not the Italian mountain and plain in generic terms but, rather, the unique economic and social milieu formed by the mountain of Amiata and the Maremma plain below.

From the point of view of primary production, the mountainous regions of medieval Italy were characterized by the dominant activities of forestry and animal-herding.[1] The mountain zone in Tuscany and elsewhere was, on the whole, a poor community with very little social stratification based on landed property. Nonetheless, the presence of the forest encouraged the development of artisan crafts; woodworkers and blacksmiths can be identified in fairly large numbers. The rest of the mountain population of Italy was comprised of shepherds, swine herders, small landowners, woodcutters, and charcoal workers. One encounters only rarely land owned by city dwellers, who tended to prefer the lands of the foothills or plains that were more fertile and more readily organized into farmsteads. Here the pattern of dispersed settlement that characterized much of the rest of the region was virtually absent. Finally, one notes that properties exploited collectively survived longer in the mountainous zone, and the structures of communal life proved more resilient than in the areas closer to the city, which experienced the contemporaneous diffusion of sharecropping contracts (*mezzadria poderale*).[2]

A close examination of the society of Amiata and the Maremma reveals many similarities but also many contrasts with this generally accepted picture. In terms of physical features, the volcanic mountain of Amiata was an isolated cone-shaped projection in southern Tuscany, surrounded by hills of medium to high altitudes that were only sparsely inhabited along the extensive leeward slopes facing the Maremma coast. The confines of the Pisan and the Sienese Maremma were defined by the course of a modest stream called the Cornia. South of it the Tyrrenhian littoral gave way to a series of alluvial plains, where a number of waterways merged into more-or-less extensive marshes and stagnant pools before emptying into the sea. From the Maremma one can trace the beginnings of the climatic line that divided the peninsula, ultimately ending in the Abruzzi. To the north and south of that line, the prevailing conditions were modified by local variations in physical features, elevation, or soil types.[3]

In the late Middle Ages the vegetation of Amiata was distributed in fairly well-defined sectors corresponding to altitude: orchards, vineyards, and fields planted with cereal crops below; chestnuts in the intermediate zone; and beech trees at the top.[4] This contrasted with the much more varied landscape of the Appenines, which included forests, thickets, pasture, cultivated fields, and orchards.[5]

There were also significant differences in settlement patterns. A map of parishes in the Tuscan countryside between the end of the thirteenth and the beginning of the fourteenth centuries reveals a relatively dense network of settlements in the Garfagnana, the Pistoiese mountains, the Mugello, and the Casentino, with population centers distributed at frequent intervals along the main arteries of traffic.[6] In Amiata, by contrast, there was a more dispersed pattern of settlement. The population was concentrated in large *castelli* that circled the crown of the mountain at altitudes between six-hundred and eight-hundred meters.

The Maremma plain was much less densely populated. Even if the lakes and marshy pools were not totally unproductive, owing to the exploitation of fisheries, the numerous water courses impeded the cultivation of a relatively large expanse of potentially fertile land. At the same time, the stagnant basins offered an ideal breeding ground for malaria, aptly called *influentia maremanna* in Sienese documents. Thus, conditions in the plains contributed to an increased density of population in the hills. The parish map mentioned above confirms that, at the end of the thirteenth century, the Maremma was characterized by a network of settlements that became gradually more diffuse, especially in the dioceses of Massa

Marittima, Grossetto, and Sovana. Moreover, among the small Maremma towns, perhaps only Massa—the principal mining center of southern Tuscany—had a population that exceeded one thousand between 1200 and 1400, reaching four to five thousand inhabitants at the peak of its expansion.[7]

The cultivated areas around the *castelli* of Amiata were characterized by a paucity of grain crops, and, indeed, the production of cereals proved inadequate for the needs of the local population. The inhabitants of the mountain claimed that this situation was the result of several factors: the infertility of the soil; the limited extension of the *corti* (the territory under the immediate jurisdiction of the communes) relative to the population of the *castelli* and the productivity of the land; and, finally, the establishment by Siena between 1300 and 1400 of the *Dogana dei Pascoli* that sanctioned the utilization of large expanses of land for pasture.[8] At times not only grain but also vineyards and orchards were lacking.[9] In contrast to the situation in the Casentino from which wine was exported as far as Rome, there are only a few examples of communities of Amiata that specialized in viticulture, an activity that might have provided a supplementary income to a population that could not adequately support itself solely by agriculture.

Low yields on fields sown in wheat were offset primarily by the production and consumption of chestnuts. Also compensating for low wheat yields was the proximity of the granary of southern Tuscany, the Maremma. Thus, while agriculture never reached its full potential in this zone, it still represented one of the principal resources of the area.[10]

The natural enemies of an improved agricultural utilization of the Maremma were, as noted earlier, the extension of swampy tracts and the prevalence of malaria. These conditions forced the population to live in the hills and harvest grain in the plains. A second obstacle, closely related to the above, was the restricted number of agricultural laborers and, in general, the low population density of the region. Thus, Siena's attempts to colonize the area without undertaking basic reclamation projects resulted in demographically fragile communities whose inhabitants were soon overtaken by malaria and poverty. In 1370 and 1378 Siena explicitly acknowledged that the population of the Maremma had declined precipitously and with it agricultural output. Blame for this was attributed to the ruinous fiscal policy of Siena that contributed to the dispersal of the inhabitants. Since labor at the time was a highly valued resource, migration from one commune to another in search of employment was expressly prohibited.[11]

Despite this legislation and notwithstanding the lack of capital investment in the improvement and expansion of cultivated lands, cereal production continued to represent one of the principal sources of income in the Maremma and a major item of export to the Tuscan towns. However, progress toward an agrarian restructuring that would have insulated the region from the negative effects of demographic fluctuations was impeded by the victualing policy of Siena, which, like other cities, inhibited free trade in grain. Thus, when the population contracted in the second half of the fourteenth century, the role of transhumance in southern Tuscany was accentuated. In 1477 Grossetto was said to be "given over to stock-rearing and cereal culture."[12]

The Maremma sent the bulk of its grain to Siena via the intermediary grain markets of Amiata. It is necessary to examine the integration between the two zones of Amiata and the Maremma on both the economic and the social levels in order to understand the traditional patterns of mobility of the inhabitants of the mountain (or at least those on the Maremma side) who descended into the valley to sow and harvest their crops and to lead livestock to winter pastures. While this movement obviously involved individual workers, it also encompassed seasonal migrations of entire families.[13]

Following the plague of 1348, inhabitants of the community of

Civitela in the Maremma complained to the commune of Siena that many lands remained untilled because "cultivators inhabit the remote wooded districts." In 1400 some communities in the Maremma attempted to secure provisions of wine in substantial quantities because without it the "seasonal" laborers, indispensable for sowing, would not present themselves for fear of coming down with malaria by drinking contaminated water.[14]

The integration of the populations of Amiata and the Maremma was also promoted by those who accompanied the ascent and descent of the livestock, in September and May, along the transhumance tracts that crisscrossed the mountain in the East before finally turning to the West. Furthermore, for the flocks and shepherds coming from the territory of Arezzo, Amiata was one of the most frequent way stations, certainly the most important one, before the descent into the Maremma plain.[15] The direct linkage between Amiata and the extensive Maremma pastures and the relative proximity to their own homes differentiated the shepherds of Amiata from those of the distant Tuscan Appenines. The latter had to contend with the problems of supplies, of contacts with one's original home and family, of the possibilities of starting new families, and generally of going it alone. On the one hand the practice of transhumance detached people from their homes and their families, but on the other hand it also facilitated new relations with other population groups.

The availability of summer and winter pastures was such that the inhabitants of Amiata possessed considerable quantities of livestock, including sheep, goats, oxen, and swine. Nevertheless, some communities appear to have been more involved than others in animal husbandry. This is true, for example, of the inhabitants of Abbadia San Salvatore, who, in addition to other livestock, maintained large numbers of swine, owing to the abundance of chestnuts. They also produced chestnuts and a considerable amount of salted pork.[16]

That the organization of livestock rearing was undergoing a

transformation is clearly indicated by evidence from the community of Arcidosso. Even as late as 1433 the residents can be seen attempting to save their own livestock from the depredations of warfare by removing the herds to the Maremma. However, not much later, these independent operators appear to have been transformed in large part into shepherds of livestock owned by others. Almost at the same time, inhabitants of other communities of Amiata professed that they no longer owned their livestock. Paralleling this process of impoverishment through the 1400s there was an increase in urban capital invested in contracts of *soccida* in Amiata.[17]

What had taken place? With the gradual organization of the *Dogana dei Pascoli* from the mid-fourteenth through the beginning of the fifteenth centuries, the exploitation of communally held lands was increasingly restricted, thereby increasing the costs of stock raising for the inhabitants of the communities of Amiata and the Maremma. Thus, these rural dwellers were progressively forced to seek work as shepherds for third parties.[18] The availability of an impoverished and inexpensive labor force contributed to the rapid diffusion of contracts of *soccida* offering substantial profits with low risk to urban investors. The full impact of these contracts on the Sienese countryside, however, merits further investigation.

Thus, by the end of the Middle Ages, the combined flow of urban capital into the territory and the economic difficulties that afflicted large areas of the Senese (wars, famines, "evil storms") accelerated a process whereby most of the inhabitants of the *contado* were transformed into laborers dependent upon the residents of the city: either *mezzadri* in the hilly farming zones, where small peasant-held properties disappeared, or shepherds in the mountains and in the Maremma, where the small holding persisted but only as a marginally productive unit below a reasonable level of subsistence.

Nevertheless, the economy of Amiata and the Maremma cannot be totally defined by either agriculture or animal husbandry. As noted earlier, the topographical features of the zone gave rise to a significant development of artisanal occupations in Amiata that were connected to the transformation of forest products, to the utilization of hydraulic power in the zone, and/or to the caloric energy of charcoal produced from burning chestnut wood. Amiata produced a considerable quantity of high-quality charcoal, which in the mid-fourteenth century was traded as far as Siena.[19] In fact, by the beginning of the fifteenth century the activities of charcoal-makers resulted in the deforestation of large tracts of chestnut groves in the mountains to such an extent that the government of Siena was compelled to restrict new clearings.[20]

Woodcutters and carpenters worked side-by-side with the charcoal producers. The abundance of chestnuts not only provided feed for swine but also favored the collateral activity of meat curing. Moreover, the presence of goats and cattle allowed some communities to specialize in the production of shoes in sufficient quantities to supply the entire mountain zone. The availability of wool and goats' hair also created employment opportunities for carders, beaters, fullers, and weavers.[21]

One of the most widespread artisan crafts seems to have been iron-working, which was located outside the walls of the *castelli*, where the utilization of hydraulic power made possible the mechanization of the various stages of production. An initial examination of the documents—which require integration with on-site studies and archeological data—suggests something more. In 1318 near Seggiano, there were two constructions called *fabbriche* located respectively below and above the course of a torrential stream known as the "Vivo."[22] The term *fabbrica* would appear to indicate a fairly sophisticated workshed where one or more blacksmiths utilized hydraulic power to operate hammers and bellows. In 1366, in the same locality, we are informed of the smelting of iron ore in a blast furnace. Indeed, there is explicit mention of *unius ignis qui vulgariter dicitur il fuoco di sotto*.[23] Thus, on the mountain of Amiata, the first smelting of iron ore may well have taken place as early as the fourteenth century.

In the *castello* of Archidosso the situation was similar. In the mid-fourteenth century there were two fully equipped *fabbriche* there. Although the details of their activity are not recorded, we know that by 1429 several smiths had been operating there for some time with hydraulically operated wheels and hammers.[24] However, on the nearby torrent there were larger and more substantial forges called *fabbriche grosse* or *difitii da fare ferro*, which were quite different from the simpler workshops noted in this zone. Thus, also at Arcidosso, we can confirm the presence of blast furnaces (*bassi fuochi*) in which iron ore was smelted.[25] In 1429 Siena officially halted the activities of these large establishments (*fabbriche grosse*) and imposed severe penalties on those utilizing charcoal, the main fuel of this area, for smelting. The community of Arcidosso requested an exemption for at least twelve smiths who together accounted for the bulk of the artisan activity of the locality and who furnished iron to the entire Sienese territory.

At the end of the fifteenth century production of iron was also going on at Piancastagnaio. In that year a Sienese citizen constructed a forge (*ferraria*) or a building to house a forge (*hedificium actum ad ferrari*) along the nearby torrential stream.[26] At Abbadia a forge was similarly operating, albeit intermittently, in 1472. In the same territory, at the beginning of the seventeenth century, there were still a number of active shops devoted to the working of copper, iron, and wire. Between the seventeenth and the eighteenth centuries ironmongering was likewise present at Casteldelpiano and Santa Fiora.[27]

At the present time we do not know the origin of the iron ore worked on Amiata. While we cannot exclude the nearby mines of the Maremma as a source, it is more probable that local craftsmen used the mineral resources of the mountain itself. Evidence in support of the latter hypothesis comes from the term *Vena*, used to indicate the site of a forge in Piancastagnaio in the fifteenth century.

Even more explicit testimony derives from a sixteenth-century document that describes Amiata as rich in mineral outcrops. Finally, toward the end of the fifteenth century, there appeared makers of firearms (*scoppietti*), who worked for foreign markets and used not only locally produced iron but also, probably, nitrate that was still extracted in this zone as late as the eighteenth century.[28]

A combustible substance, minerals, and water were three resources capable of promoting activities of an "industrial" nature on Amiata and, in their wake, an influx of urban capital. As noted, the Sienese invested their capital in the fertile lands of the hilly zones closest to the city, which gave rise, in turn, to a profound restructuring of the landscape. By contrast, on the mountain, urban investors tended to channel their capital into *soccida* contracts of livestock or partly into enterprises that involved the working of minerals. Thus citizens became the partners of local residents in shares of property. We are dealing, therefore, with shares of capital from different contributors. At least in the early phase, this pattern of investment suggests that Sienese citizens who entered partnerships brought with them managerial skills indispensable for organizing the purchase, production, and transportation of the final product.

While the discovery of an "industrial" Amiata is a totally new hypothesis, we have known for some time that mineral extraction was a major resource of the Maremma in the medieval period. In fact, southern Tuscany contained extensive mineral deposits: copper, silver, iron, gold, lead, alum, and sulfur. In 1334 Simone di Giacomo Tondi, charged by the commune of Siena with the preparation of a report on the mineral deposits of the Sienese subsoil, described the rich veins of the Maremma in Argentario, Massa Marittima, Monterotondo, Prata, Roccastrada, Boccheggiano, and Montieri, thereby demonstrating that the mining district of the Sienese territory was one of the most important in Tuscany. The richest extractive site of this zone was that of Massa Marittima.

Siena played a crucial role in its development by directing toward this small mining community a steady stream of private capital that permitted the financing of exploration, the intensive exploitation of the mines, and the commercial distribution of the products. The discovery of new veins of copper and silver at Roccastrada just when those of Montieri were running out produced a veritable "gold rush" in the first half of the fourteenth century. Many merchants, including some who were quite prosperous, abandoned their shops and dedicated themselves to exploration with "the aim of earning an enormous profit."[29]

The importance of the Maremma in the field of mineral extraction is also confirmed by the fact that the first systematic codification of mining laws in medieval Europe, dating from 1310, is from that district.[30] The key clauses are the separation of land ownership from the rights to the subsoil (which allows the deposits to be exploited by a person other than the owner of the property) and the possibility that exploitation can be undertaken by several persons in partnership, who adopt a capitalistic structure comprised of partners, salaried workers, and "magistri" or directors of the enterprise. The above clearly demonstrates that non-agricultural and non-pastoral activities played a significant role in the economy of the Maremma and of Amiata in the late Middle Ages, despite the fact that, given the present state of research, precise figures are lacking on the number of people employed in these sectors.

Nor are we yet in a position to describe in detail the distribution of wealth. At most, we can extrapolate from isolated data the basic parameters by which wealth was measured in these localities. Clearly, taking charge of the livestock of Sienese citizens implied for the inhabitants of these zones a life of hardship and privation, "fatigued day and night looking after the stock of another."[31] Being in debt may well have necessitated sleeping on straw and earth, drinking water in place of wine, and hiding in the forest. Eating chestnuts was not only synonomous with the life of mountaineers, as the citizens maintained, but it also conjured up specific images of poor mountain dwellers, constrained to consume chestnuts in the same fashion as animals ("like swine") to avoid dying of hunger.[32] Thus, the dominance of chestnuts in the diet of mountain communities was more an expedient of the poor than simply a culinary tradition.

In sum, what was keenly sought was not merely wealth but the means to obtain it, specifically, physical strength, a willingness to work, and the possession of a productive plot of land.[33] From this point of view, despite close social connections to the Maremma plain, Amiata represented a true micro-region characterized by a substantial social homogeneity at its base. Not only are we confronted by a form of egalitarianism on the lower levels of society, but we also know that the inhabitants of Amiata compared their wealth and status to that of other communities within the mountain zone. Thus, the poverty of Casteldelpiano was said to be known "to the entire mountain of Amiata"; the sterility of the soil made Arcidosso different from the other *castelli* of Amiata that were reputed to be wealthier; and Montegiovi claimed that it no longer possessed communal lands like those of the neighboring *castelli*.[34]

The society of Amiata further demonstrates an underlying homogeneity in the endemic state of violence that pervaded the area. Given its border location, it was a frontier zone whose insecurity was heightened by long-running conflicts with the feudal lords of the district. Virtually all the communities of Amiata complained about the prevailing lack of security and the continuous exposure to wars and raids. Piancastagnaio, in particular, was referred to as the "key and gateway" of the Sienese district, underlining the fact that the *castello* was both an obligatory transit point and a border post of the Sienese.[35] The devastations suffered by the communities of Amiata in times of warfare were repeated at frequent intervals in the fourteenth and fifteenth centuries.[36] The most serious problem was theft of livestock, whose protection at one point became organized when the populace, at the first hint of war, routinely moved the flocks to the Maremma.[37]

The forests of Amiata provided a place of refuge in difficult times, even for those under the ban who were hiding from creditors. Among the refugees it proved easy to recruit mercenaries for armed conflicts, raids, and expeditions.[38] Thus, between the fourteenth and the fifteenth centuries, several generations were raised in military encampments. In this environment betrayals, homicides, rapes, and family feuds found their way into the official documentation. Among the many reported incidents was an episode that occurred at Piancastagnaio, where, in 1423, the death sentence was instituted as punishment for homicide.[39] In this same place three years later, the commune officially prohibited a traditional game that involved the division of the inhabitants into two opposing teams (called *del fiore* and *della verdura*) because it became the source of hostilities, anger, and malice.[40] In 1443 the same *castello* was occupied for a considerable time by Sienese troops engaged in border wars. Less than one year later, there was an official report of the rape of the daughter of a smith by a young soldier accustomed, we are told, "to follow his own desire rather than the dictates of reason." This incident provoked an armed response from the victim's brothers, who, in defense of family honor, pursued the rapist with the intention of intimidating and threatening him; but, when they ultimately overtook the culprit at Santa Fiora, they killed him on the spot.[41] Again at Piancastagnaio, in 1456, another youth could think of nothing better to do than accuse his rival in love of treachery toward the commune of Siena, thus injecting a note of private revenge into the violent incidents that occurred in a community where political crises frequently ended in exiles and hangings.[42]

Let me not linger over this last point. I might note only that in the mid-eighteenth century the population of this mountain was known as a "daring, quarrelsome frontier people" and also as "undisciplined, profligate, abusive, gamblers." They were further described as "rash, insolent, sanguinary, and prone to crime despite the presence of the Duke who maintains a fine palace there, and they are accustomed to acting as the bosses in that locality."[43] The characteristic fierceness of the inhabitants of the mountain was a continuous source of turbulence in the society of Amiata, even when the new ducal organization of the modern age was superimposed upon the old boundary lines.

NOTES

1. For an overview of the basic features of agriculture in mountainous regions, see G. Cherubini, *L'Italia rurale nel basso medioevo* (Bari, 1984), esp. pp. 94–95, on the role of chestnuts in the Italian mountain economy. See also, by Cherubini, "La civiltà del castagno in Italia alla fine del medioevo," *Archeologia medievale: cultura materiale, insediamenti, territorio*, 8 (1981), 247–80.

2. Cherubini also considers the low standard of living of mountain populations to be characteristic of the entire peninsula; see his *L'Italia rurale*.

3. P. Jones, "La storia economica dalla caduta dell' Impero romano al secolo XIV," in *Storia d'Italia*, II (Turin, 1974), p. 1556.

4. Pius II (Aeneas Silvius Piccolomini), *I Commentari*, vol. 3, ed. G. Bernetti (Siena, 1972–76), pp. 163–64; I. Imberciadori, ed., *Statuti di Casteldelpiano sul Monte Amiata (1571)* (Florence, 1980), Introduction, pp. 41–50; and G. Pinto, *La Toscana nel tardo medioevo: ambiente, economia rurale, società* (Florence, 1982), p. 31.

5. A clear account is provided by G. Cherubini, *Una comunità dell'Appennino dal XIII al XV secolo: Montecoronaro della signoria dell'abbazia del Trivio al dominio di Firenze* (Florence, 1972), p. 55.

6. The parish map is published in *Rationes decimarum Italiae: Tuscia*, 2: *Le decime degli anni 1295–1304*, ed. M. Giusti and P. Guidi, Biblioteca apostolica

vaticana (The Vatican, 1942).

7. Pinto, *La Toscana*, pp. 3–92.

8. These statements are taken from the collection of petitions presented to the commune of Siena by the communities of the *contado* and preserved in the *Fondo Concistoro* of the *Archivio di Stato di Siena* (subsequently cited as *A.S.S.*): *Concistoro* 2126–31, fifteenth century. Among the communes that repeatedly complained about the infertility of their lands were Abbadia, Piancastagnaio, Arcidosso (which stressed this point), Montelaterone, and Monticello; see *A.S.S.*, *Concistoro* 2126, c. 47; 2128, cc. 39 and 74; 2130, c. 62; 2131, c. 14; 2133, cc. 62 and 103; and 2134, c. 66. The communal statutes of Abbadia include a provision from 1449 to "affocolar tucti e' paesi sterili"; see *A.S.S.*, *Statuti dello Stato* 3, c. 82.

9. "Quella terra è differentiata dalle altre imperochè per la sua sterilità non si ricogle grano, nè vino, nè niuno fructo"; and again "nè grano, nè vino, nè biado alcuno"; and, also, "nè grano et altri fructi se non castagnie"; see *A.S.S.*, *Concistoro* 2134, c. 66 (1 June 1475); 2132, c. 14 (28 May 1460); and 2128, c. 39 (28 September 1433).

10. Pinto, *La Toscana*, pp. 93–140.

11. D. Marrara, *Storia istituzionale della Maremma Senese: principi e istituzioni del governo del territorio grossetano dall'età carolingia all' unificazione d'Italia* (Siena, 1961), p. 243.

12. Pinto, *La Toscana*, p. 63.

13. *A.S.S.*, *Concistoro* 2117, c. 137 (29 August 1474); *Concistoro*, 2128, c. 38 (28 September 1433); *Consiglio generale* 223, c. 114', cited by Pinto, *La Toscana*, p. 423.

14. *A.S.S.*, *Consiglio generale* 145, c. 49 (29 December 1349).

15. See the discussion in D. Barsanti, *Allevamento e Transumanza in Toscana: Pastori, Bestiami e Pascoli nei secoli XV–XIX* (Florence, 1987).

16. *A.S.S.*, *Concistoro* 2130, c. 27 (10 January 1445).

17. *A.S.S.*, *Concistoro* 2132, c. 14 (23 May 1460); 2133, c. 55 (7 November 1466); and 2134, c. 4 (18 May 1470).

18. *A.S.S.*, *Concistoro*, 2133, c. 62 (16 April 1462); Mario Ascheri, ed., *Abbadia San Salvatore: Comune e monastero in testi dei secoli XIV–XVIII* (Abbadia San Salvatore, 1986), p. 25; and Imberciadori, *Statuti*, pp. 387–88.

19. In 1364 a Sienese merchant purchased chestnut wood "ad carbonem ad usum contrate" from an inhabitant of Arcidosso; see *A.S.S.*, *Notarile ante-cosimiano* 155, cc. 20–21 (15 August 1364). In 1429 the commune of Arcidosso regulated the cutting of chestnut trees used to produce charcoal for industrial purposes; see *A.S.S.*, *Concistoro* 2127, c. 70. At Abbadia, beginning in 1432, it was prohibited to produce charcoal "in monte"; see *A.S.S.*, *Statuti dello Stato* 3, c. 67^v.

20. The elevated consumption of charcoal produced from chestnut trees for use in ironworks damaged the population of Arcidosso to such an extent that it was said that "essi castagni tagliati era el tollare la vita ale persone di quella terra." Only small independent smiths who worked with their own hands—"i fabbri da mano"—were exempted, upon request, from the prohibition that remained in force for the *fabbriche grosse* ("che essi maestri per fare esso loro mestiero manuale possino fare carbone per loro tanto lograre . . . nel tagliare d'essi castagni, che saranno l'anno picciola cosa"; *A.S.S.*, *Concistoro* 2127, c. 79 [17 March 1429]; and 2128, c. 19 [1 December 1430]).

21. See, for example, *A.S.S.*, *Statuti dello Stato*, 3, cc. 74, 81^v, (1437, 1439); 99, cc. 64–66, (1416); *Concistoro*, 2127, c. 7 (17 March 1429); 2130, c. 27 (10 January 1445); 2132, c. 56 (28 December 1463); 2134, c. 4 (18 May 1470); *Consiglio generale* 224, c. 143; 230, cc. 74^v–75; and Pinto, *La Toscana*, p. 448.

22. *A.S.S.*, *Estimo* 73.

23. *A.S.S.*, *Notarile ante-cosimiano* 156, c. 43^v (30 March 1366).

24. *A.S.S.*, *Consiglio generale* 134, cc. 53^v–54 (25 June 1344); and 136, cc. 35–36 (13 April 1345).

25. See *A.S.S.*, *Notarile ante-cosimiano* 309, c. 71^v (24 June 1418) where a locality called *Sopra la fabrica* is mentioned. In an entry of 1429 one reads: "che i

castagnieti et castagni d'essa comunità et homini si tagliavano per fare carbone per difitii da fare ferro et che quelli erano venuti in forma che in brev tempo no vi sarebbe rimasto castagno ricto; et avuto loro notitia che essa comunità et huomini si governano d'esse castagne a tempo di pace sey mesi dell'anno et a tempo di guerra la maggiore parte dell'anno, et videro che essi castagni tagliati era el tollare la vita ale persone di quella terra"; see *A.S.S.*, *Concistoro* 2127, c. 79 (17 March 1429).

According to a similar statement in 1430, "nella decta terra sempre per cagione di grande copia d'aque di fiume che sono nella decta corte ànno auto sempre buonissimi maestri fabbri da mano, maestri d'ogni ferri, e' quali per le ruote d'acqua che ivi sono, sempre sonno stati et allevati e' quali forniscono la città e contado d'ogni ferri tagliatori et altri ferri come è noto" and that "essi maestri per fare esso loro mestiero manuale possino fare fare carbone per loro tanto lograre et che quello nel tagliare d'essi castagni che saranno l'anno picciola cosa non possino fare se non con licentia de Podestà et de' Priori d'esso luogo che per li tempi saranno, acciò non si tagli se non quanto sarà abastanza per logro d'essi fabbri a mano." A notation in the margin reads: "Nec locum habeat pro fabricis grossis"; see *A.S.S.*, *Concistoro*, 2128, c. 19 (1 December 1430).

26. The notice is contained in the record of a reunion of the Council of Pian-castagnaio "super materia ferrarie fiende in districtu et iurisdictione Plani Castagnarii in loco dicto la Vena," which was held to approve that "sit danda et concedenda dicto Paulo [Vannoccii, a Sienese citizen] facultas, licentia et ius faciendi et fieri faciendi dictum hedificium actum ad ferrari et ferreriam et omnia necessaria ad ipsam ferreriam perficiendam et ius lignandi circumcircha ipsam ferrariam et in curia, territorio et iurisdictione dicti castri et suis silvis et quod nemo possit aliquod hedificium facere super dicta aqua quod impediat eius hedificium." The decision was remanded to the Priors; see *A.S.S.*, *Notarile ante-cosimiano* 783; c. without pagination.

27. Ascheri, *Abbadia San Salvatore*, pp. 64, 71.

28. In 1471 there is a notice of master arms makers: "videlicet scoppiettos et balistas in dicta terra Plani"; see *A.S.S.*, *Statuti dello Stato* 99, c. 11ᵛ. For mineral extraction in the sixteenth century, see *Biblioteca Comunale di Siena, Autografi Porri* 4, insert 113, 27 December 1589.

29. For an overview and bibliography on mineral extraction in Tuscany, see D.

Balestracci, "Alcune considerazioni su miniere e minatori nella società Toscana del tardo medioevo," in *Siderurgia e miniere in maremma tra '500 e '900* (Florence, 1984), p. 193.

30. A. Lisini, "Notizie delle miniere della maremma toscana e leggi per l'estrazione dei metalli nel Medioevo," *Bullettino Senese di Storia Patria*, 6 (1935).

31. *A.S.S.*, *Concistoro* 2132, c. 14 (23 May 1460).

32. *A.S.S.*, *Consistoro* 2128, c. 39 (28 September 1433); 2132, c. 17 (8 June 1460); and 2134, c. 111, (9 February 1478).

33. For the description of an inhabitant who was considered to be indispensable owing to his possession of these qualities, see *A.S.S.*, *Concistoro* 2131, c. 26 (10 November 1451).

34. *A.S.S.*, *Concistoro* 2128, c. 3 (11 April 1430); and 2134, c. 66 (1 June 1475).

35. *A.S.S.*, *Capitoli* 176, c. 7^r–^{v} (6 February 1445); *Concistoro* 2130, c. 6 (24 November 1443); and *Consiglio generale* 195, c. 96 (22 August 1386).

36. *A.S.S.*, *Concistoro* 2126, c. 47 (7 April 1405); 2128, c. 39 (28 September 1433); *Capitoli* 176, c. 7^r–^{v} (6 February 1455); and *Consiglio generale* 180, c. 12^r–^{v} (1 February 1370).

37. *A.S.S.*, *Concistoro* 2128, c. 39 (28 September 1433), where it is said that the livestock "per la guerra proxima passata l'e stato quasi tucto tolto perche la terra e molto vicina a' vostri et lor nemici Orsini et loro, per esso conservare, lo tenevano in quello di Cana dove lavoravano a tempo di pace e ine ne lo fu assai tolto"; see also *Consistoro* 2130, c. 6 (24 November 1443); and *Capitoli* 176, c. 2^v (1454).

38. *A.S.S.*, *Concistoro* 2132, c. 14 (23 May 1460); and 2133, c. 64 (12 September 1467).

39. *A.S.S.*, *Statuti dello Stato* 99 c. 39 (25 April 1423).

40. According to the Statute: "De pena nominantis partes Floris vel Viridure. Pericunda consuetudo que ex antiquorum usu originem traxit. Due quidem sotietates temporibus certis oriuntur in terra Plani Castagnarii sub spe sollaczii, guadi vel trepudi quarum sotietatum una appellatur sub regimine Floris et alia regimine Viridure. Et sic ex rabie propie partielitatis animi iuvenum instigantur et inanimantur unus contra alterum et later contra alterum, in tantum quod multotiens sunt et est in punto desolationis et destruxtionis dicte terre Plani, ex ind olim inimicitie multe orta sunt et scandala infinita, ideo cupientes veteros abusus repellere statuerunt et ordinaverunt quod nulla persona cuiuscumque qualitatis vel status existat, audeat vel praesumat quoquo tempore ullo modo vel aliquo quesito colore facere seu ordinare partem vel partialitatem uti flores aut verdure, ad penam quinque librarum de facto solvendarum"; see A.S.S., Statuti dello Stato 99, c. 43ᵛ (1426).

41. A.S.S., Concistoro 2130, c. 33 (24 November 1444).

42. A.S.S., Concistoro 2133, c. 31 (21 June 1456).

43. Pietro Leopoldo d'Asburgo Lorena, Relazioni sul governo della Toscana, ed. A. Salvestrini (Florence, 1974), pp. 598, 602.